BIBLICAL BACKGROUNDS

BIBLICAL
BACKGROUNDS

J. McKee Adams
Revised by Joseph A. Callaway

 BROADMAN PRESS

Nashville, Tennessee

DEWEY DECIMAL CLASSIFICATION: 220.9
Library of Congress catalog card number: 66–10023
Printed in the United States of America

To

John Richard Sampey
Archibald Thomas Robertson

distinguished members of the faculty
of Southern Baptist Theological Seminary
who served their students
and their denomination well

Preface to the First Edition

The purpose of this book is to set forth the relationships existing between the narratives of the Old and New Testaments, on the one hand, and the physical backgrounds which constituted such an important part of the development described therein, on the other. Happily, it is no longer felt that one may dismiss the subject of these relationships as having no particular bearing on a proper or intelligent understanding of the Bible. The most notable contribution in the wide field of recent scientific investigation has been to emphasize biblical orientation as one of the imperatives of biblical study. This is a solid conclusion. It means simply that the Bible will never be known in the most appreciative way, until it is approached in the light of its *geography*, its *languages*, its *history*, and its *archaeology*. This book is an attempt to contribute to the first of these requirements of balanced study, its province being the biblical countries and special areas that entered so largely into the progressive unfolding of the Bible story.

The method of approach followed herein in the treatment of biblical backgrounds is adopted for the first time. It is not historical, though a skeleton of contemporary events is given for the sake of a general outline. Nor is it chronological, if by that is meant a comprehensive sweep of world movements in point of their occurrence in various countries. Specifically, this survey of the biblical backgrounds is confined to the principal lands of the Bible as they appear in the progressive realization of the redemptive movement, beginning with Abraham and Israel in the ancient world, and culminating with Jesus and the apostles in the Roman Empire.

Properly defined, the geographical background is the natural framework in which human factors have been brought together to form an intelligent picture of relations existing between environment and life. On this view biblical geography becomes the physical setting for the sacred scriptures. These narratives cannot be removed from their original conditions and be fully understood. An Egyptian obelisk looks beautiful in New York, in Rome, in Istanbul, but it looks *natural* only in Egypt. The obvious inappropriateness of an Egyptian monument in a foreign setting, however, is no more pointed than the futile effort to understand the Bible in an environment to which it is alien, though its spiritual treasures are applicable to all ages and may be at home anywhere.

It is clear that understanding must precede both interpretation and application. The matchless story of the Lost Sheep, the bold metaphor of the Good Shepherd, and other incomparable utterances of the Master, all came out of a definite background of oriental character and complexion. The significance of all his teaching is heightened, widened, and deepened when we understand what he meant. The same principle applies to every part of the Bible story. It is an oriental book, from an oriental environment, and to the East we must go to get its meaning.

J. McKee Adams

Preface to the Revised Edition

With the expiration of copyright privileges of the second edition of *Biblical Backgrounds*, it was decided in consultation with Broadman Press and Mrs. J. McKee Adams to extensively revise the book since it has maintained over the years a constant usefulness to students and ministers. Changes have been made in the text to reflect accurately the progress in scholarship since the second edition was published. Chapters one and two, dealing with Mesopotamia, have been combined. Chapter twelve, which was not in the original edition, has been omitted, and the chapter on New Testament Jerusalem has been completely rewritten in the light of recent research.

The original text has been cut to a minimum to allow wider use of illustrative material. New photographs have been secured and used in a larger format to make them more meaningful to the reader. The sketch maps preceding each chapter have been replaced by more simplified maps which deal only with the subject matter of the relevant chapters. And sixteen colored maps have been added to make the detailed study of biblical geography more attractive.

I am indebted to C. S. Hammond and Company for permission to use the colored maps, and to the Department of Missionary Education and Promotion of the Southern Baptist Foreign Mission Board for permission to use the photographs. Mr. Fon H. Scofield, associate secretary of the Division of Visual Education, supplied the photographs from his files. Acknowledgment is gladly made for the visual dimension given to this revised edition by Mr. Scofield.

To Mrs. J. McKee Adams, whose abiding interest in Southern Baptist Theological Seminary is a constant source of encouragement, I am indebted for permitting the revision of *Biblical Backgrounds*. And to Broadman Press I must express gratitude for continued interest and helpfulness in every effort to make the revised edition most useful for students, pastors, and laymen.

JOSEPH A. CALLAWAY

Contents

Illustrations and Maps

Illustrations and Maps

Illustrations

Line Maps

Colored Maps

(following page 112)

Acknowledgments of Illustrations

Gerald Harvey, numbers 11, 12

Marc Lovelace, number 10

Frank K. Means, number 45

Milton Murphey, numbers 61, 63, 64

Fon H. Scofield, Jr., numbers 1, 2, 3, 4, 5, 6, 7, 8, 9, 13, 14, 15,
16, 19, 20, 21, 22, 23, 24, 25, 26, 27, 30, 31, 32, 33, 35, 36, 37,
38, 39, 40, 41, 42, 43, 44, 46, 48, 49, 51, 52, 53, 54, 57, 58, 60,
62, 65, 66, 67, 68

Al J. Stuart, Jr., numbers 17, 18, 28, 29, 34, 47, 50, 55, 56, 59

Introduction

The modern student of the Bible usually dismisses right away the childish fancy of the medieval cartographer who, actuated more by theological controversy than geographical knowledge, dared to represent the world as a great circle whose center was Jerusalem. Although at first glance the conception seems elementary, judged from the standpoint of the actual course of world events, it has had an amazing confirmation. And, if the cartographer had confined his representation to the biblical world, particularly to those areas which witnessed the beginning and the culmination of the biblical revelation, his central point would have been approximately correct.

A circle drawn with a radius of fifteen hundred miles from Jerusalem would include, not only every principal country mentioned in the Old and New Testaments, but a vast stretch of territory at no time associated with the people of Israel. The western portion would take in Rome, the capital of the Caesars; the eastern would encompass Chaldea, Persia, Media, and Scythia. In the southern part of this circle would fall the whole of the Arabian peninsula and the unex-

plored regions of Ethiopia. A similar line on the north would enclose lands of which nothing was known even as late as the Hebrew monarchy, for the horizon of the Hebrew world faded out along the shores of the Euxine [Black] Sea and the hinterlands of the Hittites in Asia Minor.

Contract the circle, and other significant relations appear. Athens, for example, was hardly more distant from Jerusalem than Ur of the Chaldees; Thebes and Babylon were almost equidistant from Jeremiah's town. Memphis on the Nile and Hamath on the Orontes were located only 300 miles from the City of David, while almost due west, at practically the same distance, stood Alexandria, founded by the great Macedonian who saw in it the possibilities of an emporium for three continents. Damascus, the marvelous oasis city, the gift of Mount Hermon to the Syrian desert, was situated just 160 miles northeast of Jerusalem, being both the beginning and the terminus of every oriental trail. Finally, within the short sweep of a similar circuit were enclosed the borders of the land of Goshen in Egypt, the wilder-

1

ness of Paran in the Sinaitic peninsula, and Sela, the rock city of the sons of Esau in Mount Seir.

The purpose of this survey, however, is not to dwell on Jerusalem and Canaan as the recognized geographical centers of the biblical world. Rather, it is our intention to trace in successive order the countries as they appear in the framework of biblical history. Regarded in this manner, Canaan does not stand in the foregrounds of the biblical narratives but is pictured as a land to be reached in the course of a journey.

Abraham could travel from Babylon to Bethlehem in a hurried trek of forty-five days, but to reach it by the way of promise the journey would require two thousand years. We elect to follow the latter method in order to become familiar with the numerous way stations and arresting experiences that constitute such an important part of the biblical background of both Abraham and his descendants, the Chosen People. Furthermore, this method of approach, while providing a more vivid conception of the environments associated with peoples of the Old Testament, takes into consideration the changes wrought in the New Testament period of expansion when the horizon was gradually pushed backward to include the whole of the Roman Empire.

Expressed in terms of longitude, the principal countries of the biblical world lay well within the arcs representing 55° East and 5° West, the territory thus embraced extending from the Persian Plateau to the Straits of Gibraltar. Correspondingly, this geographical area falls within North Latitude 20° and 45°. Expressed in terms of continents, the

1. **Mosaic map of Madeba. An ancient map of Jerusalem (oval circle) and Judah built into the floor of a sixth-century Byzantine church in Moab.**

biblical backgrounds were restricted to the northern portions of Africa, western Asia, and southern Europe. The Old Testament world found its horizons marked by five great bodies of water: the Euxine Sea, the Caspian Sea, the Persian Gulf, the Red Sea, and the Mediterranean Sea. The heart of the territory lies along the eastern Mediterranean, an area commonly called the Fertile Crescent.

The New Testament world, on the other hand, included all of this Near East sector of Egypt, Palestine, Syria, and Asia Minor, but it also extended westward through Macedonia, Greece, and Italy, touching the islands of Cyprus, Crete, Samothrace, Rhodes, Malta, and Patmos.

Again, in terms of rivers the Old Testament world ran along the courses of seven historic waterways: the Nile in Egypt; the Jordan in Canaan; the Leontes, Orontes, and Abana in Syria; the Euphrates and Tigris in Mesopotamia. However, the New Testament world was featured by only three important rivers: the Jordan, which witnessed the beginnings of the Christian movement; the Orontes, its expansion; and the Tiber, its culmination in the first century.

Finally, great cities stand out in the Old Testament backgrounds: Ur of the Chaldees, Babylon, Nineveh, Susa, Haran, Carchemish, Hamath, Damascus, Tyre, Sidon, Jerusalem, Shechem, Bethel, and a hundred other significant places. While the New Testament adopts some of these ancient cities, it presents its own list of commercial, social, religious, and educational centers whose culture far surpassed that of the older communities: Alexandria in Egypt, Antioch in Syria, Tarsus, Ephesus, Smyrna, Philadelphia, Pergamum, Troas, Philippi, Amphipolis, Thessalonica, Athens, Corinth, and Rome. These are almost selected at random; the Roman Empire was literally dotted with flourishing cities which reflected the maximum achievements of the Greco-Roman civilization.

Now, in describing these biblical backgrounds, it is not our purpose to deal at length with areas incidentally connected with the biblical narratives. Rather, we shall seek to set forth the larger aspects of the geographical environment of these principal countries whose horizons successively marked the progress of the Chosen People. Accordingly, in this order of development, our first interests will be found in the southern and middle Mesopotamian sections which witnessed the ancestral beginning of the patriarchs. In upper Mesopotamia we sojourn with Abraham in the land of Aram-naharaim, the early home of the Aramean, Mitannian, Hittite, and Amorite peoples, whose territories extended from the country of the twin rivers to the Mediterranean coasts. Following the old world trails, the journey is continued toward the south, passing east of the Anti-Lebanon mountains to reach Damascus, the gateway to Canaan.

In our first view of Canaan, the Land of Promise, strong emphasis will be placed on its central geographical position in the biblical world, and on the significant results which grew out of that relationship. From Canaan we descend into the land of Egypt, the house of bondage. In quick succession we will then present the geographical backgrounds of the Exodus, from the passage of the Red Sea to Mount Sinai, the sojourn at Kadesh-barnea, and the arrival in the Plains of Moab beyond Jordan. At this point we shall examine in detail the topographical features of Canaan, including the Coastal Plains, the Shephelah, the Western Plateau, the South Country, the Jordan Valley, the Eastern Plateau, and the Plain of Esdraelon.

With these geographical divisions clearly defined, we will then proceed with the Hebrew invasion, conquest, and settlement in Canaan. Two chapters give the backgrounds of the Hebrew kingdoms and the scattered nation. In the transition from the Old Testament to the New Testament scene, our survey deals with the Hellenistic East and Herodian Palestine. At this juncture, because of its great importance in the biblical narratives, we shall present a study of Jerusalem during the era of the New Testament. Finally, we will consider a description of the changing horizons in the period of missionary expansion when Asia Minor, the bridge to Europe, was crossed, and when, throughout the Empire, the outstanding Greco-Roman centers were enlisted to secure the permanent establishment of the Christian religion.

It is hoped that no essential element will have been left out of this survey. Our desire is that the whole work may serve as a basis for forming a composite of biblical backgrounds in which the narratives of the Old and New Testaments will be seen in a new light and with a new understanding.

1
Mesopotamia:

Land of the Two Rivers

Mesopotamia is a country of absorbing interest to every student of the Bible. The name, signifying "between the rivers," was used by the Greeks and Romans to designate the territory lying adjacent to the two great rivers, the Tigris and Euphrates, and stretching from the foothills of the Armenian Taurus range to the Persian Gulf. The earliest references to Mesopotamia suggest that it extended as far north as the Massis [Ararat] Mountains, while in New Testament citations the area is made to include Babylonia and Ur of the Chaldees.

From a geographical standpoint, the country falls into three natural divisions: southern, middle, and northern, which in turn are further described as Sumer, Akkad, and Aram. No emphasis should be placed on the adoption of the foregoing names, however, since other appropriate and generally accepted terms are used to designate these particular sections.

We are told that Abraham, the father of the Hebrew people, lived in the two extremes of the Mesopotamian country: first at Ur of the Chaldees, later at Haran in the north. From this latter place he proceeded on his trek to the Land of Promise (Gen. 11:31; 12:5). It is, therefore, primarily because of this beginning and the far-reaching results involved that we make further inquiry into the general characteristics of Mesopotamia and its relationships to border territories.

Geographical Description

The geographical location of Mesopotamia may be defined roughly as lying within North Latitude 30° and 38° and East Longitude 38° and 48°. Viewed from the north, the country extends in a southeasterly direction, following the winding courses of its great rivers. In form Mesopotamia resembles a wedge thrust in between the Syro-Arabian Desert on the west and the foothills of the Zagros Mountains on the east. The top is placed immediately to the south of the Taurus and Masis ranges, and the point is at the Persian Gulf. The territory embraced is 600 miles in length and 300 in breadth, making a total of approximately 180,000 square miles. The modern state of Iraq is practically co-extensive with ancient Mesopotamia, excepting the northern portion now incorporated in Syria.

The percentage of acreage subject to cultivation at present is very small, whereas in ancient times practically all of this region was utilized in agricultural projects. Now the land under cultivation is restricted largely to the immediate borders of the river courses, while the remainder is arid or semidesert. This situation is not one of necessity, however, for nature provides a gently sloping terrain from the Euphrates, which is slightly higher than the Tigris throughout middle and southern Mesopotamia, thus making possible irrigation projects of great magnitude. Mesopotamia was at one time featured by a regular network of canals, the outlines of which can still be traced. This will be discussed more in detail later, but at this point it needs only to be stated that where the land is cultivable, it may be classed with the delta regions of the Mississippi and the Nile, some of the most fertile soil in the world. This, of course, is made possible in Mesopotamia by the two great water courses, the Euphrates and the Tigris, which give to the country its name and its life.

The Euphrates, meaning "that makes fruitful," has its sources in the northern foothills of the Armenian Taurus Range. It flows in a winding course, encompassing the fertile plains of Mesopotamia for a distance of 1,780 miles, and empties into the headwaters of the Persian Gulf south of the present port of Basra. The Babylonian name for the Euphrates was Purattu, the name being reflected in the Arabic word Al Furat. On the other hand, the Tigris takes its name from the straight course which it follows for 1,060 miles, from the southern slopes of the Armenian Taurus, to join its twin river before entering the Persian Gulf. The word Tigris means "arrow." Modern Arabs call the river Ed-Dijla. The junc-

tion of the Tigris and Euphrates is near the city of Korna, and from this point the twin rivers receive the name of Shatt el Arab, "the great Arabian River."

Mesopotamia is the product of its rivers just as Egypt is the gift of the Nile. Throughout the region the soil is remarkably fertile, though only a small portion is now under cultivation. The country lies in practically the same latitude as the southern part of the United States. While the annual precipitation in the Mesopotamian area is only ten inches, as compared with approximately sixty inches in the southern United States, or twenty-five in Palestine, this is no serious drawback in view of the irrigation possibilities.

At a very early date the inhabitants of this area harnessed the water power at their disposal. By a system of canals they converted Mesopotamia into the most attractive portion of the Fertile Crescent. The eyes of neighboring peoples were continually fixed on the gardens of Mesopotamia. From the Arabian Peninsula, the plateaus of Assyria, Media, and Persia, warlike and adventurous hordes descended to conquer and to rule.

Early Settlers and Settlements

The earliest villages are found in northeast Mesopotamia, along the foothills of the Kurdistan Mountains. East of Kirkuk, the site of Jarmo was settled about 7000 B.C. and rivaled in antiquity the Neolithic town of Jericho in the Jordan Valley. However, Jarmo was not a walled town like Jericho. Another Neolithic settlement founded later than Jarmo was Hassuna, located south of Mosul and west of the Tigris River.

In lower Mesopotamia the earliest site

2. The land of Ur. The flat country around Ur as seen from the top of the temple tower, or ziggurat, dating from the time of Abraham or earlier.

known was Eridu whose lowest levels date about 4500 B.C. The Sumerian list of Kings gives Eridu as the place where kingship was "first lowered from heaven." During the long period between the founding of Eridu and the establishment of the First Dynasty of Ur, about 2500 B.C., many prehistoric towns were settled in the marshy lowlands near the Persian Gulf. Little is known of the first inhabitants of the region, but it is known that the Sumerians, a non-Semitic people, developed the first great civilization of the region. They developed a system of cuneiform writing, a city-state form of government, and an elaborate religious ritual complete with temples and a priestly hierarchy.

Possessed of a high degree of initiative, the Sumerians applied themselves to the physical development of lower Mesopotamia. Two difficulties blocked the way to agricultural projects on a large scale: (1) the absence of sufficient rainfall to insure successful farming; (2) the delta lowlands, flooded annually by two great rivers, retained a considerable portion of flood waters shut up in lagoons with no natural outlet, thus converting many sections of the river country into marshlands. There was no possibility of affecting the rainfall, but the Sumerians set themselves to the problems of flood control and irrigation.

Early Mesopotamians were not confronted with exactly the same problem as that faced by the Egyptians, that is, a period of Nilotic inundation followed by very low waters, for there was sufficient water in the Euphrates and Tigris throughout the year. Accordingly, the Sumerian solution took the form of a vast system of irrigation canals which resulted, not only in the draining of

3. The ziggurat at Ur. The reconstructed south face and monumental stairway of the temple tower at Ur.

swamps and marshlands in the lower delta area, but converted the higher arid sections into most productive soil. Canalization had its inception with the Sumerians who, having developed the system highly, passed it on to the early Babylonians who brought it to a state of perfection.

While the present barrenness of a large part of Mesopotamia (Iraq) is observed by all, it is not always recalled that this is exactly the reverse of its astonishing productivity under the Sumerians and the Babylonians. The country is as fertile as it ever was in ancient times. Approximately 7,000,000 people, distributed through a territory of 171,600 square miles, constitute the population of modern Iraq. There was a day when this same territory, intelligently irrigated and farmed by the Babylonians, supported 20,000,000 people. Thus all Semites and Aryans who subsequently came into this Mesopotamian garden reaped abundantly from the wisdom, foresight, and honest toil of the early Sumerians. The canal system broke down after the Moslem conquest in the seventh century, and a great part of the country reverted to desert and became depopulated.

Among these Sumerians there was a political conception which probably became the forerunner of the city-state idea which the Greeks brought to perfection fifteen hundred years later. Numerous Sumerian settlements in southern Mesopotamia were, in their beginnings, independent communities. The existence of these autonomous city kingdoms in the valley region, their rapid development, and later on their disappearance can be partly explained on geographical grounds. At the time of the Sumerian advent physical conditions in the gulf coast lands were not conducive to the establishment of any central government. The existence of marshlands and

lagoons, corresponding approximately to the bayou regions of southern Louisiana, had the effect of dividing the country into patches or detached areas.

The establishment of a particular center promoted all of the interests of the group, while further providing economic advantages for adjacent territory. Lines of communication were possible, of course, but contacts were of such slight importance that no confederacy resulted. With Sumerian progress in canalization, however, physical barriers became less noticeable, and larger activities were engaged in as common projects. Hand in hand with this advanced step came the opportunity for outstanding rulers to exercise authority over associated cities and, finally, to establish kingdoms inclusive of the whole valley area.

Located immediately to the north of Sumer was the territory of the Semitic Akkadians whose numerous cultural centers were in competition with the Sumerians for many centuries, and whose kings finally triumphed over the Sumerian states. Thus, in southern and middle Mesopotamia these two peoples, the Semitic Akkadians and the Sumerians, came to grips in a racial and cultural combat, with the result that the Sumerians were vanquished and absorbed, although the cultural contribution made by these unique people remained. The struggle, however, was not terminated until after long eras of city-state rule among Sumerian independencies, especially Uruk, Kish, Erech, and Ur.

Abraham and Ur

Ur was a great city of Sumer, at least a thousand years before the time of Abra-

4. Babylon. Base of the temple tower, or ziggurat, of ancient Babylon seen as an island. This has been associated with the Tower of Babel in Genesis 11.

ham, the patriarch. Sir Leonard Woolley excavated the remains of the ancient center of moon worship and found the "royal" cemetery of the First Dynasty dating to about 2500 B.C. The tombs were vaulted rooms of brick and stone in which multiple burials accompanied the interment of important or "royal" persons. Cylinder seals identify two of the significant burials as those of Abargi and Lady Shubad.

The tomb of Lady Shubad was especially rich in objects of gold and precious stone. A beautiful fluted gold cup lay in the tomb by her hand, and some nine yards of gold band decorated with gold flowers having lapis lazuli centers made up her elaborate headdress. Large, hollow gold, crescent-shaped earrings and a golden decorative comb were also a part of her adornments. The shocking thing about the burial was that some twenty-five attendants seem to have been sacrificed to accompany Lady Shubad into her existence beyond death. This barbarous custom seems to have been common. The bodies of more than sixty people were found in a "death pit" associated with the tomb of Abargi, and one other pit contained the bodies of six men and sixty-eight women. Even chariots loaded with treasures were driven into the pits and buried with the people. Some scholars believe that the apparent sacrifice of numbers of people at one time may have been part of fertility rites in moon worship, and that the so-called "royal" persons were actually priests or priestesses associated with the temple at Ur.

Although the First Dynasty tombs date long before the time of Abraham, they indicate the wealth and splendor of Ur and suggest something of its influence as a religious center. The Third Dynasty of Ur, dating in the twentieth century B.C., flourished briefly before the Elamites stormed down out of the hills and sacked the capital city and took Ibi-Sin, the

king, captive about 1960 B.C. If Nelson Glueck is correct in associating Abraham with the nomadic Amorites who migrated to Palestine in the twentieth century B.C., it is possible that the patriarch was influenced by the political events of the fall of Ur. He may have felt the effects of the occupation of the land of Sumer and Akkad by Amorite forebears of the old Babylonian kingdom which rose to greatness under Hammurabi about 1700 B.C.

Perhaps the most significant monument of the Third Dynasty of Ur was the great Ziggurat of Ur-Nammu completed by his son Shulgi. The ziggurat was a solid mass of brickwork 200 feet long by 150 feet wide and some 70 feet high. It was crowned with a shrine to the moon-god Nanna, and its stepped terraces were probably planted in green plants in a kind of garden of the god. Remains of the ziggurat, rebuilt by Nabonidus, king of Babylon in the seventh century B.C., may still be seen at the site of Ur. It has been estimated that the 150 acre city of Ur was populated with about 24,000 inhabitants in the days of its glory under the Third Dynasty.

The biblical accounts of Abraham give no indication that he was influenced by the advanced culture of Ur. It is probable that his contact with the Sumerians was slight, since he is represented as a wanderer of Semitic background (Deut. 26:5), whereas the Sumerians were non-Semitic. The real affinites of Abraham were with the Aramean tribes of northern Mesopotamia around Haran. W. F. Albright has shown from both biblical and extrabiblical evidence of the patriarchal period that Abraham probably engaged in caravan trade first in the Mesopotamian area, then in the land of Ca-

5. The Tigris River in ancient Assyria. Ruins of the city of Asshur are in the foreground.

naan, where he moved about in the region between Canaan and Egypt. But even after he settled in the land of Canaan, Haran was to the patriarch "my country," the land of "my kindred," and of "my father's house" (Gen. 24:4,7).

Physical Characteristics of Aram Naharaim

The physical features of northern Mesopotamia have little in common with the extreme southern portion of the same strip of territory lying at the headwaters of the Persian Gulf.

The contour of Aram varies from that of Sumer and Akkad in two important respects. First, for the want of a better term, it is the plateau section between the rivers. It is interesting to observe that the term Aram itself might have risen out of geographical usage, signifying high or elevated land. Beginning at the borders of Akkad, to the north the country takes on the appearance of uplands whose western and eastern edges slope gradually to the lowlands of the river courses. About one half of the territory is from 328 to 984 feet above sea level, while the remainder varies from 984 to 1,640 feet. Haran, the principal city of Aram, stood just on the edge of the higher elevation, approximately 1,000 feet above the Mediterranean.

The lay of the land offered, of course, no inducements for irrigation projects. However, the country, on the whole, was well watered and fertile. On the other hand, its undulating plains, rising up into the Massis and Taurus piedmont, provided attractive regions for the shepherd and his sheep. In addition, these uplands were a paradise for hordes of nomads who poured into northern Mesopotamia from all sections of the Middle East. Along the great watercourses of the Tigris, Euphrates, Khabur, and lesser perennial streams cutting across the rolling country, pastoral life flourished from

a very early period. From the Genesis records we understand that that was the type of life followed by Abraham and others of the patriarchs. At any rate, all of the biblical pictures of Aram center around these great shepherds of the East.

Aram in the Patriarchal Age

The patriarchal narratives in Genesis 12 to 35 were written against the background of a continuing relationship between Abraham and his descendants and their relatives around Haran. Descendants of a later time were taught to say: "A wandering Aramean was my father" (Deut. 26:5, RSV), preserving the ancient tie of the Israelites with their background in Aram. Later the Arameans became known as great traders and were able to build a state with its capital at Damascus. But what do we know of the people of Aram during the age of the patriarchs?

The towns of Aram.—Discoveries in the excavations at Mari on the Euphrates, south of Aram, reveal interesting relationships with the patriarchs. The Mari tablets, found in the library of the ancient city, name several towns in the region of Aram with names equivalent to those of relatives of Abraham. For instance, a brother of the patriarch is named Haran (Gen. 11:27), the same name as that of the town from which Abraham moved in his journey to Canaan. References in the Mari archives indicate that Haran was a flourishing town in Aram in the eighteenth and nineteenth centuries B.C.

A second brother of the patriarch is called Nahor, and it was to the city of Nahor that servants were sent to find a wife for Isaac (Gen. 24:10). The city of Nahor is known in both the Mari records

6. The Euphrates River between Babylon and Ur.

and Assyrian documents, and although the actual city mound is not yet identified, it is in the vicinity of Haran. Also, the name of Terah, father of Abraham, is reflected in Til-Turakhi, another town near Haran. West of Haran was Sarugi, a town of the same name as Serug, the grandfather of Terah. And near the juncture of the Khabur and Euphrates Rivers, south of Haran, was the town of Phaliga, a name similar to Peleg, another ancestor of Abraham.

The names of Abraham's relatives and ancestors reflected in the names of towns around Haran suggest two things. First, the land of Aram is much more closely associated with the family background of the patriarch than is the land of Ur in lower Mesopotamia. Genesis 24:4, which points to the Haran area as the "country" of Abraham and his kindred, supports this conclusion. Second, the towns of Haran must have borne the clan names of Abraham's kindred, which would establish the area as one in which his ancestry was rooted instead of merely a stopping place on the journey from Ur to Canaan.

The journeys of Abraham from Ur to Haran and from Haran to the land of Canaan followed established caravan routes. And further movements into the Negeb and Egypt were along established routes, which suggests that the patriarch engaged in caravan trade with the peoples of his time. It is quite possible that his associations with Ur, which receive little emphasis in the Bible, were as incidental as his contacts with Egypt, and that the real ancestral roots of Abraham were in Aram. Thus, his most significant migration was probably to the land of Canaan from Haran.

Peoples of Aram.—About 1960 B.C. the great Neo-Sumerian period was brought to an end by invading Amorites. Pouring out of the semiarid fringes of the Arabian Desert, their shadow fell across the

Fertile Crescent and initiated a "dark age" in which the older, established cities and kingdoms fell. Subsequently, a semi-nomadic culture was imposed upon the ruins of the former civilization. But the Amorites were not a people without culture, because the great city of Mari on the Euphrates, south of Haran and north of Babylon, rose as the cultural center of northern Mesopotomia.

Before the reign of Hammurabi of Babylon (*ca.* 1728–1686 B.C.), Mari was the leading center of culture and political power in Mesopotamia. It was proba-bly during this period between the fall of the Neo-Sumerian kingdom (*ca.* 1960 B.C.) and the conquest of Mari by Ham-murabi (*ca.* 1700 B.C.) that Abraham lived in Aram and migrated to Canaan. Thus he belongs in some sense with the Amorite movements which penetrated Palestine in the nineteenth century B.C., and his racial stock probably should be traced back to a group within the Semitic Amorites.

Scattered throughout the northern area of the Fertile Crescent during the patriarchal period was a people called

the Hurrians. Their original home is to be sought in the region of Armenia. But by the time Mari became a flourishing city on the Euphrates, Hurrian influence in the region of Aram-Naharaim was considerable. In fact, the region around Haran became the center of the Mitanni Empire, in which the Hurrians were a dominant cultural element. However, the Mitanni Empire was formed after the patriarchal period and flourished during the fourteenth and fifteenth centuries B.C. The Hurrians were a non-Semitic people who mingled freely with the Amorites. They even exerted an influence upon the religion and language of the Amorites.

Another non-Semitic people, the Hittites, inhabited the central plateau of Asia Minor and extended their culture to the borders of Aram even in the patriarchal age. A Hittite king, Mursilis I, led an expedition through Aram into lower Mesopotamia about 1550 B.C. and captured the city of Babylon, bringing to an end the Old Babylonian Dynasty of which Hammurabi was the sixth king. During the time of Abraham the Hittites were not an international power, however, and contacts with them in the vicinity of Haran were only cultural.

The fact that Abraham mingled freely with both Hittites and Hurrians in the land of Canaan suggests that they were a cultural component of the land of his youth.

7. The law-code of Hammurabi. Upper part of the law-code of Hammurabi shows the king receiving the laws from the sun-god, Shamash, dating to the patriarchal period.

2
Canaan:

Land of Promise

Geographically, the land of Canaan was situated practically midway between the great river basins of the Tigris-Euphrates and the Nile. It was the natural causeway over which the armies of the Egyptians, Assyrians, and Babylonians passed in aggressive campaigns, the coveted object of their political and military strategy. Its northern and southern frontiers were virtually fortified outposts marking the boundaries of hostile neighbors, while on its eastern and western borders were the forbidding barriers of desert and sea. Through the central plateau region and the coastal plains ran the international trade routes connecting the fertile valleys of Egypt and Mesopotamia.

Accordingly, Canaan was not an isolated country. Instead of being in the backwaters of ancient affairs, it was located in the main currents of the world's life. The people who dwelt here, the least of all lands, were inseparably connected with the interests of Asia, Africa, and Europe. Their country became a buffer state between competing civilizations and dominant world powers. Indeed, all recurrent changes in Ca-

naan's political, religious, and economic history relate principally to this central and strategic geographical position. It was no-man's-land only in the loose sense that it was everybody's. Its neutrality meant nothing to overpowering enemies.

Early records, particularly those which come out of the early Babylonian and Tell el-Amarna eras, reveal Canaan as a helpless dependency, dominated by foreign interests. It was always subject to the peril of invasion. Hemmed in by the Syrian and Arabian deserts on the east, the Great Sea on the west, and by powerful neighbors on the north and south, it could ill afford to be aggressive in relations involving other peoples. As a consequence, the status of Canaan was never definitely fixed. The annals of the country are filled with dreary monotones of wars and rumors of wars, with menacing threats of oriental despots bent on conquest and spoil.

However, it is significant that the im-

8. Shechem. The great east gate at Shechem dating to the time of Joseph. The gate was destroyed about 1550 B.C.

portance of Canaan's world relations does not pertain, in the first instance, to its unequal contacts with domineering empires. Rather, it grows out of implications of the pronouncement made to Abraham in Ur of the Chaldees: "Get thee out of thy country . . . and come into the land which I shall shew thee" (Acts 7:3). Henceforth, in the light of that divine declaration, Canaan is regarded as "the Promised Land" or "the Land of Promise." It was invested with a significance altogether out of proportion to the position that it occupied as a small territorial unit in the political affairs of the ancient world. Accordingly, its subsequent history, properly regarded, is the record of a religious development which came to full realization in the mission of Abraham, the Hebrew. Although the Bible is not concerned primarily with the bare events of that record, it is of the utmost importance to know Canaan as the immediate background in which these events took place, from Abraham to the Christian era.

Territory Included

The territory embraced within the boundaries of patriarchal Canaan was practically coextensive with the area of modern Palestine. Ideally considered, Canaan extended from the River of Egypt (Wadi el-'Arish) to the "entrance of Hamath" (Num. 34:8), but actually that vast territory was never connected with the dominions of Israel except during the reign of Solomon. Strictly regarded, the land of Canaan had for its western border the Mediterranean from the Leontes to the River of Egypt; its eastern border was the Jordan Valley from the Hermon foothills to the lower reaches of the Dead Sea area. To the north were the highlands of Galilee, and on the south was the great Negeb or South Country, centering around the oasis of Kadesh-barnea.

The territory now designated Transjordan was not a definite part of patriarchal Canaan, although there is an implication in the Genesis account that the area would be included ultimately in the dominion of Israel. It is of interest to note in this connection that there is probably no record that Abraham ever traversed the country "beyond Jordan toward the sunrising." It is true that the descendants of the patriarch came into a larger inheritance, but to Abraham, Canaan was the narrow stretch of territory reaching from Dan to Beer-sheba, and from the Jordan to the Great Sea. This is the promised area referred to repeatedly in the records describing its conquest.

Relation to Highways

The route of Abraham from Ur of the Chaldees to the Aramean city of Haran in all likelihood followed the great international highway along the Euphrates. His journey from Haran into Canaan was probably made along the western extension of this ancient trade route by way of Carchemish. From Carchemish the modern road, with slight variation, runs in the same general direction as the old caravan trail, passing through the important centers of Aleppo, Hamath, Homs, and Damascus. While we may not claim positively that the itinerary of Abraham took in each of these cities (the Genesis narrative does not give specific details until the arrival in Canaan), yet we may propose the route with a high degree of probability. The highway is still there, following its ancient course.

Aleppo, the gate city of Syria and northern Mesopotamia, from time immemorial has been the converging point

9. Bethel. Stony ruins on the site of ancient Bethel, where Jacob lay with his head on a stone for a pillow and had a vision of the angels ascending and descending from heaven.

of numerous caravan routes. The ancient mounds of Hamath and Homs frown down on bustling communities which have neither the desire nor the fortitude to dig into their secrets of the ages. From Aleppo and "the entrance in at Hamath" recurrent traditions and landmarks indicate with pride various incidents associated with the trek of Abraham from Mesopotamia to Canaan. There is clear evidence of Damascene contacts in the reference to Eliezer of Damascus, the chief steward of Abraham's household who, before the promise and birth of Isaac, was regarded as the legal heir of the patriarch. At all events the journey of Abraham would have included Damascus, for all highways between East and West commenced and ended in this marvelous oasis of the Syrian desert.

The main trade route leading out of Damascus for Egypt goes through northern Galilee. It crosses the Jordan about two miles south of the Waters of Merom (now drained by the Israeli Government), almost due east of Hazor. From this point roads radiate into all sections of northern Canaan, particularly southwestward into the great Plain of Esdraelon and the valley of Jezreel. The great Canaanite fortresses of Jokneam, Ibleam, Taanach, and Megiddo lay in full view, disputing the passage of invaders headed for the interior of Canaan and the coastal plains.

The middle fork of the highway leaving the Plain of Esdraelon follows a comparatively straight course through Dothan, Samaria, Shechem, Bethel, Jerusalem, Hebron, and Beer-sheba. This branch thus cuts through the heart of the central plateau of Canaan. From Shechem, this route is certainly the way followed by the patriarch in his sojourning in the land of Canaan. The descent of

10. Oaks of Mamre. Ancient oaks growing on a site near Hebron.

Abraham into the kingdom of the Nile was made by the same roadway which crawls from Beer-sheba through the midst of the burning wastes of the desert and wilderness of Shur to the delta pastures of Goshen.

Corresponding to that international line of communication, both in age and importance, is the alternate route from Egypt to Mesopotamia. This one leaves the junction point near the borders of Lake Timsah and takes its course through the northwestern portion of the wilderness of Shur, joining the way of the land of the Philistines at Gaza. From the latter point, hugging the eastern coastline of the Mediterranean, it extends to the foothills of the Carmel range, where it abruptly turns to the northeast, entering the Plain of Esdraelon at Megiddo. The journey out of Esdraelon may be continued along the route already described, which leads across Galilee by way of Hazor to Damascus and the East. At Megiddo, however, there is a branch highway, the most important of all to ancient monarchs, which returns to the coastline through the maritime Plain of Acre, and extends to Tyre, Sidon, Beirut, the perilous pass at Dog River, Tripoli, Homs, Hamath, and Aleppo.

The eastern approaches to Canaan were no less important. Out of Damascus went a beaten trail paralleling the borders of the Syrian and Arabian deserts. This is the present Hedjaz Route which ends at Mecca, the most sacred shrine of Islam. Two branches of this famous highway lead into Canaan across the Jordan. The first, the northern road, leaves the main route about five miles north of Ramath-mizpeh, and from there it goes by way of Abila, Gadara, Beth-barah, and Beth-shan to Shechem. The second, or middle approach, comes by way of Jerash (Gerasa) or the more southerly route from Rabbath-Ammon to Es-Salt, then over the Jordan ford to Jericho.

In addition, other less conspicuous roads are contributory to these main lines. For example, the King's Highway, the thoroughfare of romantic name and association, which touched the southern borders of Canaan from the East by way of Ma'an, Petra, and Kadesh-barnea, joins at Lake Timash the International Highway and the way of the land of Shur into the Nile Valley. Finally, from Ma'an to the Gulf of Aqaba, then across the great wilderness of Paran, runs the oriental trail connecting Arabia and Egypt.

The Significance of Canaan's Central Position

From this summary, it is obvious that Canaan sustained vital connections with the major trade routes of the ancient world. Its intermediate position, its openness to bordering peoples, converted it into a kind of halfway house between the great river basins, thus making numerous contacts with other sections of the East inevitable. Many attempts have been made to set forth in an adequate manner this strategic situation. Situated midway between the two great empires of the ancient Oriental world, it was both the high road and the meeting place of the civilizations of Egypt and Babylonia. It was a "highway for the civilizations of other peoples," a "causeway," "harbor," "pasture," "field of the world," "battleground of nations," "a land of seclusion and opportunity," and, finally, "a bridge" which connected the extremes of the Old Testament world.

The figure of a land-bridge is used perhaps more frequently to describe Canaan in old world contacts, but its inadequacy is apparent. It may be granted at once that armies, caravans, migrations, and invasions have utilized Canaan as a bridge in international movements, but if that had been its only function the history of the country would have been entirely different. Its relations with outside peoples were never incidental, but inevitable. In the days of the patriarchs the country sustained vital connections with Babylonians, Amorites, Hittites, Egyptians, and Arameans, only to be touched by the powerful empires of Assyria, Persia, and Macedonia in subsequent centuries. In the last stages of its unequal struggles it was vanquished by the formidable hand of Rome.

Canaan was never simply passive. This land was unable to assume the role of an onlooker when invading hordes approached its borders; its position involved it in the maelstrom of world movements. Indeed, the country promised to Abraham was so related to the biblical world that it could never be wholly detached from the restlessness of the nations.

Situated at the crossroads of the ancient world, Canaan early became the melting pot of a variety of religious conceptions which based their chief appeal on the weakness of human nature. No cult hesitated to make commerce with vice. Baalim, Ashtaroth, Asherim, idols, altars, and sacred groves all combined to form the grossest aspects of an earthy religion that sought to minister to men's material needs at the expense of the spiritual. From the time of Abraham's first stop at Shechem, the sordid religious practices of the land of Canaan were a challenge to all moral and spiritual ideas of the God of Israel.

The geographical position of Canaan determined to a considerable extent its political status also. Lacking natural wealth and extensive space for habitation, it cringed in the midst of competing world powers which overran the territory almost at will. Canaan never enjoyed autonomy for any great length of time. Thus the rulers of the land developed great talent in intrigue and political subterfuge, because their existence depended upon maintaining alliances with the dominant powers that continually made Canaan the arena for military debate.

Amalgamation of races was a consequence of the central location of Canaan. Settlers were invited from every quarter, and many came uninvited. Indeed the racial makeup of the land had the name of legion. We are able to distinguish the Canaanites who dwelt in the lowland cities; the Amorites who settled in the central highlands; the Hittites who dealt with Abraham at Mamre; the Hurrians who are represented by the Jebusites in Jerusalem; the Hivites, Perizzites, and Girgashites who inhabited the land before the conquest by Joshua. Then there were the apparent newcomers to the land during the last half of the second millennium B.C. whom we know as the Habiru, from the Amarna tablets, and the Philistines and Hebrews known in the biblical narratives.

In Canaan, peoples who traveled in peace or with malicious intent came from north, south, east, and west and hammered out a social complexion which converted Canaan into an epitome of the larger world of which it was a vital part. It was in this environment that the biblical revelation came in a covenant with the Chosen People. We may perceive the wisdom of the divine counsels in planting this people in the midst of the nations, because it was a revelation ultimately for the uttermost parts of the earth.

3
Egypt:

House of Bondage

In the Vatican treasures salvaged from the ruins of the Old World there is a piece of sculpture by an unknown Alexandrian sculptor representing Egypt and the Nile. It is a statue of a giant around whose reclining form happy children are playing, and in whose hand are the ripened fruits of the Nile Valley. In the foreground appears the crest of the annual flood laden with alluvia from the south. Crouched before the great figure, with features expressive of confidence and satisfaction, is an androsphinx representing Egypt. The whole work is symbolic of the regard in which Egyptians of all ages have held their life-giving waters. It is also in complete harmony with the facts from a natural standpoint, for Egypt is the Nile.

If this famous watercourse were diverted from the land of the Pharaohs, within a short period all life would cease and the entire area would be reclaimed by the Arabian and Libyan deserts. Indeed, its bold course through the heart of burning sands is the perpetual emblem of its function to give and preserve life in the face of death. One of the strange enigmas of Egyptian scientific investigation, however, is found in the fact that, although there was such a vital connection between the Nile and Egypt, the ancient inhabitants sought no explanation as to the regularity with which the river rose and fell. But the absence of scientific inquiry did not imply indifference. It was sufficient that the waters did not fail, that the river-god Hapi did not forget to bring the season of inundation.

The Nile River System

Unlike the great Missouri-Mississippi river system whose headwaters are increased all along its course by numerous tributaries, large and small, the northern portion of the Nile River for fifteen hundred miles consists of one deep channel into which are brought the waters of northeastern and central equatorial Africa. One might think of the Nile from Atbara to Cairo as a great natural canal with no tributaries and no outlets except those artificially designed for irrigation. In the Sudan many small streams find

11. The great Pyramid of Cheops at Giza, Egypt.

their way into the Nile basin, flowing from the western and northern watersheds of the highlands. However, it is from the Abyssinian plateau that come the Baro, the Blue Nile, and the Atbara, the three principal tributaries of the Nile.

The northern portion of this mighty waterway is flanked by arid regions, beginning with the Sahara and Nubian deserts in the Sudan. Then come the Libyan and Arabian sands throughout upper, middle, and lower Egypt where everything is barren waste except the ribbon territory of the Nile Valley itself and the great delta section hugging the coasts of the Mediterranean. Rain in Egypt proper is extremely rare. Consequently the Nile receives no increase in its volume from any part of this territory; its only function is to distribute its waters as widely as possible either by flood, irrigation, or infiltration.

The main source of the Nile is Lake Victoria, a very large body of water located approximately 3° south of the equator within east longitude 30° and 35°. Abundant showers fall here practically throughout the year, causing the lake to receive a regular supply of water. From this tremendous reservoir the Nile, in turn, is given a comparatively constant amount of water which enables it to maintain a certain level throughout the year. In addition to Lake Victoria, there are other connecting lakes which also serve as vast storage basins for the Nile supply. But if the river had no other sources, floods would never occur in lower Egypt. All of these waters from the lake reservoirs, being practically free from alluvia, are of a grayish-green color, giving the southern half of the river the name of the White Nile.

As the Nile continues its flow northward through Sudan, it is joined by its three principal tributaries. The first of these, the Baro, has its source in the

Abyssinian highlands about 100 miles west of Addis Ababa. It is the smallest of the three streams and plays no prominent part in Nile changes. The second tributary, flowing clear and blue for 480 miles, comes from the region of Lake Tana in the Abyssinian uplands. In the plateau area this river is called the Abbai, but as it flows westward across the borders of the Egyptian Sudan it becomes the Blue Nile, the name being derived from the color of its waters. The junction point of these two rivers is a little south of Khartoum.

One hundred miles north of Khartum is found the mouth of the third main tributary of the Nile system, the Atbara. The sources of the Atbara are also in the plateau regions of Abyssinia in the immediate vicinity of Lake Tana. The Atbara is hardly more than a wadi (dry river bed) during the greater part of the year, but after the heavy May rains in the highlands of Abyssinia, the stream becomes a raging flood with a channel more than 1,800 feet wide. Its waters, laden with rich alluvial deposits, sweep on to northern or lower Egypt to fertilize as well as to irrigate. Here is one of the compensations of nature—from the fertile soil of Abyssinia (most of which produces two crops a year), from the rich silt of its forests, woodlands, prairies, steppes, and savannas there comes an annual renewal of soil for a country constantly menaced by the deserts. "For Egypt," says Herodotus, "is the gift of the Nile," and ultimately, one might add, of Abyssinia.

The White Nile, practically constant throughout the year, is joined by these upland waters of the Blue Nile and the Atbara to make the great Nile, which has no other tributary for the last 1,500 miles of its course to the Mediterranean. It is the inrushing of the Abyssinian flood-

12. The Great Sphinx at Giza, Egypt.

waters, through these tributaries, which constitutes the excess supply in the White Nile, thus creating the overflow which reaches the lowlands of Egypt during the summer and fall of every year. This periodic inundation begins in June and continues until the latter part of July when its increase becomes very rapid.

About the middle of September the Nile reaches a high level which it maintains for almost a month. Reinforced by the floods, late in arriving, the Nile suddenly increases to reach its crest. It is during September that the river attains its greatest height, when the whole valley is flooded with waters laden with richest detritus. The alluvial deposits are left throughout the lowlands thus effecting an annual renewal of the soil. During the month of December the Nile is once again within its normal channel, and the adjacent territory commences to dry out in preparation for seedtime and harvests.

The Nile Delta

At Cairo the Nile begins to spread out like a fan, the bulk of its waters going into two branches: the Rosetta, which empties near Alexandria; and the Damietta, which reaches the sea near Port Said, the Mediterranean end of the present Suez Canal. In addition to these two main branches, there are five other estuaries which traverse the whole of this lower portion of Egypt. The district enclosed within and lying adjacent to these river channels is called the delta, one of the most fertile parts of which is the land of Goshen, stretching northeast from Cairo and On.

The whole delta territory extends for almost 125 miles, north and south, its greatest width being about 115 miles. Built up by the accumulation of Nile silt, the delta was converted into a garden by the inhabitants of Lower Egypt and ultimately became the granary of the biblical world.

Political Divisions

Hand in hand with this production of fertile soil, the Nile also determined in large measure the southern boundary of ancient Egypt. Between Aswan and Khartoum there are six cataracts which serve to mark the limits of river traffic and communication. The Egyptians developed the sailing vessel quite early, and engaged in maritime business along the inland waterways. But they never sailed beyond the first cataract of Aswan in their traffic southward. The granite ledges over which the Nile floods rushed with slight impression constituted a natural and effective barrier against commerce. In like manner, the first cataract marked the usual southernmost limit of Egyptian political and social unity.

Ancient Egypt, accordingly, lay between Aswan and the delta, a strip of country approximately 675 miles in length, the fertile portion ranging from 2 to 30 miles in width. There were two great centers—Noph (Memphis) and No-Amon (Thebes), which alternated as capital cities of the dual kingdom. In the Old Testament, Egypt is called Mizraim, a term signifying the two lands or two divisions of the north and south. The rulers are designated Pharaohs, an official title conveying the idea of "The Great House." According to Manetho, an Egyptian court historian of the third century B.C., the unification of these two kingdoms was effected at a very early date and continued practically uninterrupted until the Roman conquest in 31 B.C. There is, of course, no division of the kingdom in modern periods, since the whole of the territory up to the Sudan is under one ruler whose capital is at Cairo.

Natural Barriers

In addition to these characteristic features of the Nile Valley, the lateral areas constituted an effective barrier against invasions from either the east or west. More forbidding than seas and mountains were the Libyan and Arabian deserts. The sands of Egypt constituted its bulwark. With the exception of the sporadic raids of Libyans, Nubians, and Ethiopians, Egypt's immediate danger was never in the territory adjacent to the Nile valley; its fortifications provided by nature on the east, west, and south were almost impregnable.

Toward the north, on the other hand, lay its weakness, that is, the approaches to the Sinaitic peninsula and the land of Canaan. Accordingly, the Pharaohs were not slow in throwing across this territory a line of artificial defenses, or "migdols," which disputed the advance of Asiatic invaders. In the immediate vicinity of these fortresses there were the storehouse-cities, or granaries, which held sufficient supplies for Egyptian garrisons and constituted their bases for expeditions into the north. Apart, however, from this particular northeastern area, Egypt was practically isolated.

The effect of this was to leave the Egyptians to apply themselves to their own problems and development. This they did until the regimes of the Eighteenth and Nineteenth Dynasties when ambitious rulers carried the Egyptians far beyond the Nile Delta in campaigns which reached even to the Euphrates. The imperial policies of Thutmosis III, Seti I, and Rameses II were successfully carried out, and affected a vast territory which was disjointed and cumbersome. In the long run, however, it was these campaigns which proved the undoing of Egypt. The empire of Egypt was unwieldy; the forces required to hold it intact drew heavily on the manpower of the kingdom. Most of all, these military aggressions provoked wars of retaliation on the part of the Mesopotamian rulers, who finally plundered the Egyptians and destroyed the Nile kingdom itself.

Egypt and the Old Testament

It is not within the scope of this work to canvass the military operations between Egypt and Mesopotamia, although they did have a bearing on the developments narrated in the Old Testament. It will be sufficient here to give a brief summary of events in Egypt relating to the Old Testament from the time of Joseph to the bondage under a "Pharaoh who knew not Joseph."

The story of Joseph who was sold into slavery by his jealous brothers is well known. He rose to be chief of the Egyptian royal household, and when famine in the land of Canaan drove his brethren to Egypt for bread, Joseph generously sent for the entire family to join him. Seventy persons of Joseph's kindred settled in the land of Goshen, the rich delta plain on the eastern frontier of lower (northern) Egypt.

With the death of Joseph, and the coming of a Pharaoh who "knew not Joseph," the Israelites were enslaved. The bondage of serving Egyptian taskmasters became increasingly oppressive until Moses was raised up as a deliverer by Yahweh, the God of Israel. The experience of deliverance from bondage in Egypt under the leadership of Moses imprinted itself indelibly upon the memory and religious consciousness of Israel. The Exodus became a spiritual as well as a physical deliverance which served as the heart of Old Testament faith. Egypt then provided the background for the most significant religious experience in Old Testament religion. Three important elements in this background are related to the biblical narratives in Genesis 37 through Exodus 12.

The Hyksos and Joseph.—According to Manetho, a priest of the temple of Heliopolis, Egypt was ruled during the Fifteenth and Sixteenth Dynasties by Hyksos kings who were Asiatics. He called them "shepherd kings," and his record of the devastation wrought by the invaders was preserved by Josephus.

The term Hyksos is now thought to be a corruption of an Egyptian expression meaning "ruler of a foreign land" or "rulers of foreign lands." It occurs in the Beni Hasan panel as a designation of Absha, the chief of a band of thirty-seven nomad metalsmiths who came peaceably into Egypt to sell their wares about 1900 B.C. Thus it was the name applied to Asiatics from Palestine who overwhelmed the defences of Egypt about 1720 B.C. with a revolutionary new weapon of war, the horse and chariot. A capital, Avaris, was established in the delta, and upper Egypt was placed under tribute.

Before the Hyksos were driven out of Egypt about 1570 B.C., a golden age of prosperity was brought to the land of Canaan through trade and cultural interchange. The Semitic kinsmen of the "shepherd kings" had freedom apparently to move freely from the region of Syria-Palestine into Egypt. Strongly fortified cities were built at Shechem and Jericho, and the country seems to have been organized into a city-state system. Canaanite culture in Palestine reached its zenith during the Hyksos period, but for the proud Egyptians it was a dark age of oppression by the hated foreigners.

Several lines of evidence suggest that Joseph went down into Egypt during the Hyksos period, probably about 1700 B.C. The biblical narratives indicate that the court of Pharaoh was near Goshen in the delta region (Gen. 46:28 ff.). The capital city of the Hyksos was Avaris,

northwest of the land of Goshen. Prior to the coming of the Hyksos, the Middle Kingdom had its capital at Thebes in Upper Egypt, and after the Hyksos were driven out, the capital was again established at Thebes. The Genesis narratives indirectly support the interpretation that Joseph went down into Egypt and rose to prominence at a time when possible Semitic kinsmen of his ruled the land from Avaris.

Another line of evidence that associates Joseph with the Hyksos is the statement in Exodus 12:40 that "the time that the children of Israel dwelt in Egypt was four hundred and thirty years" (ASV). If the Exodus occurred sometime about 1300 B.C., as many scholars now believe, the descent into Egypt 430 years earlier would date Joseph to the early part of the Hyksos period.

The land of Goshen.—Jacob and the kinsmen of Joseph were settled in the land of Goshen in Egypt (Gen. 46:26 ff.), and there they tended their flocks and herds (47:1). The name "Goshen" is not known from Egyptian records, but the region is generally understood to have been the area around the modern Wadi Tumilat in the eastern part of the Nile Delta. Wadi Tumilat is a narrow valley some forty miles long connecting the Nile Valley with Lake Timsah, now a part of the Suez Canal. Another name for the area in biblical times was probably "the land of Rameses" (v. 11), a name belonging to the time of Moses instead of Joseph, or "the field of Zoan" (Psalm 78:12), a name occurring in Egyptian records with reference to the Wadi Tumilat region.

The fields to the north of Wadi

13. The Land of Goshen. An irrigation wheel or pump operating in the fertile Nile delta region where the Israelites served a Pharoah who "knew not Joseph." The ox is blindfolded.

Tumilat are among the richest in Egypt, both in ancient and modern times. In 1838 the pioneer explorer Edward Robinson reported that more flocks and herds were to be found in that area than in any other part of Egypt. Also, he noted that the population was largely nomadic in character, moving about with their flocks and herds along the eastern fringes of the desert and into the rich delta plain. To the pastoral Hebrews, the land of Goshen was "the best of the land," and it was there they dwelt until Moses led them out of bondage some four centuries later.

The bondage in Egypt.—In the biblical narratives the enslavement of the Hebrews is attributed to a Pharaoh who "knew not Joseph" (Ex. 1:8). The implication here is that during the rule of Joseph, and for a period subsequent to his day, the liberties of the Hebrews were respected and that in the pursuit of their pastoral activities they were unmolested. The question then arises: who was the Pharaoh who placed the descendants of Joseph in bondage, and who was the Pharaoh of the Exodus?

Following the expulsion of the Hyksos about 1570 B.C., the great Eighteenth Dynasty of Egypt established its capital at Thebes, hundreds of miles up the Nile River from Goshen. An effort was made by the proud Egyptians to erase the humiliating memory of Hyksos domination. Inscriptions on monuments were erased, and royal lineage was traced back to the rulers of the Middle Kingdom, bypassing the Hyksos period as though it did not exist. We may infer that the wrath of the new kingdom would fall upon any people, especially non-Egyptians, who enjoyed favors from the despised Hyksos rulers. Quite likely the Hebrews were placed in bondage in the wake of this new nationalism. The aggressive new rulers saw that they could erase a threat to the new kingdom, secure

cheap slave labor for new building projects, and at the same time vent the wrath of injured national pride upon the hapless Israelites. Thus the people of Israel possibly felt the iron heel of oppression soon after 1570 B.C. By the time of the dramatic emergence of the powerful Eighteenth Dynasty upon the international scene, the kinsmen of Joseph were certainly groaning under the whips of the taskmasters of Egypt.

After Jacob went down into Egypt, the Bible is silent concerning the activities of the Israelites until near the end of the period of bondage. And even when it takes up the events leading to the Exodus, they are not related to persons specifically named in Egyptian history. The name of the Pharaoh who knew not Joseph is not given, and the Pharaoh who strove to prevent the children of Israel from leaving Egypt is not identified. Therefore, any identification of the Pharaoh of the Exodus would be based on indirect evidence.

We are told that the Hebrews were forced to build for Pharaoh certain store cities called "Pithom and Raamses" (v. 11). Pithom is a name possibly derived from *pr-Itm,* "house of Atum," the sun-god. It was probably a town in the Wadi Tumilat region, because two sites are pointed out today as ruins of Pithom. In the two sites, buildings of stone and brick were erected by Rameses, and there was a cult of the god Atum associated with the sites. "Raamses" probably designates the rebuilt site of Avaris which Rameses II made into a royal city and named after himself. A monument from Beth-shan in Palestine mentions the royal buildings at Raamses, or Rameses. There was no city of Rameses before the Nineteenth Dynasty came to power about 1300 B.C. The store cities Pithom and Raamses suggest that Rameses II of the Nineteenth Dynasty was the Pharaoh of the Exodus.

Furthermore, the account of the birth and preservation of Moses (Ex. 2:1–10) and the accounts of visits to the court of Pharaoh by Moses (chaps. 5–12) suggest that the royal household was in the delta region near Goshen. The Nineteenth Dynasty was the first to build a capital in the delta since the Hyksos period. And the capital was then located on the site of Avaris, renamed Rameses. It would seem that Rameses II, who engaged in extensive building projects with the use of slave labor, and who built his capital at the edge of the land of Goshen, would be the most likely candidate for the Pharaoh of the Exodus.

4

The Great Wilderness:

Land of Refuge and Wandering

Deeply embedded in the historical narratives of the Old Testament is found the account of centuries of humiliating bondage visited upon the sons of Jacob in the land of the Pharaohs. Inseparably connected with those records is the memory of a great deliverance at the Red Sea—an event unparalleled in the experiences of any other people. This occasion was followed by a series of miraculous interventions to preserve the Hebrews through a period of forty years of wilderness wanderings and, finally, to conduct them into the land of Canaan.

We now turn to the problem of the route followed by the Hebrews in the crossing of the Red Sea and the march through that "great and terrible wilderness." This would include information relating to the general background of the Exodus from the departure out of Egypt until the arrival in the Plains of Moab. However, it is not necessary that one engage in an effort to determine specific sites or places, the exact locations of which will probably never be known, nor, on the other hand, to labor under the obsession that where so little is known nothing can be certain. This is

an extremely difficult field where probabilities rather than exactness must play a large part. For convenient study the various regions are presented in the order of their occurrence.

The Red Sea

While Egypt lay under the last and most terrible of the plagues, the children of Israel left the land of Goshen and began the initial stages of their journey out of the land of bondage. According to the account in Exodus 12 to 14, the Israelites journeyed from "Rameses to Succoth" (12:37) and from there to "Etham, in the edge of the wilderness" (13:20). Then, they encamped "before Pi-ha-hiroth, between Migdol and the sea, over against Baal-zephon" (14:2). At this point the Egyptians caught up with the fleeing Israelites and deployed forces which trapped them with their backs to the sea. But the children of Israel were delivered from the army of Pharaoh when the waters of the sea were swept back by a strong east wind which blew all night (v. 21) and enabled the Israelites to walk across to the safety of the wilderness of Shur. The Egyptian

36

chariots failed to negotiate their way through the sea (v. 25), and Israel was delivered from danger when the returning waters overwhelmed the pursuing forces in the sea (v. 27 f.).

Most of the place names associated with the journey to the Red Sea and the site of the crossing are imprecise, and archaeological evidence from places excavated in the region does not provide adequate information. The word succoth (12:37), which means "the tabernacles," is often used as a place name. Likewise, Etham (13:20) derives from an Egyptian word meaning "wall" or "fortification," and is a general term. Pi-ha-hiroth (14:2) can mean "house of marshes," a name suggesting a location in the marshy area north of the Gulf of

Suez, but this is imprecise as far as locating a specific place is concerned. Migdol is a general term for "fortification" or "tower" in biblical usage and may refer to any of a series of "migdols" built by the Egyptians along the course of the present Suez Canal to guard the eastern frontier of the land of Goshen. Baalzephon means "Baal of the north," referring probably to a shrine to the Baal of Canaan which must have been located on a route leading toward the land of Canaan.

The term Red Sea in Exodus 13:18 and 15:22 is vague in that the Hebrew term *yam suph* is more accurately translated "marshy sea" or "sea of waterplants." *Suph* can mean reeds, or marsh grass, or even seaweed as in the case of

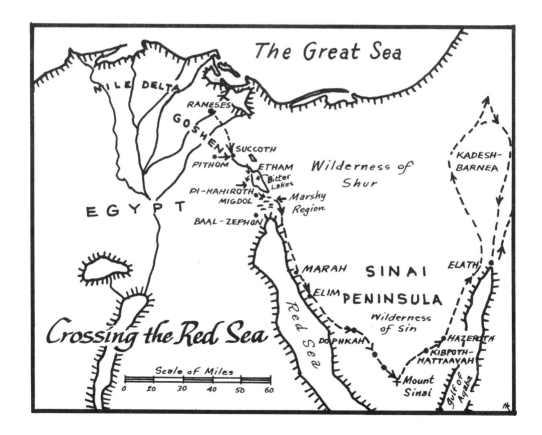

Jonah who said in his prayer from the belly of the fish, "The weeds [*suph*] were wrapped about my head" (Jonah 2:5). But the translation "sea of water-plants" does not settle all the problems of locating the site of the crossing by the children of Israel, although it does add some understanding to that provided by the place names along the route. The Bible knows the Gulf of Aqaba as *yam suph*. In the case of the Exodus crossing, *yam suph* could by itself mean the marshy area between Lake Timsah and the Gulf of Suez, or it could refer to the Gulf of Suez. The probable site of the crossing of the sea must be located in the light of combined evidence, and not on the evidence of *yam suph* alone.

The first stage of the journey, from "Rameses to Succoth" (12:37), probably was from the site of Rameses, capital of the Nineteenth Dynasty, to a place in the land of Goshen. Modern Tell el-Maskhutah is suggested as a possible location of Succoth, in the east central part of Goshen. Succoth was a rallying point from which the children of Israel would depart for the eastern trek out of Egypt. The decision there was to avoid the heavily traveled northern route along the Mediterranean coast (the way of the land of the Philistines, 13:17), because Egyptian border garrisons would challenge passage by the Israelites and there would be fighting. Thus, they struck out eastward toward the wilderness (desert) and encamped "in Etham, in the edge of the wilderness" (v. 20).

Apparently Etham was one of the Egyptian border strongholds, the ruins of which are known today along the ancient border from the lake area north of the Gulf of Suez to Pelusium on the

14. Oasis in the Wadi Gharandel, "The Wilderness," near Sinai. This may be Elim, where the Israelites stopped on the way to Sinai.

Mediterranean coast. The Hebrews did not challenge the border patrols at Etham. Instead, they turned back apparently to the southwest and encamped "before Pi-ha-hiroth, between Migdol and the sea" (14:2). This would be in the region of the Bitter Lakes which were connected in ancient times with the Gulf of Suez by a lagoon-like marshy region.

Pi-ha-hiroth and Migdol are places mentioned in Egyptian inscriptions, although the exact locations have not been identified. Likewise, Baal-zephon is known from a Phoenician letter, but its exact location is not certain. Nevertheless, these are definitely historical places which belong in the eastern frontier region of Egypt between the Gulf of Suez and Pelusium. When this is considered, along with the evidence that the children of Israel turned back from the fortified area and encamped in the vicinity of the marshy region (in front of Pi-ha-hiroth —Ex. 14:2), where the Egyptians would see no need for fortifications, the bearing of the Hebrew term "sea of water-plants" takes on significance. The biblical statement that a "strong east wind" blew all night and caused the waters to go back (v. 21) suggests strongly that the crossing was in the normally impassable shallows north of the Gulf of Suez, and either south of the Bitter Lakes or in the region south of Lake Timsah a little further to the north.

Delivered from the pursuing Egyptians, the children of Israel entered the wastes of the Desert of Shur and turned southwards toward Sinai.

The Wilderness of Shur

In the biblical narratives there are several general references to the wilderness of Shur, although none of them provides us with definite information concerning either its boundaries or its extent. It is probable, however, that the wilderness covered a considerably larger area than is usually assigned to it, certainly more than the little strip of seaboard at the northeastern corner of the Gulf of Suez. From the notice preserved in the Exodus account, we can infer the approximate position of the territory in relation to Egypt, since it is said that the children of Israel passed directly from the Red Sea into the wilderness. They journeyed through its desolate wastes for three days, probably going toward the south (15:22). This southern extension of Shur would, therefore, include Marah and Elim and, on the basis of Numbers 33:10-11, perhaps the camp by the sea also.

In general, then, we may regard the wilderness of Shur, at least in its middle and southern portions, as including the area in the vicinity of the eastern coasts of Lake Timsah and the Gulf of Suez as far as the traditional site of the camp by the sea. Its northern borders, on the other hand, are more difficult to define. Did the wilderness extend as far as the Mediterranean, to Pelusium and the adjacent territory of the Serbonian Bogs, through the lower borders of which ran the Way of the land of the Philistines? This is not altogether improbable, since the position of Shur is defined as being opposite Egypt on the way to Assyria. This means, of course, the great territory stretching from the Plain of Philistia to the Nile Valley, and lying between the River of Egypt (Wadi el-'Arish) and the Pelusiac branch of the Nile. Its eastern extension is merely hinted at in passages describing the journeys of Abraham and Hagar from Hebron, when both travelers are represented as being in the wilderness, on the way to Shur, between Kadesh (Ain Kadeis) and Egypt (Gen. 16:7,14; 20:1). It is likely that other portions of its eastern borders merged with the wilderness of Paran.

The foregoing description of the wilderness of Shur has been based entirely on scriptural passages referring to it. From Egyptian records regarding this particular area, however, we obtain additional information which enables us to interpret the significance of the wilderness in its relation to biblical backgrounds.

First, the whole of the western border of Shur, extending from the Pelusiac Branch of the Nile to the Gulf of Suez, constituted a menace to dwellers in the delta from earliest times. It was exposed to nomadic tribesmen who were continually being pushed from arid steppes and burning deserts toward the inviting fields of Goshen. As a consequence, this area became the camping territory of all invading hordes. Through this region the Asiatics, or Hyksos (the Hyksos were called "Asiatics" by the Egyptians), made the invasion which resulted in the subjugation of the delta and, later, the gradual conquest of upper Egypt. Apparently the center of the wilderness was near the headwaters of Lake Timsah, immediately opposite the Wadi Tumilat, the natural gateway to Egypt. All of the great international highways which reached Egypt from the extremes of Arabia, Mesopotamia, and Asia Minor converged here. These included the famous roadway from Elath on the Gulf of Petra in the hills of Edom; the way of Shur from Kadesh-barnea and Beer-sheba; and finally, the way of the land of the Philistines, the great way of the sea. Shur was accordingly a buffer region between the East and the West.

Second, the strategic position of the territory, plus the memories of disastrous invasions which had formerly come from this section, led Egyptian rulers to erect along their border a series of artificial

15. Mount Sinai. The traditional mountain of Moses in Sinai, viewed from a trail leading to its summit.

defenses. The main purpose of these barriers was to stop marauding hordes from the East.

In all probability, therefore, the wilderness of Shur derived its name primarily from the fortifications or "walls" which guarded the approaches to Egypt from Pelusium to the Gulf of Suez. This is evidenced by the fact that "migdols," or "towers," were built on the eastern borders of Egypt, from the vicinity of Lake Timsah to the neighborhood of Tahpanhes, for military purposes. It should be remembered that the so-called "storehouse cities," or granaries, were also located in this area, and that they were probably built as supply bases for Egyptian expeditionary and defensive forces. Finally, the word Etham is used synonymously with "Shur," a term definitely connected with an Egyptian fortress located on the eastern borders of Egypt in the region of Lake Timsah.

The Region of Sinai

The territory of the Sinai Peninsula proper is more definitely fixed than the wilderness of Shur, its exact position being between the Gulf of Aqaba on the east, the Gulf of Suez on the west, and the great wilderness of Paran on the north. During the flourishing years of some of the Egyptian dynasties, especially the Twelfth, Eighteenth, and Nineteenth, the peninsula was regarded as a vital part of the empire and a most valuable foreign possession. From numerous references to the region, we know that the Egyptians engaged in extensive mining operations in various parts of the country with great success. From these mines they obtained supplies of turquoise and copper. Also, from the highly developed quarries of the western area came the red granite and pink gneiss, used so extensively in Egyptian public buildings and sculpture.

The whole region has been explored many times. Most of the exploration reports conclude that the modern peninsular area is the same as that referred to in the biblical narratives about the Exodus and the wanderings of Israel. With few exceptions, its general divisions and boundaries may be reasonably indicated, although specific names and places are determined with more difficulty.

One problem is the specific location of Mount Sinai. In this case it is likely that the traditional view, which identifies Mount Sinai with Jebel Musa, will prevail. This view has a long and honorable history in Jewish and Christian thought. It meets all of the requirements indicated in the Old Testament, a condition of tremendous importance in determining the identification of any site.

The rival claim, which insists that there is not conclusive evidence for placing Mount Sinai in the Sinaitic peninsula, holds that the Hebrews left Egypt by the northern route to Kadesh (Ain Kadeis), and from Kadesh made a pilgrimage to Mount Sinai which was somewhere in or near Edom. This, however, seems untenable in the light of the biblical writing which places Horeb (Mount Sinai) eleven days journey from Kadesh-barnea by the way of Mount Seir (Deut. 1:2). Estimating a day's journey at 14 miles, the total distance from Kadesh to Sinai would be approximately 150 miles, which is the actual distance between the traditional Sinai and Kadesh on the borders of Edom. This early Hebrew source, plus the general implications of references in Exodus and Numbers in particular, provides a high degree of probability in favor of the traditional site.

In addition to this, however, there is

16. Wadi Feiran in Sinai, a part of the desolate route traveled by the Israelites on the way to Sinai.

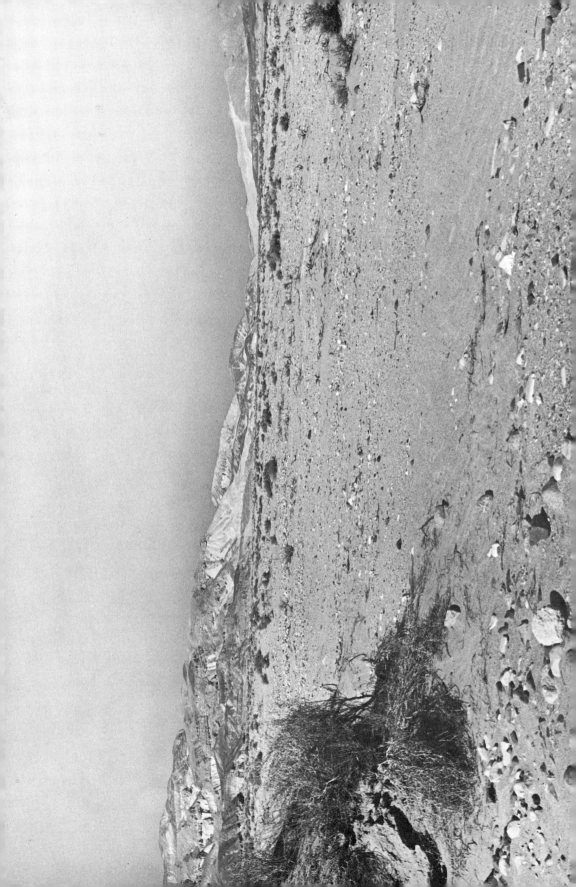

other evidence which carries weight in the determination of the locality of the sacred mount. For example, Josephus, whose testimony comes from the first Christian era, may be said to represent the current Jewish view as to the location of Sinai when he places it in the Sinai Peninsula. From the Christian standpoint, there is an unbroken tradition supporting this site which goes back to the fourth century, to Eusebius and Jerome. Finally, it is not without significance that practically all explorers, who have made intimate and exhaustive researches on the grounds, have been impressed with the correspondences between this region and the biblical references to the Sinaitic territory and to Mount Sinai.

Thus, while the location of the sacred area is not of the nature of a demonstrable proposition, there is a high degree of probability that the earliest traditions among Jews and Christians, now supported by scientific investigation, point to Mount Sinai or Jebel Musa in the peninsula of Sinai as the place where the covenant was made with Israel. Accepting, then, this territory as the area visited by the Hebrew refugees under Moses, we may distinguish the following sections: The wilderness of Sin (Ex. 16:1); the Oasis of Rephidim (Ex. 17:1); the wilderness of Sinai (Ex. 19:1); and Sinai, the Mount of God (Ex. 19:2 ff.).

The wilderness of Sin.—This section lay along the western borders of the peninsula, exactly opposite Mount Sinai, and extended north and south, probably a little lower than Elim, down to the tip end of the Sinaitic region. For the most part, it consisted of sandy wastes thrown broadside to the Gulf of Suez, with a few hills of inconsiderable elevation scattered through the plains. Toward the east, however, the piedmont section begins and gradually ascends to the mountain range heading up to the splendid peaks of the Sinaitic Jebel et-Tor, sixty miles to the southeast. The Hebrews reached this wilderness one month after their departure from Egypt.

It is likely that the camp by the sea was located in this section, near the present Wadi Taiyibeh (the goodly valley). There the foothills creep close to the coast and form such an attractive camping place that nomads, through the centuries, have continued to use it as one of the chief watering places between Egypt and Sinai. In the immediate vicinity of the wilderness of Sin, toward the northeast, were the ancient mining sites of the Egyptians. Located here were the mines at Serabit el-Khadim where many Semitic inscriptions have been found, some of which are dated as early as 1500 B.C. The presence of these mines on the way to Sinai has been used as an argument that the Hebrews would hardly have followed a route which thus exposed them to Egyptian garrisons and that, consequently, they made their Exodus from Egypt by a more northerly way. The objection is not a formidable one, however, since the garrisons were isolated outposts and would not have been able to obstruct the Hebrew advance (cf. Ex. 17:13).

The Oasis of Rephidim.—Strictly regarded, this is not a detached region but an integral part of the Sinaitic stronghold. It is only fifteen miles from Mount Sinai, and is the natural approach to the mountain from the northwest. The name Rephidim (meaning "refreshments") suggests the nature of the environment and echoes the remembrance of special provisions made for Israel at this point. Dotted with palms and tamarisks, the knolls and slopes

17. The desolate Negeb Desert between Kadesh-barnea and Sinai.

around the oasis were once occupied by an ancient monastery. Its purling brook, only a few inches in depth, still runs cool, clear, and refreshing. It was in this vale that the Amalekites, nomad tribesmen of the great wilderness of Paran to the north, disputed the advance of the Hebrews, and Israel won its first battle in the open field (vv. 8–16).

The wilderness of Sinai.—This area need not be restricted to the southern portion of the Sinaitic peninsula, since it is probable that it included all of the surrounding territory of which Mount Sinai was the center. It is, of course, in the heart of a mountain region whose physical characteristics include outstanding peaks, low-lying hills, vales and ravines, innumerable wadies, with adjacent valleys quite sufficient to accommodate the Hebrew refugees who camped in the region for almost a year. The whole situation is one of awful ruggedness, and yet of unsurpassed splendor. Adequate water supplies are to be found in the neighborhood of Jebel Musa. Several streams of running water are fed by springs, and numerous wells have been dug in the mountainous district. The wilderness of Sinai thus provided a safe place of refuge and supplies of food and water while Moses regrouped and organized his unstable band of refugees.

Sinai, the Mount of God.—The traditional mount of God is Jebel Musa which stands with imposing grandeur in the midst of the Sinaitic wilderness. The mountain is 7,370 feet high. It does not stand alone but is one of a series of peaks whose majestic heights range from 4,000 to 8,550 feet. This group of mountains is called Jebel et-Tor by the Arabs, the term being a general description applied to any hill of considerable height. Although not the highest peak in the vicinity, Jebel Musa is the most conspicuous and imposing because of its position at the head of the broad plain which opens before it to the northwest. Every indication suggests the probability that it was here that God said to Moses, "Draw not nigh hither: put off thy shoes from off thy feet, for the place whereon thou standest is holy ground" (3:5). It was here, after the Exodus from Egypt, that "the glory of the Lord abode upon mount Sinai, and the cloud covered it six days: . . . And the sight of the glory of the Lord was like devouring fire on the top of the mount in the eyes of the children of Israel" (24:16–17).

Sinai, as a desert or a mountain, is referred to thirty-five times in the Old Testament narratives; in seventeen other passages the name Horeb is applied to the same mountain or territory. The terms are used interchangeably in Exodus and Deuteronomy, while the name Sinai is employed in the other books of the Pentateuch. It is evident that both terms refer to the same place. The view that the Mount of God was a part of the Seir range, located on the eastern or western borders of Edom, has little to commend it. Nor is there any proof that it was located somewhere in Midian, east of the Gulf of Aqaba. Furthermore, Deuteronomy makes identification with Mount Seir seem improbable, providing a definite statement as to its distance from that range (1:2).

Jewish and Christian traditions combine in support of this identification of Jebel Musa with Mount Sinai or Horeb. It should be stated, however, that from the distinctively Jewish standpoint, none of these traditions was ever framed with any purpose of investing Sinai with sanctity apart from the actual experiences of Israel. No proposal was ever made to convert it into a shrine for devout pil-

18. Wasteland at the south end of the Dead Sea near the probable location of Sodom and Gomorrah.

grimages, such as Mecca and other holy places, in spite of the fact that Sinai was the sacred mount of the Law and the covenant. It was no Mecca for Israel at any period, and one looks in vain for pilgrimages, apart from the extraordinary experiences of Elijah (1 Kings 19:8) and, perhaps, Saul of Tarsus (Gal. 1:17).

The Wilderness of Paran and Zin

The central and northeastern area embraces the wilderness of Paran (Desert et-Tih) and the wilderness of Zin. The whole territory might be regarded as the heart of the Sinaitic peninsula from a geographical standpoint, since it is the middle section. Its southern boundaries merge with the wilderness of Sinai, the western with the wilderness of Shur, and the northern with the Palestinian South Country. The eastern boundaries of this area are sharply marked by the Mount Seir range and the upper waters of the Gulf of Aqaba. It is practically coextensive with the western portion of Arabia Petraea. Within this area there are few subdivisions, only one of which is of any great significance, that is, the wilderness of Zin.

Biblical references bearing on the territory of Paran and Zin do not clearly differentiate their borders. From the narrative in Numbers 13:3,26 the spies were sent out from Kadesh in the wilderness of Paran, and after their visit to Canaan they returned to Kadesh to make a report. In Numbers 20:1, on the other hand, Kadesh is definitely described as in the wilderness of Zin (cf. Num. 27:14; 33:36; 34:4; Deut. 32:51). It is probable that Zin was a division of a larger area, the wilderness of Paran, which extended southwest of the Dead Sea to Mount Sinai along the western borders of Edom and the Gulf of Aqaba. It is a high plateau region composed chiefly of limestone formation and char-

acterized by almost interminable wastes, broken here and there by refreshing oases. Through the heart of this great desert runs the Haj Route from Cairo to Elath, an ancient highway connecting the Arabian peninsula with the Mesopotamian valley.

Over all this unattractive region roamed the rough Bedouin tribes of Amalek, Ishmael, Esau, and Midian. In particular, it was the range of the Amalekites who, because of unyielding hostility in disputing Israel's encampment at Rephidim, were doomed to destruction. Their somber story is told in the narratives of the Old Testament (Ex. 17:8,16; Judg. 7:12; 1 Sam. 14:48; 15; 27:8; 30:17). Here the nomadic clans of Ishmael and Esau wandered at will; here they still roam in open and unhindered spaces. Rugged sons of the desert, practically untamed, they never yielded to Egypt, and today they are largely a law unto themselves.

On leaving the wilderness of Sinai, it is likely that the Hebrews set out toward the northeast, following as closely as possible the coast line of the Gulf of Aqaba. This general direction is certainly called for by a passage in Numbers 33:35 ff., describing their arrival at Ezion-Geber at the northern end of the sea. From Ezion-Geber they turned to the north and northwest through the borders of Edom and the wilderness of Zin, arriving ultimately at Kadesh-barnea, one of the most attractive oases in the whole Desert of Paran.

The arrival of Israel at this oasis, forty miles south of Beer-sheba, was probably regarded as the last encampment preliminary to the final advance on Canaan and the Amorites. There is positive evidence

19. The Wadi Zered with Moab on the right and Edom to the left. The wadi flows into the south end of the Dead Sea.

in the mission of the spies that some form of invasion was contemplated from Kadesh-barnea. The biblical accounts portray the reasons why the southern offensive was never carried out, ascribing it not only to the adverse report of the spies but to the consequent unbelief of the people.

Kadesh-barnea was accordingly the sector where the forces of Israel were defeated by demoralization and not by force of arms. It was also the scene of another defeat, and one just as pathetic —the collapse of the commanding figure of Moses at the waters of Meribah in Kadesh. The hopes, aspirations, and almost superhuman struggles through forty years of leadership were blasted here by a momentary display of arrogance which permanently removed from the great lawgiver any possibility of entering Canaan. And, finally, it was here at Kadesh-barnea that a new nation was born to become heirs of the old promises made to Abraham, Isaac, and Jacob. This rebirth of Israel was accompanied by all the sacred memories of recent bondage, deliverance, and wanderings, but above all there was a new spirit as they moved forward once more to the Land of Promise in what was to be their final advance.

The Borders of Edom and Mount Seir

The eastern boundary of the great wilderness area was coextensive with the territory of Edom which lay immediately southeast of the Dead Sea, stretching south to the headwaters of the Gulf of Aqaba. The whole of this region, composed primarily of the massive and imposing range of Mount Seir, was the mountain fortress of the Edomites. It lay partly in the deep depression of the Arabah, or rift, extending from the Jordan Valley to the Gulf of Aqaba, with its watershed located practically in the middle portion. The depression on the west borders of Edom has the effect of accentuating the height of the Seir range, which varies in elevation from six hundred to approximately six thousand feet above sea level. On the eastern slopes, however, the country assumes more of the nature of a plateau which loses itself in the Arabian Desert. At the northwestern angle of Edom there is a plateau section which provides spacious pasture lands for nomadic tribesmen, and in the vicinity of which was the oasis of Kadesh-barnea.

During the Greco-Roman period, when the Edomites where driven from their strongholds by the Nabataeans, the whole southern portion of Palestine and the Negeb territory were occupied by the Edomites, and the name of Idumea applied to the area. The Edomites were, of course, closely related to the Israelites, tracing their direct line of descent from Esau, the son of Isaac and the father of Edom (Gen. 36:9). Perhaps it was the survival of the ancient feud between Esau and Jacob which led the Edomites to refuse flatly the request of Moses to allow the sons of Jacob to pass through their territory en route to Canaan. Blood relationship between these descendants of Isaac explains, too, the positive command that not a foot of Edom's soil was to be subdued: "Contend not with them; for I will not give you of their land, no, not so much as for the sole of the foot to tread on; because I have given mount Seir unto Esau for a possession" (Deut 2:5, ASV).

Israel's request for passage through Edom by way of the King's Highway was dispatched to the King of Edom from Kadesh. At the same time a similar petition was sent to the King of Moab whose territory was adjacent to Edom on the way to Canaan (Num. 20:14–16; Judg. 11:17). The refusal on the part of both peoples, Edomites and Moabites, together with the abandonment of any idea of an invasion of Canaan from Kadesh-barnea, explains fully the route now specified for Israel's advance:

Then we turned, and took our journey into the wilderness by the way to the Red Sea, as Jehovah spake unto me; and we compassed mount Seir many days. And Jehovah spake unto me, saying, Ye have compassed this mountain long enough: turn you northward (Deut. 2:1–3, ASV).

The topography of the country from Kadesh to the Arabah allows a natural approach to the foothills of Mount Seir at the very portals of Petra. The route of Israel, therefore, would have followed the Wadi as it inclines a little south of east but, in the vicinity of Petra and Mount Hor, abruptly turns to the south. It was at this point that Israel came into actual contact with the borders of Edom. Here they commenced to pass through the territory of their brothers, the Edomites, whom they had been commanded to leave alone. After the death of Aaron, the route of Israel continued toward the south until they came to the end of the Seir range near the Gulf of Aqaba. The open country was now before them. Swinging to the north, along the ancient King's Highway connecting Ezion-geber with Bozrah, Kerak, Dibon, and Damascus, the Hebrews once again turned their faces to the Land of Promise.

According to Numbers 33, Moses led the people northward at least part of the way in the Arabah (Valley). Past the mining center of Punon, they crossed eastward at the northern border of Edom to avoid traversing their land. Following the Zered Valley eastward, Moses again turned northward along the border of Moab and arrived "on the other side of the Arnon, which is in the wilderness, that cometh out of the border of the Amorites; for the Arnon is the border of Moab, between Moab and the Amorites" (Num. 21:13, ASV). Finally, from the Arnon the Israelites made their way to the top of Pisgah, where the Land of Promise lay before them.

5

A Geographical Survey
of Canaan

A view of Canaan from Mount Nebo constitutes a most beautiful and inspiring panorama. No doubt its impressiveness is heightened by the lights and shadows associated with the people of Israel, but the view itself is attractive and arresting. Topographical features, consisting of watercourses, hillsides, dales, and plains, are thrown together in a relatively limited field of vision to make a lasting impression. Perhaps in no other part of the world could one obtain a glimpse of such marked changes in landscape as are presented here within a distance of hardly one hundred miles.

A discriminating observer would be interested in noting the variations in topography as shown in high mountains and great depths, plateaus and valleys, foothills and rolling plains, snowcapped peaks and lowland pastures, sea of death and waters of life, trackless wilderness and desert sands, extensive fields and undulating seabeds, rocks and slime pits, abrupt precipices and deep ravines. But that is not all. If the observer were making his survey in early spring, overhead would appear the glory of Syrian skies, underneath a carpet of grass and flowers.

Indeed, in this view from the top of Nebo, nearly four thousand feet above the surface of the Dead Sea, one surveys a panorama in which earth, sea, and sky are joined to produce variety, beauty, and inspiration. In every direction there is the mark of difference; yet, over the whole, there hovers an abiding sameness: the lure of a land which through centuries has found expression in a people's hopes and struggles, "a goodly land flowing with milk and honey."

Although not as extensive as the rolling valleys of the Tigris-Euphrates area, nor as fertile as the delta in the region of Goshen, the land of Canaan gathers up into its picturesque landscape all of the imagery of Mesopotamia and Egypt. To this it also adds its own distinctive features. In a sense it is an epitome of the world, for there is hardly a characteristic of the earth's surface but that a limited correspondence might be found in Canaan. For this reason, perhaps, the land

20. The Jordan Valley, the Dead Sea, and the land of Canaan stretch away in the haze as seen from the summit of Mount Nebo.

has become a metaphor of human hopes and aspirations, a representation of unbroken rest after earthly struggles, a land of abiding peace and happiness before whose spiritual gateway rolls the river Jordan, the great divide.

But Canaan is more than a glorified ideal. On all the surface of its hills and plains are permanently recorded the historical experiences of a people who made it their home, whose agelong struggles in spiritual warfare have hallowed every foot of its soil. It is more than a promised land, more even than a land of promise: Canaan is the physical complement of the divine purpose announced first to Abraham and subsequently confirmed to his descendants. It is only when the land and the promise are properly equated that we get the real meaning of Canaan. Accordingly, as one looks into the heart of the country, he knows that his eyes are resting on holy ground. In his vision of those plains and tablelands one feels that something is suggested, not only of the depths of God's love, but of the height of his thoughts for the human race.

The earliest attempt to describe the general divisions of the land of Canaan is preserved for us in a passage in Deuteronomy, where Moses is pictured ascending Mount Nebo to view for the last time the Land of Promise. There was, perhaps, no thought on the part of the author that he was making the first contribution to biblical geographical backgrounds, but the remarkably condensed survey which he has given serves as a standard for all who would undertake to set forth the physical features of the land of Canaan.

Subsequent writers on biblical geography have made their distinctive contributions, but each has largely followed the biblical writer. There is variation in terminology when designating the several parts of the country, as might be expected, but in general the original outline has been preserved. This, however, was inevitable. If one is to treat Canaan as it is, there is no occasion to improvise new or arbitrary regions or zones. The topographical features of the land are well defined and call for natural separate divisions.

Thus viewed, the country has for its natural boundaries the Negeb and the River of Egypt (Wadi el-'Arish) on the south, the Mediterranean on the west, the river Leontes and Mount Hermon on the north, and the deep depression of the Jordan Valley on the east. The eastern range, practically coextensive with modern Transjordan, was not a part of early Canaan, although it was conquered by the Israelites and given to the tribes of Reuben, Gad, and East Manasseh. Subsequently it was identified with the affairs of the Northern Kingdom. Canaan properly lay between the Jordan and the Mediterranean, and from Dan to Beersheba, in length about 150 miles. Its greatest width, including the eastern plateau, was approximately 100 miles. Situated midway between the river basins of the Tigris-Euphrates and the Nile, Canaan formed a part of the Fertile Crescent, a narrow stretch of country extending from the southern section of Canaan through the coastlands of Syria, the valley of the Lebanons, and the three divisions of the Mesopotamian area (Aram, Akkad, and Sumer) to the headwaters of the Lower Sea (the Persian Gulf).

The physical features of the country call for five longitudinal divisions. Beginning with the Mediterranean seaboard and going eastward, these come as follows: the Maritime Plain, the Piedmont or Shephelah, the Western Plateau, the Jordan Valley, and the Eastern Plateau. In addition to these five distinct regions running north and south, there are two lateral zones which cut across the country westward: The Plain of Esdrae-

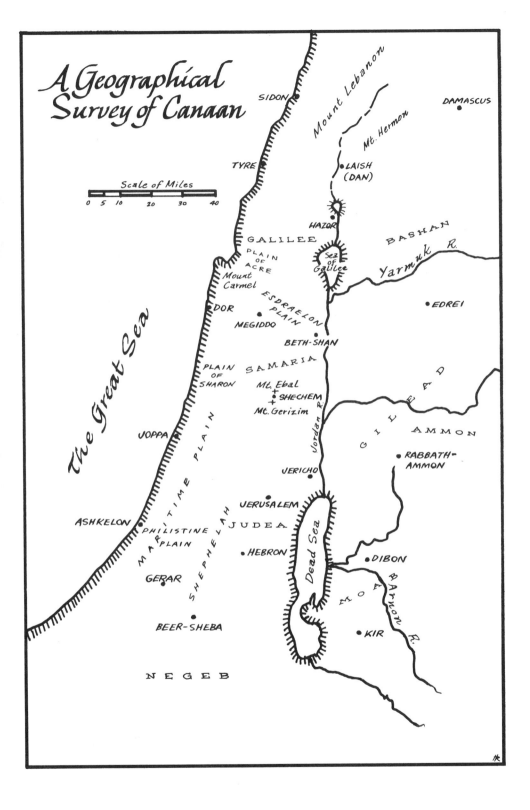

lon, from the Jordan Valley to the Mount Carmel range; and the Negeb, from the Arabah of the Dead Sea to the River of Egypt.

The Maritime Plain

The coastal region of Canaan extends from the River of Egypt at Rhinocolura, about forty miles southwest of Gaza, to the Ladder of Tyre (Ras en-Naqura), fifteen miles south of the city of Tyre. The length of this strip of land is 140 miles. The width, however, varies considerably, being merely a fringe of territory in the extreme northern portion. A few miles north of Carmel it broadens into a beautiful plain that reaches inland from 5 to 10 miles at various points. South of Carmel, the coastal region commences to cut into the interior, reaching its greatest breadth of a little more than 25 miles in the extreme southern portion. All of this coastal area was at one time a seabed. The soil is made up of a thin strip of sand dunes created by the northern currents of the Mediterranean from the coasts of Africa, but beyond this the soil is composed of the fertile deposits which, by erosion and other natural causes, have gradually increased at the expense of the plateau section. The interior of this maritime area from north to south offers a large part of the most desirable land in Canaan. The whole coastal region readily lends itself to a threefold division: the Plain of Philistia, the Plain of Sharon, and the Plain of Acre.

The Plain of Philistia.—This section begins at the boundary line of Canaan, the Wadi el-'Arish, and extends to the Nahr el-'Aujah, five miles north of Joppa. The distance between these two extremes is about seventy miles. The heart of the territory lies south of Joppa and includes Gaza and its vicinity, reaching a maximum breadth of about twenty-five miles between Gaza and Beer-sheba. The plain has a good watershed which

stands in the interior about five hundred feet above the sea. In this section are found several outstanding cities which flourished during the biblical period.

This plain is of special interest, however, because of its Philistine connections. It was in the most fertile portion of this area that the newcomers settled. Having overwhelmed the native Canaanites in their strongholds, and having organized the great Philistine Pentapolis, consisting of Gaza, Ashkelon, Ashdod, Gath, and Ekron, the Philistines dominated the area for a considerable period. They repeatedly threatened the independence of the Hebrews. The political importance of these five cities was doubtless heightened by their strategic position at the entrance into Canaan, but the agricultural possibilities of the Plain of Philistia gave them an economic prestige in addition.

Apart from the great triangular territory at the foothills of southern Galilee, there was no portion of Canaan which offered such promising acres as the Plain of Philistia. Also, there was no other section which was characterized by such natural advantages. Thus, it was inevitable that the people who held this section securely would also exercise a dominant influence over their neighbors. On the other hand, its natural exposure to the north and south, its openness to invading armies from Egypt and Syria, constituted its weakness. The Plain of Philistia was an inviting field for conquest, and it was so situated that no enemy could afford to leave it unsubjugated. As a consequence, Philistia was continually despoiled, and its people were gradually reduced to various amalgams. In spite of this weakness, or probably because of it, the primacy which nature gave to Philistia is still reflected in the name applied

21. The Plain of Sharon, near the head waters of the Yarkon River.

to the whole of Canaan—Palestine, the land of the Philistines.

The Plain of Sharon.—This section constitutes the second division of Canaan's coastal area. The southern boundary of Sharon is marked by the Nahr el-'Aujah, which empties into the Mediterranean near Joppa. Its northern part, if one includes the coast of Dor, extends to the foothills of the Carmel range which slowly bend to meet the sea at the modern city of Haifa. The length of the plain is fifty miles; its breadth varies from six to twelve miles. While the limits of the plain are sharply determined by these mountains on the north and east, the southern boundary is quite arbitrary, since there is no perceptible difference between the rolling plains of Philistia and Sharon at this point. It is even likely that Sharon was an integral part of the conquest effected by the alien Philistines and, during their ascendancy, was counted in the Plain of Philistia.

In the Old Testament period, however, the Plain of Sharon was clearly regarded as a separate region (cf. Isa. 65:10). Its attractiveness, for the most part, is just as pronounced as the country of the Philistines, although its fertility in the narrow coastal region of Dor is marred by the encroaching sand dunes and the rugged nature of the foothills of Carmel. The slope of the land is toward the west, the elevation ranging from sea level to five hundred feet above the Mediterranean. Sharon is amply supplied with water for, in addition to an annual precipitation of twenty-five inches, there is the runoff from the central highlands. This water slowly returns to the sea through several perennial streams in the lowlands, including the 'Aujah, Iskanderuneh, Mefjir, and Zerka.

The abundance of water in the Plain of Sharon converted the region into a most attractive place, providing luxuriant vegetation and extensive pasturage (cf. 1 Chron. 27:29). During the period of Philistine occupation, it is thought that much of Sharon consisted of forests and woodlands, although at present, aside from isolated palm trees and reforestation projects, the region is practically destitute of woods.

The Plain of Acre.—This area has its beginning at the foothills of the Carmel range, from which it extends along the coast for a distance of about twenty miles to the promontory of Ras en-Naqura, the Ladder of Tyre. The plain lies broadside to the hills of the Central Plateau, varying in breadth from two miles in the north to approximately ten miles in the southeastern section. Here it is separated from the interior by a narrow pass between the hills of Galilee and Carmel. Two small streams—the Nahr Namein and the ancient watercourse, the river Kishon, flow through the Plain of Acre, with their sources in the central section. As at other points along the Mediterranean coast, the sea has thrown up vast sand dunes which render a good deal of territory useless. Also, this condition obstructs the outlets of numerous small streams and creates water-soaked lands along the seaboard. However, the interior of the plain is very fertile, particularly the northern and southern portions where villages have flourished through all the centuries.

The whole area of Acre, plus a considerable part of Sharon south of Mount Carmel to Dor (Tantura), originally belonged to the Phoenicians, whose dominions were confined to the narrow littoral from Carmel to the mouth of the river Orontes in the north. The territory from the borders of Tyre and Sidon to Mount Carmel was assigned to Asher as a part of his possession, but Asher was never able to withstand successfully his more powerful neighbors and finally disappeared in a racial amalgamation.

Acre, Tyre, and Sidon never became Israelite cities, though they figured prominently in Phoenician affairs. Acre, located on the coast fifteen miles north of Mount Carmel, was not only the chief city of the Plain of Acre, but it was the strategic point into the interior of Canaan, and to the southern coastlands of Sharon and Philistia. Its importance is noted in the New Testament in connection with Ptolemais.

The Shore Line.—One other characteristic feature needs to be emphasized, that is, the straightness of the shore line of the Maritime Plain, and the consequent absence of natural harbors. If the interior of the coastal plains offered unusually attractive fields to farmers and shepherds, the inhospitable seaboard quickly discouraged maritime enterprises on the part of the coast dwellers. Canaan's western boundary, the Great Sea, remained practically impassable throughout the Hebrew period.

On the other hand, as one travels north along the Mediterranean seaboard he observes promising harbors at Tyre, Sidon, Beirut, Gebal, Tripoli, and many other less important places. Even in Egypt, Alexandria was not devoid of haven facilities, while Port Said is today one of the principal ports in the Mediterranean area. Apart, however, from the semblance of a harbor at Acre, and the artificial haven at Haifa involving a great expenditure of money and labor, there is hardly a recess along the whole coast of Canaan that offers a suitable place for port facilities.

Joppa, from earliest times the principal port of Jerusalem, does not have the natural characteristics of a haven, its roadstead being completely exposed to the Mediterranean. Although it is true that ancient seagoing vessels were much smaller than the modern ships and required less depth of water in making port calls, no ship would have been safe at Joppa and other open ports, unless beached. At Caesarea, the principal port of Jerusalem during the Herodian period, there were no natural features to offer safe moorings, nor was the port of Caesarea superior to that of Joppa.

Herod the Great, for political purposes, converted Caesarea (formerly known as Strato's Tower) into a beautiful Greco-Roman city, and invested it with great significance as an administrative center in the Roman provincial system. Thus rendered politically important, Caesarea quickly won the commercial prestige for which it had been prepared by the erection of an artificial harbor whose quays and wharves, though in ruins, are still visible. At the southern end of the seaboard stood Gaza, strategically located in the Plain of Philistia. It was the point of departure and arrival for all caravans moving east and west. But the importance of Gaza was not derived from its maritime advantages, which were negligible. Whatever port facilities the city might have enjoyed were nullified by deposits of sand brought by Mediterranean currents from the Nile and Africa.

As a consequence, the Hebrews made no ventures by the sea. As a rule, they were not the men who went down to the sea in ships, but rather they gave themselves to the less exacting pursuits of an agricultural and pastoral existence. Solomon's navies and his maritime interests were not on any great scale. Being limited to commercial activities, they were probably connected with the neighboring Phoenicians, the outstanding maritime people of the ancient world. To Israel, the coastal area became not only a boundary but a barrier, effectively restricting her material interests to the land of Canaan. With the passing of the centuries, however, her spiritual interests broke over the shore lines to the islands and mainlands of the Gentile world.

The Piedmont or Shephelah

Between the coastal plain and the higher plateau section west of Jerusalem are the low foothills of the Shephelah. This is a well-defined section, and it is mentioned in the Old Testament in many passages. The term Shephelah, or lowlands, is rendered variously in English versions, for example: "plain," "valley," "low country," "the vale." But in recent versions the word "lowlands" has been used consistently. The average height of these low hills ranges between five hundred and one thousand feet, although at a few points the elevation would be approximately fifteen hundred feet above the Mediterranean. The soil is not characterized by the rich loam found in the plains of Philistia and Sharon, nor by the abundance of moisture which marks the coastal region from Gaza to Mount Carmel.

The territory is peculiarly suited to olive cultivation, grapes, and pastoral activities. Considerable grain is grown in the Shephelah, especially in its valleys, but the broad fields of the plains are naturally better adapted to this aspect of agriculture. The whole area is very desirable. By virtue of its location midway between the plains and the plateau, it became debatable ground between the lowlanders and the highlanders. This was especially true during the early Israelite occupation, when Hebrews and Philistines struggled for its possession.

The general limits of the Shephelah are usually represented as being within the stretch of territory extending from the valley of Aijalon, five miles northwest of Jerusalem, to Debir in the extreme south. This area is inclosed by the

22. A crusader castle in the harbor of ancient Sidon, the city from which Jezebel came to Samaria during the time of Ahab.

lateral divisions of the Philistine plain and the Judean highlands. Its total length would be about fifty miles, that is, from Aijalon to Debir, while its width would never be more than a few miles. At no time did the Shephelah include the Plain of Philistia, nor was the term ever used to designate that plain in the Old Testament.

The valley of Aijalon.—Approaches to the southern and western part of the hill country led through the Shephelah. There are four very important passes, the northernmost of which is the valley of Aijalon. This historic approach figures largely in Israel's experiences from the beginning to the end of the conquests in Canaan. It is a natural gateway to Jerusalem from the Plain of Sharon and the Shephelah. Aijalon begins near Gibeon, five miles northwest of Jerusalem. By a series of descents, frequently abrupt and through narrow defiles, it issues in the lowlands at Lower Beth-horon, on the edge of Sharon. The valley was easily defended. Joshua's pursuit of the Canaanite confederates took place in this region, while centuries later Judas Maccabeus demonstrated here his superiority in mountain warfare in a series of victories over Syrian forces. As a strategic point in the defenses of Jerusalem, Aijalon was guarded with great care by the Hebrew rulers. Solomon erected fortresses at several crucial points in his territory, and in his scheme of national defense Lower Beth-horon, near Aijalon, was of prime importance.

The valley of Sorek.—The second approach to the hills of Judea through the Shephelah lies immediately west of Jerusalem and issues into the Plain of Philistia near the ancient cities of Gezer and Ekron. It is well known because of the exploits of Samson and the Philistines. The modern railroad from Lod to Jerusalem follows, in the main, this narrow valley to the tablelands by way of

Beth-shemesh, Zorah (the birthplace of Samson), Artuf, and Eshtaol. The vale of Sorek lies well within the territory of the Shephelah, and is one of its most fertile parts. Being open to the Philistine plains, it was also strategic.

The valley of Elah.—The third of these approaches to the central range is found in the valley of Elah. The head of this valley is a little south of Bethlehem, where it looks out upon the historic battlefields of Beth-zacharias on the open road to the city of Jerusalem. Its western extension passes the imposing mound of Zakariyeh, situated in the Shephelah, and issues in the undulating Plain of Philistia at Tell es-Safi (Libnah). The importance of this approach is readily seen. The situation of Libnah at the mouth of Elah constituted an imminent danger to the interior. In all probability Tell Zakariyeh is the ancient Azekah, in the vicinity of which Israel and the Philistines were encamped, and where David conquered Goliath. Azekah was converted into a fortress by Rehoboam, together with a number of other cities whose positions were vital in the defense of Jerusalem. The valley of Elah was, accordingly, a very important passage into the highlands. Although it was not as frequently used as the valley of Aijalon, it was the most logical approach to Jerusalem from the maritime plains.

The valley of Zephathah.—In the vicinity of Beit Jibrin a fourth approach, the valley of Zephathah, has its beginning. Being considerably removed from Jerusalem, it played no active part in the city's defenses, although it did constitute a possible source of danger. To approach the heart of Judea by this passage involved not only the conquest of Hebron

23. The ruins of Lachish, located at the edge of the Shephelah, southwest of the hill country of Judah.

but the fortress of Beth-zur which guarded the highroad to Jerusalem.

It was inevitable that the people who fortified and held these four southern passes would control the highlands of central Canaan. Likewise, it was inevitable that the Shephelah, the immediate approach to these passes, would constitute disputed territory and a battlefield. The history of the region is a story of continual struggle, gathering around the names of Philistines, Hebrews, Greeks, Romans, and others who dared to invade the hill country of Judea, or conversely, to descend from the highlands in formidable attacks on the plainsmen.

The Western Plateau

The third great longitudinal division of Canaan is the Western Plateau, which stands intermediate between the coastal plains, the foothills, and the Jordan Valley. It is by far the most important section of the country in biblical interests, and is inseparably connected with every phase of its checkered history. As one surveys Canaan from the top of Mount Nebo, the western horizon is filled with a massive range of hills. With the exception of the broad plain at the foothills of Galilee, the range takes on the appearance of a great plateau, extending from the slopes of the Lebanons, slightly west of Dan, to Beer-sheba, 150 miles south.

In the southern portion of this highland area are the bulwarks of Judea; in the middle section, the more scattered hills of Samaria; and in the northern extension, the gradually ascending region of Galilee. Although regarded loosely as a compact area, the three divisions of the Western Plateau are essentially different in every aspect. The nearest general correspondence is found in the matter of elevation, which ranges from two thousand to four thousand feet above the Mediterranean. The topographical features vary, from the relatively compact tableland of Judea to the isolated hills of Samaria and the series of steppe elevations in Galilee. Accordingly, the Western Plateau must be studied in the light of its definite characteristics.

Galilee.—The northern portion of the Western Plateau forms the backbone of Galilee. In biblical times it was environed on the west by the coastal plains of Acre and Phoenicia, on the north by the river Leontes and the Lebanon ranges, on the east by the beautiful valley of the Jordan, and on the south by the rolling Plain of Esdraelon. Beginning from the Lebanon hills, the plateau descends to Esdraelon in a series of steppe formations composed of two divisions: upper Galilee, and lower Galilee.

In upper Galilee the hills, ranging from east to west, rise to high elevations, that is, 2,000 to 4,000 feet. These hills were heavily wooded in biblical times. In lower Galilee there is a series of long parallel ranges, all below 1,850 feet, with broad valleys between them. They cross from the plateau above Tiberias to the maritime Plains of Haifa and Acre. The whole region is well supplied with water, produced not only by an annual precipitation of 25 inches but by the heavy mountain dew and the unseen waters of Mount Hermon. As a consequence, the fertility of its tillable soil was proverbial, and constituted a standing challenge for restless neighbors bent on invasion.

The variety of its soil ranged from volcanic hills to alluvial plains, extensive fields to sloping hillsides, all of which offered unlimited opportunity for farmers and shepherds. Grains were grown in abundance; grapes, olives, and nuts were products of the soil of Canaan. Attractive in its agricultural and pastoral possiblities, and crisscrossed with highroads leading into all parts of Canaan, Transjordan, and Syria, Galilee was overrun

with foreign peoples. Their coming not only liberalized the religious prejudices of its population but produced a cosmopolitanism more pronounced than that of any other part of Canaan. Galilee had no closed doors; its approaches were inviting, open, and easily accessible.

Samaria.—The middle portion of the Western Plateau is made up of the broken hills and valleys of Samaria. Although not as accessible as the open highlands of Galilee, the Samaritan hill country was equally exposed to invasions, both commercial and military, and was just as inviting. Its sloping countryside and foothills offered grazing for herds and flocks, while its numerous glens, vales, and plains lured the agriculturist by granting rich rewards for his labor. It was in Samaria that the disciples at Jacob's well were commanded: "Lift up your eyes, and look on the fields, that they are white already unto harvest" (John 4:35, ASV).

There are two plains, or fields, of special importance within this section. First, there is the Plain of Dothan that surrounds the ancient site of Dothan, where Joseph was sold into bondage to Midianite merchants from the Transjordan country, and where much later Elisha was besieged and delivered. Second, there is the Plain of Moreh at the foothills of Ebal and Gerizim, the site of the old Shechem, where Abraham sojourned on his arrival in Canaan, and where the Samaritan woman was enlightened at the well of Jacob. The whole of this latter territory throbs with historic interest, from the days of the patriarchs and the conquests down to the modern Samaritan colony on the slopes of Gerizim. It was at Shechem that Israel was brought

24. The Esdraelon Plain, stretching away toward Mount Tabor and the hills of Galilee, in the distance, from Megiddo, in the foreground.

together to receive the farewell message of Joshua and the exhortation to faithfulness (Josh. 24:1 ff.). It was also at Shechem that Israel, assembling after the death of Solomon, received the royal announcement which created two kingdoms, Judah and Israel, and two kings, Rehoboam and Jeroboam (1 Kings 12:1 ff.).

Throughout its history Samaria acted the part of a liberalizing force in Hebrew affairs, thereby estranging itself from the strictly orthodox of Judea. Their open attitudes were the result of unobstructed communication and contacts with foreign peoples and influence, especially those of the Phoenician coastal region. Across its center and along its boarders went highroads to the East and the West. These afforded inevitable contacts and conflicts with alien cultures and interests. The result on Samaria was the weakening of its orthodox beliefs and, finally, the collapse of its faith. Calf worship at Bethel and Dan, Baal worship at Carmel, and other phenomena connected with Israel's religious life were encouraged by alien contacts. These activities far surpassed anything that ever occurred in Judea.

Judea.—The third division of the Western Plateau consists of the highlands of Judea. The extent of this tableland, beginning at Bethel and reaching to Beer-sheba, is approximately 60 miles. Its elevation ranges from 2,000 to 3,300 feet above the Mediterranean, attaining about 2,600 feet at Jerusalem and more than 3,300 feet at Hebron. A slow descent is made from the latter point until, south of Beer-sheba, the plateau sprawls out into the hot sands of the Negeb country. On its western border was the Shephelah area where the hills are lower than the highlands of Judea. From this

25. The hill of Samaria, where Omri built the Israelite capital.

territory Judea was approached by the four mountain passes already described. On the eastern side, however, the descent into the Jordan Valley is more precipitous. In this area is found one of earth's phenomenal depths, that is, the water line of the Dead Sea, lying 1,292 feet below the Mediterranean. From the headwaters of the Dead Sea to the Mount of Olives, 18 miles to the west, the line of elevation attains a maximum of 3,892 feet.

This extraordinary descent, or ascent, produced two important topographical results on the eastern borders of Judea. First, the rapid descent into the valley provided a natural playground for the heavy winter rains of the hill country. As the waters rushed down the steep slopes toward the Jordan, their channels were converted into deep gorges or ravines. Innumerable wadies, dry for the greater part of the year, were thereby created. The Wadi Kelt descends through one of these deep gorges to reach the Jordan near Jericho. Unlike other wilderness streams the Kelt is perennial, and is supposed to have been the watercourse by which the prophet Elijah rested. Second, the quick fall into the lowlands renders the entire plateau region inaccessible, unless approached by three passes leading out of the Plain of Jericho.

The first of these approaches is that which goes up from the Jordan region on the upper side of the Wadi Kelt and slightly to the northwest. It proceeds by way of the pass and city of Michmash to Ai and Bethel, where it reaches the high elevation of the plateau, ten miles north of Jerusalem. This was an old commercial route from the Jordan to the interior of Judea, and it figures prominently in Israel's later history, particularly in the struggles with the Philistines. Along this historic pass Joshua led the armies of Israel into the hill country.

The second of these strategic ap-

proaches to the highlands begins due
west of the ancient city of Jericho. It is
extremely difficult. Because of its numerous gorges and narrow defiles, this route
was practically impregnable. In a distance of approximately 18 miles from
Jericho to Jerusalem, the road maintains
an average grade of 190 feet per mile. No
invading army could possibly have succeeded in forcing the passage, if seriously
opposed. It was along this trail, fre-
quented by robbers, that Jesus laid the
scene of the story of the Good Samaritan.
Along this trail, now converted into a
Roman road, came the great pilgrim processions from Galilee to Jerusalem. The
building of this highway was quite an
engineering accomplishment. It was so
well made that the modern road follows
the old route for a considerable distance,
utilizing the ancient foundations. In case
of any emergency, caused by cloud burst
or other acts of nature, traffic is diverted
to the old Roman passage. By this approach, one comes to Bethany, then over
the eastern slopes of the Mount of Olives
to the city of Jerusalem.

Finally, the third route leading from
Jericho into the interior takes a more
southerly direction to make its point of
contact with the Kedron Valley in the
wilderness of Judea. There it turns to the
northwest to arrive at Jerusalem from
the south. The entire road is wild and
dangerous. It is also more precipitous
than the middle road to Judea. Thus, it
is seldom used. At the junction of the
Kedron, alternative approaches are
offered: (1) one route leads by way of
Bethlehem to Jerusalem, and (2) another makes a wider detour to include
the Oasis of Engedi, and then goes to the
city of Hebron, the highest point of the
southern plateau, eighteen miles from
Jerusalem.

The Judean highlands, although
difficult to approach, were not completely detached from the common interests of Canaan. Forbidding passes do
not necessarily mean inaccessibility.
Judea was neither unassailable nor un-
conquerable. The history of its principal
city, Jerusalem, is conclusive proof that
the whole region was always within reach
and near the heart of things. This was
certainly true after the city became a
hallowed religious center. The difficulties
of access were brushed aside by men of
violence who frequently sought to take
the territory by force.

The Jordan Valley

The fourth longitudinal division of
Canaan, the Jordan Valley, is one of the
most picturesque and fascinating areas
on the surface of the earth. Within a
short distance of only 150 miles the territory associated with this valley presents
the extremes of height and of depth.
Mount Hermon, standing at the head of
the Jordan Valley, gradually rises to the
elevation of 9,166 feet above the Mediterranean. At the southern end of the
Jordan system lies the Dead Sea, 46 miles
long and about 10 miles wide. The surface level is 1,292 feet below the Mediterranean, while the actual depth of the sea
adds approximately 1,300 feet to the depression.

Properly regarded, the Jordan Valley
includes not only all of this area through
which the Jordan flows both in its upper
and lower reaches, that is, from the
slopes of Mount Hermon in the north to
the depths of the Dead Sea in the south,
but the valley itself is a part of a greater
territory. In the late Pliocene age this
larger area was subjected to a tremendous upheaval of nature affecting the
whole of the Lebanon area, the land of
Canaan, and the country as far south as
the Gulf of Aqaba or Red Sea. It will be
of interest to look at the great depression
as a whole, beginning in the northern
part of Syria.

In the vicinity of Hamath on the

Orontes, the range of hills running parallel with the Mediterranean throughout Syria and Palestine is supplemented by another series of elevations slightly removed to the east. Strictly regarded, these two ranges constitute the Syrian Lebanons. The western range consists of the Lebanons proper, while the eastern series is called the Anti-Lebanons. The western range is marked by a few points of unusual elevations, such as at Kurnat es-Sauda, northwest of Baalbek, where the hills attain more than 11,000 feet, and at Jebel Sunnin where the height is 9,022 feet. The eastern range, on the other hand, is at first a series of low elevations, frequently broken off from the main ridge, but subsequently it takes on the appearance of a massive mountain and rises to the splendid heights of Mount Hermon, southwest of Damascus.

Between these parallel ranges lies an extensive region characterized throughout by great fertility but especially productive in the vicinity of Baalbek and Reyak. The beginning of this territory may be regarded as in the region of Hamath or, using the Old Testament geographical phrase, "the entrance of Hamath." The whole area is designated as the valley of the Lebanons, but it might just as appropriately be called the valley of the Leontes and Orontes, since the two rivers, flowing in opposite directions from the center of the country, water the entire territory. In the Greco-Roman period it was called Coele-Syria, or the "hollow area."

In the region of the Lebanons and the Anti-Lebanons, hills are seemingly thrown across the valley from east to west. Here the Leontes is diverted through a narrow ravine to find its outlet in the Mediterranean between Tyre and Sidon. Beyond Coele-Syria and the apparent junction of hills, the valley reappears to continue its course to the Dead Sea and the Gulf of Aqaba. From this point the depression is flanked on the east by the plateau of the Hauran, the long range of Transjordan highlands, the tablelands of Moab, and the Mount Seir range. The western extension includes the hill country of Galilee, the mountains of Samaria, and the steep bulwarks of Judea which gradually descend into the wastes of the South Country.

Between these mountains, tablelands, and plateaus south of Mount Hermon, the Jordan River takes its course. Following the basin of the great rift, the river hastens on by a series of rapid descents to reach the Dead Sea, from which there is no exit except by evaporation. The whole valley takes on the appearance of a great basin, gradually deepening until it reaches its lowest levels in the Dead Sea. From there it slowly ascends by way of the Arabah, south of the sea, to its watershed opposite the ancient city of Petra. It is probable that the entire basin, during the pluvial period, constituted a great inland sea extending north to Galilee. In the southern part of the valley, especially in the vicinity of Jericho, the entire floor of the depression resembles an old sea bottom, with fantastic marl formations appearing everywhere in a scene of desolation.

Although this great depression reaching from Hermon to the Dead Sea, and from the Dead Sea to the Gulf of Aqaba, is continuous, it does not have the same topographical features or geographical characteristics throughout. A closer study reveals that the area naturally divides itself into five distinct parts: (1) the upper Jordan Valley, or northern Arabah; (2) the Sea of Galilee; (3) the Ghor, or middle Arabah; (4) the Dead Sea; and (5) the southern Arabah. An examination of these divisions will set forth the principal characteristics of each.

The upper Jordan Valley.—This section, also referred to as northern Arabah,

begins along the western and southwestern slopes of the Hermon range and extends to sea level, a little south of the Waters of Merom (Lake Huleh). In the upper part of the valley are the three principal sources of the Jordan River. First, the Nahr Hasbani, which rises in the vicinity of Hasbeya on the western slope of Hermon, is the longest of the Jordan tributaries, but it has the least volume of water. Second, the Nahr Leddan takes its source at Tell el-Quadi (ancient Dan), gushing directly from the rocks in a stream about twelve feet wide and three feet deep. The third, the Nahr Baniyas, boils up from the southwestern ledges of Hermon at the old city and shrine of Pan. It is probable that Pan or Paneas (modern Baniyas) was the same as the Dan of the Old Testament. This is likely the site of Caesarea Philippi, the northernmost point of the ministry of Jesus. Of these three sources, the Leddan and Baniyas have always been considered the most important. Flowing down from the northwest is a fourth stream, the Nahr Bareighit, which has its source not far from the Leontes River.

These tributaries come together about five miles south of Tell el-Quadi, and from there they flow together for ten miles into the first of the inland lakes formed by the Jordan system. In the Old Testament this body of water is called the Waters of Merom. In the vicinity of Merom, Joshua won the decisive victory of his northern campaign against the Canaanite kings at Hazor (Josh. 11:1–9). It was not a very large lake, being only four miles long and three miles wide, and was very shallow. Its water level stood seven feet above the surface of the Mediterranean. The lake has been drained by the modern state of Israel, having constructed a canal immediately below its outlet which is almost on a level with the ocean. The northern approaches to Huleh offer some very desirable lands on the edges of the valley, but at the floor of the basin the earth in biblical times was converted into interminable marshes and water-soaked bogs, infested by malaria during the summer. In this region the papyrus plant flourished.

Over the whole scene of this upper Jordan area towers Mount Hermon. Then, as the Jordan emerges from Huleh, it begins a rapid descent through the narrow hills of Galilee, reaching the Sea of Galilee 20 miles to the south. The fall within this short distance is exactly 689 feet, an average of almost 35 feet per mile.

The Sea of Galilee.—This sea maintains a water level of 682 feet below the surface of the Mediterranean. It constitutes one of the most beautiful bodies of water on the earth's surface. The Sea of Galilee lies almost midway between the heights of Hermon and the depths of the Dead Sea. On the west are the volcanic hills of the central plateau, and on the east are the high tablelands of the Hauran and Gaulanitis. From the hills of Safad, 6 miles to the northwest and 2,750 feet above the Mediterranean, the view of Galilee is unsurpassed. The whole body of water can be seen. It resembles a pear in its shape, with the bulge to the northwest. The lake is 15 miles long. Its greatest width, from Magdala to the land of the Gerasenes, is about 8 miles. It is estimated that a maximum depth of about 750 feet is reached in the northern portion.

Although practically encircled by the hills and tablelands which leave only a fringe of seashore on the east and west, the open spaces to the northwest, northeast, and south make possible three long plains. A little to the northwest lies the Plain of Gennesaret, tucked away in a

26. The ruins of Hazor. Biblical Hazor stood on the mound in the center.

cove of Galilean hills. To the northeast, immediately south of Beth-saida beyond the Jordan, is an extensive plain which fulfils all of the requirements of the biblical narrative regarding the miraculous feeding of the multitudes (Mark 6:35 ff.). To the extreme south are the plains of the Jordan around the town of Semakh. At this point the valley of the Jordan is about four miles wide, but neither Semakh nor its plain is mentioned in the biblical narratives. In this vicinity stood Hippos and Gadara—two members of the Greek Decapolis.

On the northern borders of the lake there is more of a gradual slope to the heights of the Galilean mountains. The entire region is one of beauty, variety, and sharp contrasts. Just above the western coasts of the lake, the white and gray limestone cliffs and hills look down upon its surface. From the southern portion of this encircling wall come the hot waters from extinct volcanoes. The mineral springs near Tiberias, sought from earliest times, are still popular. On the eastern side, the hills creep back a short distance from the shores, then mount up to a plateau region covered with black basalt and diorite. In this area are found the fertile grain fields of the great Hauran, Gaulanitis, and Trachonitis.

Forty miles to the north, Mount Hermon, clad in its mantle of snow, dominates the whole landscape. Below, as a jewel in a setting of natural splendor, are the blue waters of the Sea of Galilee. It is a peaceful scene. One would hardly think that a body of water marked by such awe-inspiring grandeur could be lashed by sudden squalls and violent storms. Tempests, however, are of frequent occurrence, being made possible

27. Deir Alla, an ancient city mound which is a possible location of Succoth. The site is in the Jordan Valley east of the river.

by the openings in the surrounding hills through which rush the cool winds of the Mediterranean to displace the hot atmosphere hanging over the low surface of Galilee.

Around the shores of this historic lake centered the religious, social, political, and commercial life of Galilee. As early as the Old Testament period, Galilee was the circle of the nations (Isa. 9:1), placed straight across the path of all Old World relations. In the early part of the first Christian century, when Jesus and the disciples ministered to city, village, and country, the area witnessed a bustling activity unmatched in any other section of Palestine. The Sea of Galilee was in the center of the territory.

The Ghor.—This section of the Jordan Valley, also called middle Arabah, extends from the Sea of Galilee to the headwaters of the Dead Sea. The distance is approximately 60 miles in a straight line, though the course of the river Jordan, obstructed by innumerable objects, zigzags over 100 miles before it reaches the Dead Sea. The current of the Jordan increases its momentum upon leaving the Sea of Galilee and is converted into a raging torrent in flood season. The fall from Galilee to the Dead Sea is 610 feet, an average descent of 10 feet per mile. The force of the flood is so strong that a vast amount of alluvial deposit is displaced and carried south to form the Jordan delta at the northern end of the Dead Sea. As a consequence of this displacement, the narrow channel of the Jordan is constantly being deepened by the surging waters.

The average width of the Jordan is from 90 to 100 feet, but during the flood season it is considerably extended. To this enlarged flood bed of the river the Arabs apply the name "Zor." The Zor is probably the same as the Old Testament reference to the "swelling" of the Jordan. This floor of the Jordan system, including both the regular and the enlarged river bed, is a part of a wider area which extends from Galilee to the Dead Sea, and from the foothills of the Western Plateau to those of the Eastern. To all of this valley area the name of the Ghor is applied, the meaning of which is "the rift," "the depression," or "the fault." It is actually a great natural ditch, lying between two massive, bulging mountain ranges which hang over it or recede from it at various points.

Immediately south of the Sea of Galilee the Ghor, or Jordan rift, is about four miles wide. In the region of Beth-shan the valley widens to about seven miles. Fifteen miles south of Beth-shan the parallel mountain ranges come closer together, thus infringing on the valley and converting it into a strip from two to three miles wide. After this, the hills pull apart once again and the valley widens, until at Jericho it reaches about fourteen miles in extent.

Climatic conditions in this belt are not the most desirable. Temperatures ranges from 104° to 118° in the summer. The unsusually high humidity has a most debilitating and enervating effect on the inhabitants. It has not been a region that attracts the founding of numerous, or even great cities, though from earliest records we find mentioned a few important centers, such as Jericho, Adam, Zorah, Sodom, and Gomorrah. It is generally recognized that promising agricultural possibilities are present here, especially in the northern and central sections of the valley.

The Dead Sea.—The fourth division of the Jordan Valley is the Dead Sea. It is the largest inland lake of the Jordan system and, perhaps, the most valuable. The Dead Sea is sometimes characterized as a concentrated remnant of an old ocean. Its total length is 46 miles, its widest point 10 miles, and its maximum depth 1,300 feet. In all probability the

shoreline of the Sea has contracted to a considerable extent, having at one time penetrated the valley area many miles up the Jordan. This delta, of course, has been formed by the heavy alluvial deposits of the Jordan, brought down from the upper regions. In the extreme south, the Dead Sea, varying in depth from 6 to 18 feet, spreads out over a large area of saline marshes, perhaps the "slime pits" of the scriptural narratives (Gen. 14:10). In the north and northeast portions, the floor of the sea is reached at tremendous depths.

The water of the Dead Sea holds about 26 per cent of solids in solution, or almost five times as much as the water of the ocean. These consist of chlorides, bromides, and sulphates. The highest percentage is that of chloride of magnesium, followed by sodium, calcium, potassium, bromide of potassium, and sulphate of lime. In addition to these, however, other solids such as manganese, aluminum, ammonium, iron, and nitrogenous organic matter are found. The excessive saltness of the water of the Dead Sea is due principally to two causes: (1) the salt cliffs of Jebel Usdum, along the southwestern shores, have probably added immense amounts of fossil salt to the sea; and (2) the streams flowing into the Dead Sea are impregnated with various chemicals, gathered from nitrous soils, sulphurous springs, bituminous matter, and petroleum deposits.

All of these deposits are brought together in the huge basin of the sea, and there they remain. Tremendous evaporation, estimated at from six to eight million tons, takes place every day, but no solids are lifted in this vapor from the caldron. The great density of the water of the Dead Sea gives it more buoyant force than that of any other body of water. No trace of life has been found in the Dead Sea. Its chemical wealth, however, is considerable. The actual process of extracting the vast wealth is negligible.

The Dead Sea is not mentioned in the New Testament. In the Old Testament, it is associated with various events. It was in this region that the allied kings of Mesopotamia won a decisive victory over the native rulers, forcing them into the slime pits (Gen. 14:1–10). Here were located Sodom and Gomorrah, the cities of the plain, whose sites have been variously assigned to the four corners of the Sea. It is thought by some that the cities of destruction are covered by the waters of the Dead Sea. Though their sites will probably remain a mystery, the descriptions in the Scriptures call for a location in the shallow area south of the Lisan Peninsula of the Dead Sea, near Mount Sodom, a seven hundred-foot cliff composed largely of salt.

Southern Arabah.—Immediately to the south of the Dead Sea begins the fifth division of the valley, the southern Arabah. The entire region is characterized by wastes and barrenness. Journeying southward from the Dead Sea, one is conscious of a gradual ascent. Almost due west of Petra the elevation reaches 723 feet above the surface of the Gulf of Aqaba. This is the watershed of the southern Arabah. The distance to the Dead Sea from this point is 65 miles, while it is 50 miles to the Gulf of Aqaba, making the total length of the depression south of the Dead Sea 115 miles. This broad, shallow valley is a land of stones, gravel, and sand, with only a few trickling springs—a lonesome, forbidding region where heat, dust, and the Bedouin rule supreme today as they have for thousands of years.

Across this desert pass came the Hebrew refugees from Mount Sinai to the Oasis of Kadesh-barnea, and by this way they retreated to the Gulf of Aqaba to strike the northern highways to Canaan. The fertility of the region is negligible on the whole, although along the slopes and at isolated oases limited crops are grown under great difficulty. To the west of the southern Arabah lies the wilderness of Paran; to the east, the Mount Seir range; to the south, the Gulf; to the northeast, the mountains of Moab; and to the northwest, the hot country of the Negeb.

The Eastern Plateau

The Eastern Plateau, which lies broadside to the great Jordan Valley, is practically coextensive with the modern state of Transjordan, whose capital is at Amman. In the Old Testament this territory is referred to as "the land beyond the Jordan eastward toward the sunrising," or by equivalent expressions. Although not regarded as a part of patriarchal Canaan, the area was subsequently conquered by the Hebrews in their Exodus from Egypt and settled by the tribal units of Reuben, Gad, and East Manasseh. Between these eastern tribes and their fellow settlers to the west of the deep valley, there flowed the Jordan River, a great natural dividing line. In time this river affected not only their interrelations but actually produced the disintegration of the eastern units. The history of this region is that of a detached area, subjected to alien and powerful influences from the beginning.

The earliest references describe the inhabitants of the northern portion of the plateau as Amorites, those on the eastern borders as Ammonites, and the southern dwellers as Moabites. The geographical locations of these Semitic groups are fairly well fixed. Offensive campaigns were mounted against Og of Bashan and Sihon of Heshbon, the two kings of the Amorites, who were strongly entrenched in the hills of this eastern tableland. On the other hand, the country immediately south of the river Jabbok and north of the Mount Seir range was apparently held by the Moabites.

Before the coming of Israel, the Amorites had succeeded in expelling the Moabites from part of their territory and confining them to the border south of the river Arnon (Deut. 3:8). With the defeat of Sihon at Jahaz (Deut. 2:32–34), this area passed to Israel (Reuben's territory), although it was recovered centuries afterwards by Mesha, king of Moab. It is necessary to hold in mind these historical points in order to understand geographical notices frequently misunderstood, for example, "the plains of Moab by the Jordan at Jericho" (Num. 36:13, ASV). The citation is understandable in view of the fact that this was the original territory of the Moabites. In general, then, during the Old Testament period there were three main divisions of the Eastern Plateau: (1) Bashan, the northern portion; (2) Gilead, the middle section, and (3) Moab, the southern part.

The territory of *Bashan,* in its widest application, included all of the tableland south of Mount Hermon to the river Yarmuk. It stretched from the Jordan Valley and the Sea of Galilee eastward to the present volcanic wastes of El Ledja, forty-five miles from the Jordan depression. Its elevation averages about two thousand feet above the Mediterranean. The entire region is of limestone formation and is covered with volcanic deposits. Its soil is very rich. From earliest times it has constituted one of the most attractive areas for farmers and herdsmen.

There are numerous references to Bashan in the Old Testament. The region was assigned to the half-tribe of Manasseh at the time of the conquest. Its principal cities were Golan (one of the cities of refuge), Edrei, and Ashteroth-karnaim. During the New Testament period, Bashan was subdivided into four parts: (1) Ituraea in the north; (2) Gaulanitis, or Jaulan, which stretched along the Jordan Valley from Hermon to the Yarmuk; (3) Hauran, or Auranitis, which was probably the large area east of the Jaulan; and (4) Batanaea, which extended from Gilead to the wastes of El Ledja. In all probability Trachonitis included the northeastern fringe of this Bashan area, although the bulk of its territory lay southwest of Damascus between Hermon and El Ledja.

Adjoining the area of Bashan, but south of the upper and lower courses of the Yarmuk River, was the territory of *Gilead,* referred to so many times in the Old Testament narratives. The natural southern boundary provided by the depression of the Jabbok River was disregarded in determining the limits of Gilead. As a consequence, its southern border was extended below the Jabbok to a natural break in the Eastern Plateau, almost directly west of Heshbon. From the Yarmuk to the Jabbok was upper Gilead, and from the Jabbok to Heshbon, lower Gilead. The eastern borders of Gilead were determined by the territory of Bashan on the northeast, and by the upper reaches of the Jabbok in the vicinity of Rabbath-ammon, which was in the region of the Ammonites. The territory is connected with numerous persons in the Scriptures, particularly with Jephthah, Elijah, Saul, and David. In general, Gilead consists of a massive mountain ranging from 2,000 to 2,500 feet above the Mediterranean. Because of its woodlands and watercourses, its rolling acres and unusual pastures, one can well understand the tribesmen's request to remain in this section of the conquered territory (Num. 32:1–5).

During the era of the New Testament

28. The hills of Gilead in Transjordan, home of Elijah.

this territory was extremely important, being practically coextensive with the region of Perea, except in its southern reaches. From the Yarmuk to the Arnon was the actual territory of Perea which was a part of the kingdom of Herod Antipas (4 B.C. to A.D. 37). In this area were some of the important cities of the Greek Decapolis, for example, Pella, Dion, Gadara, and Gerasa. In addition, Scythopolis (Beth-shan) and Philadelphia (Rabbath-ammon) were on its borders. Other centers of great importance flourished in Gilead from earliest times. The country was criss-crossed with roads during the Greco-Roman period. It was through this territory that the great pilgrim processions came down from Galilee to attend the religious feasts at Jerusalem, thus avoiding a passage through Samaria in the Western Plateau.

Moab stood at the southern end of this Eastern Plateau. In its original extent, it probably stretched from the Jabbok River to the southern end of the Dead Sea. However, after the successful invasion of the Amorites, Moab was confined to the area south of the Arnon, "for Arnon is the border of Moab, between Moab and the Amorites" (Num. 21:13). In the Old Testament it is necessary to distinguish the territory actually occupied by the Moabites, that is, the area south and southeast of the Arnon, and the area which formerly belonged to them, that is, the country extending from the northeastern end of the Dead Sea to the river Jabbok. It is a very desirable territory.

Unlike Gilead, which is comparatively broken into a series of rugged mountains and less extensive fields, Moab is practically compact, its elevation attaining over 3,000 feet above the Mediterranean. It spreads out into a wonderful tableland area which offers unusual opportunities for pastoral and agricultural pursuits.

Moab had a strong appeal for the tribes of Reuben and Gad, and later it became their possession. Although not as well watered as Gilead, Moab was far superior in its spreading fields. Here flourished the important cities of Heshbon, Medeba, Dibon, Bezer, Rabbath-Moab, Kir of Moab, and Aroer. Also here was Mount Nebo, from which Moses viewed the land of Canaan. The camp of the Israelites was here, until the advance over Jordan. From this territory, in later years, Naomi returned to Canaan, attended by Ruth the Moabitess. And, finally, it was here that John the Baptist was beheaded by Herod Antipas in the fortress of Machaerus, east of the Dead Sea.

The whole of this Eastern Plateau section, including Bashan, Gilead, and Moab, is more abundantly supplied with water than the Western Plateau. It is a land of perennial streams. Breaking forth from tablelands, hills, and valleys, all of them find their courses bending toward the great Jordan rift and the Dead Sea. Three of these mountain streams are of primary importance. The *Yarmuk,* six miles south of the Sea of Galilee, empties into the Jordan a great volume of water gathered from the uplands of ancient Bashan and northern Gilead.

Forty miles south of the Sea of Galilee, the river *Jabbok* finds its way through the Gilead highlands into the Jordan. This historic waterway has its principal source in the immediate vicinity of Rabbath-ammon, called "the city of waters" in the Old Testament. The course of the Jabbok from Rabbath-ammon is almost due north, but a little south of Jerash it turns abruptly to the west to follow the beautiful ravines and hollows to the Jordan Valley, which is about

29. The brook Jabbok, where Jacob wrestled with the angel.

twenty miles north of the Dead Sea.

The last of these Transjordan rivers, the *Arnon,* comes down from the highlands of Moab to empty into the Dead Sea west of Aroer and Dibon. The valleys of the Arnon constitute some of the world's most beautiful and spectacular scenery. At the western end, where the multicolored cliffs hang over the river and the sea at great height, the view is unsurpassed. The valley region is about 1,700 feet deep and 2 miles wide, while the actual floor of the river is only 120 feet wide. Up through this territory Israel came to meet the Amorites at Jahaz and, finally, to camp at Mount Nebo in the plains.

One other topographical feature of this Eastern Plateau—its eastern borders—remains to be mentioned. Beginning at Damascus, in the extreme north, and extending to the headwaters of the Gulf of Aqaba, in the south, the barren waste of the Syro-Arabian desert runs parallel with all the Transjordan country. This arid region of sand slopes almost imperceptibly from the Eastern Plateau toward the east. From the Jordan Valley to the deserts, the distance varies between thirty and eighty miles. One is hardly out of the fertile tablelands of Moab when he enters the parched country of the Arabian sands. The transition is sudden and almost phenomenal.

The Plain of Esdraelon

The sixth division of Canaan is the lateral strip crossing the Western Plateau from the slopes of Mount Carmel to the upper borders of the Jordan Valley at Beth-shan. The area extends towards the northwest and southeast, and is approxi-

30. The Esdraelon Plain viewed from Nazareth in Galilee. The Valley of Jezreel leads past Mount Gilboa at the upper right toward the Jordan Valley in the distance.

mately forty miles in length. This entire territory is included in the present-day Emek Jezreel, or Valley of Jezreel. In this designation the original limits of Jezreel have been greatly enlarged, while Esdraelon has disappeared altogether. We adopt here the early Hebrew conception which regarded the great plain as divided into two parts: (1) the Plain of Esdraelon, and (2) the Valley of Jezreel.

In the Old Testament, the great *Plain of Esdraelon* is also known as the Plain of Megiddo, the name being derived from the Canaanite city of Megiddo which dominated the territory in all directions. Properly regarded, Esdraelon is triangular in shape, its lines being roughly drawn from the following points: (1) Mount Tabor in the north, by way of the slopes of the hill of Moreh, to the foothills of Mount Gilboa; (2) from Gilboa to the base of Mount Carmel, where the low hills of Galilee form a narrow pass at the entrance to the Plain of Acre; and (3) from Carmel, by way of the southern Galilean steppes, to Mount Tabor. These lines, of course, are irregular, but in general they represent the limits of the plain. From Tabor to Gilboa, the distance is about fourteen miles; from Gilboa to Carmel, twenty-four miles; and from Carmel to Tabor, fourteen miles.

The area thus enclosed is justly regarded as one of the most beautiful plains in the world. In fertility, it compares most favorably with the delta sections of the Tigris-Euphrates, the Nile, and the Mississippi. In strategic importance, Esdraelon lay across the path of all approaches to central and southern Canaan from the north. Because of its position, it became the great battlefield of the nations. Here the great Thutmosis of Egypt triumphed, carrying off fabulous spoils from Megiddo; here, by the waters of Megiddo, the stars in their courses

fought against Sisera in the victory of Deborah and Barak (Judg. 5:1–31). It was in this place that Pharaoh Necho slew the young King Josiah who sought to block his passage to Carchemish (2 Kings 23:29–30; 2 Chron. 35:20), and here opposing armies continued to meet in decisive battles through succeeding centuries. The seer in Revelation pictures the final struggle between the forces of good and evil as occurring here in the Plain of Megiddo (Rev. 16:16).

The marvelous fertility of Esdraelon is due to the decomposition of volcanic deposits washed down from the surrounding hills through thousands of years, and to the basaltic subsoil which makes its appearance at points along the edges of the plain. The plain possesses an abundance of water which, during the winter, converts the interior into an almost impassable region. The watershed is reached about twenty-four miles from Mount Carmel, just a little northwest of ancient Jezreel. The water flowing west of this shed finds its way into two unimportant tributaries of the river Kishon which unite in the vicinity of Megiddo. Here the Kishon is greatly increased by copious springs. It finally reaches the Mediterranean through the Plain of Acre.

On the southern borders of Esdraelon were situated four Canaanite towns whose strategic positions enabled them, not only to cope successfully with northern and southern invaders from the great river basins of the Nile and the Tigris-Euphrates, but through many centuries to rob Israel of the full conquest of Canaan. These strongholds of Jokneam, Megiddo, Taanach, and Ibleam proved especially strong in their opposition to Issachar and Manasseh, whose tribal territory bordered and included the Plain of Esdraelon. Not until the period of David and Solomon were these fortified strongholds brought into subjection and converted into Israelite centers.

It is clear that the position of Esdraelon in the land of Canaan assured its possessors of a practical domination over the lower parts of the country. Through the heart of this territory passed all of the coastal caravan routes, the connecting highways between the Orient and the Levant. Esdraelon lay at the door of Canaan; once beyond its fortified outposts, the invader was virtually master of the land, particularly of its middle portion.

The *vale of Jezreel,* on the other hand, was not identified with the plain of Esdraelon by the early Hebrews but was regarded as an independent area. Its watershed lies slightly northwest of Jezreel, the descent from that point being toward the deep Jordan Valley. The vale of Jezreel is a narrow stretch of fertile depression, bordered by the slopes of Moreh and the hills of lower Galilee on the north, and by the Gilboa range on the south. Its total length is about fifteen miles. Beth-shan, the principal city of the area, is located at the eastern end of the valley. It is four miles from the Jordan, its elevation being 430 feet below the Mediterranean and 300 feet above the Jordan. Accordingly, the average fall of the vale of Jezreel is about 50 feet per mile.

Through this valley flows the Jalud, a perennial stream, which has its source at Harod, east of Jezreel, where a copious spring bursts out of the side of Mount Gilboa. This is the traditional place where Gideon and his men opposed the Midianites who were encamped on the other side of the valley. In winter the Jalud becomes a raging torrent, rapidly falling toward the Jordan. At the western entrance to the vale of Jezreel is the

31. Mount Tabor, from whose peak Barak came down to battle the chariots of Sisera in the plain below.

site of the old city of Jezreel (modern Zerin), the capital of Ahab and of Jezreel (1 Kings 18:45 f.). At this point, in all probability, stood Naboth's vineyard. The plain below gives us the picturesque setting of Jehu's wild ride up from the Jordan (2 Kings 9:15 f.).

Opposite Jezreel is the ancient village of Shunem on the slopes of the hill of Moreh. In this vicinity stood the camp of the Midianites, until overthrown by Gideon's men who came from Mount Gilboa (Judg. 7:1 f.). In later centuries, these identical positions were occupied by the Philistines and Israelites when Saul and Jonathan were defeated at the battle of Mount Gilboa. On the northeastern side of the hill of Moreh was the village of Endor where Saul visited the witch.

Finally, on the southeastern spur of the Gilboa mountain stood the powerful Canaanite city of Beth-shan, where Saul's armor was placed in the temple of the Ashtaroth and his body hung on the walls of the city until recovered by the men of Jabesh-gilead. It is clear, therefore, that through all the centuries, the valley of Jezreel was of strategic importance because of its commanding position in eastern and northern approaches to Canaan. As will be seen later, it was of special significance to the cities of the Decapolis on the eastern side of the Jordan.

The Negeb, or South Country

The Negeb territory begins at the southern extreme of the Western Plateau, where the hills of Judea commence to sprawl out into the rolling plains of the great wilderness. In its southern reaches the Negeb is practically barren. However, in the northern portion, with favorable early and later rains, fairly good grain crops can be grown.

Early biblical references to the territory indicate numerous settled communities disputing the advance of the Hebrews. It will be recalled that in this section several attacks were made against the Hebrews by the Amalekites, a people who inhabited the northern and northwestern portions of the wilderness of Paran. Indeed, it is likely that the Amalekites roamed throughout the Negeb territory in search of livelihood. At present, the barrenness of the soil renders the territory practically desert, unless it is irrigated.

It is not known whether the climatic conditions characterizing the Negeb have undergone changes during the course of history. The whole region is arid today, but there is evidence that the marginal lands supported a considerable population during the patriarchal period, the reigns of the eighth- and seventh-century kings of Judah, and Greco-Roman times. Recent research indicates that past inhabitants were masters at using available water.

Whatever its potentialities or liabilities from an agricultural standpoint, the Negeb occupied a strategic position as a border territory of the land of Canaan. Bounded on the east by the difficult approaches of the southern Arabah, on the south by "the great and terrible wilderness" of Et Tih, or Paran, on the west by the desolate steppes of Shur, and on the northwest by the Plain of Philistia, the Negeb lay across the path to the hills of Judea. Desolate wastes and parched sands offer no encouragement to advancing armies or hordes. For this reason, invasions of southern Canaan never came by way of the Negeb to Beer-sheba, Hebron, and Jerusalem. Rather, they came by the easier and more inviting approaches through the coastal plains.

Two of the great highways of oriental communication passed along the borders of the Negeb, but these were principally the trade routes which have continued down to the modern era. An invasion of

Canaan through the Negeb would have been halted effectively by natural conditions. Through this territory, however, came Abraham in his journey from Bethel and from Egypt. Also in this region was Kadesh-barnea, the wilderness home of the Hebrews.

Apart from the natural protection which it afforded upper Canaan, the Negeb was of great importance in the economic life of the Hebrews. This elevated plateau, gradually rising to approximately three thousand feet above the Mediterranean and extending about seventy miles east and west, was more than a borderland. It contained deposits of copper and iron in its rugged sandstone cliffs which the more prosperous Hebrew kings, beginning with Solomon, mined and converted into profitable trade merchandise. Also the Negeb provided access to the only seaport outlet to south Arabia and the Far East at Aqaba. During the reign of Solomon, a fleet of merchant ships plied the Red Sea and brought wealth in trade from as far away as the east coast of Africa below the south coast of Arabia.

6
Conquests and Settlement in Canaan

The Israelites camped on the Plains of Moab east of the Jordan, opposite Jericho. Medeba and the territory north of the Arnon had been taken from the Amorites. Also the Transjordan regions of Gilead and Bashan were now under Israelite control. The strongholds of Og, king of Bashan, had been assaulted, and the decisive battle of the Transjordan had been won at Edrei. The new territory was given to Reuben, Gad, and Manasseh.

Joshua succeeded to the command of the Israelites after the death of Moses on Mount Nebo. Immediately plans were made for an advance across the Jordan and into the land of Canaan. In reconstructing the backgrounds of his military expeditions, our principal sources of information are the accounts preserved in the book of Joshua, chapters 2 to 12, where the conquest is described in terms of campaigns into the central and south hill country, and later to the north. The book of Judges pictures the conquest as more of an extended, piecemeal aggression which could have taken place over a century. It is likely that the sweeping campaigns described in the book of Joshua should be viewed as taking place over a considerable period of time, instead of being two or three blitz attacks in rapid succession.

The geographical areas involved in the conquest are best described within the framework of the campaigns of Joshua, and we will consider them in the following order: (1) the base of operations at Gilgal, (2) the southern campaign, (3) the northern campaign, (4) territory unconquered, (5) allotments and settlements in Canaan.

Base of Operations at Gilgal

The first encampment of the Israelites west of the Jordan was made at Gilgal, a site probably in the region of Khirbet el-Mefjir. In this region, referred to in the Old Testament as the plains of Jericho, the valley of the Jordan reaches its widest extent, the distance being fourteen miles from the foothills of Judea to the mountains of Moab.

We do not know how long the Hebrews remained at Gilgal, but evidently they derived from this territory adequate support. For all practical purposes the encampment became a permanent settlement. It was not only the base of operations against Jericho but also against the Amorite league at Gibeon and the Canaanite league at Hazor. It was the central point to and from which the forces of Joshua were continually in movement throughout their campaigns of subjugation. In particular, it was at Gilgal that Joshua received the wily ambassadors of the Hivites, who succeeded in making an alliance with Israel (Josh. 9:3–15).

The Southern Campaign

Jericho occupied a strategic position in the defenses of southern Canaan. It stood at the gateway of the three principal passes leading up from the Jordan Valley to the lower portion of the Central Plateau. Located about six miles from the Jordan, it was on the main highway connecting oriental trade routes from Gilead and Moab. Along this general route the forces of Israel advanced from the Plains of Moab, until they encamped at Gilgal in the plains of Jericho. Three miles west of Gilgal the imposing mound of Jericho could be seen. Before any advance could be made into the interior of the land, Jericho had to be conquered.

Very little remains today of the city which stood between the Israelites and the interior of Canaan. It was thought at one time that the brick walls of the city which fell before Joshua had been identified in excavations at the site. However, it is now known that the latest walls remaining on the ancient mound date at least two centuries before the time of Joshua. No walls of the city of Rahab, the harlot, can be found. The sole remains of the city that can be associated with Joshua are a fragment of a house wall, its small patch of floor, an oven, and a small pottery jug on the floor beside the wall. Also there is a possible building excavated by John Garstang

above the so-called "streak," a heavy layer of ashes and debris that accumulated between 1550–1400 B.C. when Jericho seems to have been unoccupied.

Erosion from wind and winter rains accounts for the disappearance of the city which sat on top of the high, steep-sided mound. The fact that almost all of the city eroded during the long centuries after Joshua captured it suggests that it was not as large a city as the Jericho of the time of Joseph. This also is reflected in the report of the spies, which mentions absolutely nothing of the impregnable nature of the city fortifications (Josh. 2:1–24).

The conquest of Jericho was only the first step in the destruction of Canaanite outposts. With one of the towns in ruins, however, the task appeared comparatively easy. Ai was selected as the next point of attack. The choice of Ai suggests that the Israelites proposed to reach the interior by the northern pass, rather than by the middle and southern approaches which were more difficult and more easily defended. The situation of Ai was accordingly pivotal in a network of fortified places protecting the interior. Its distance from Jericho is approximately fourteen miles. In the patriarchal narrative its position is given as east of Bethel, the exact distance between the two places being about two miles. Here on a mountain between Ai and Bethel, Abraham had pitched his camp after leaving Shechem, subsequently returning to the same place in company with Lot.

Ai was evidently a small town, judging from the small detachment of Israelites sent against it, but its situation imparted to it great importance. The narrative states that the first attack on Ai resulted in a complete rout of the Hebrew forces, the defeat being attributed to the sin of Achan. When the second assault was made a considerable body of men took

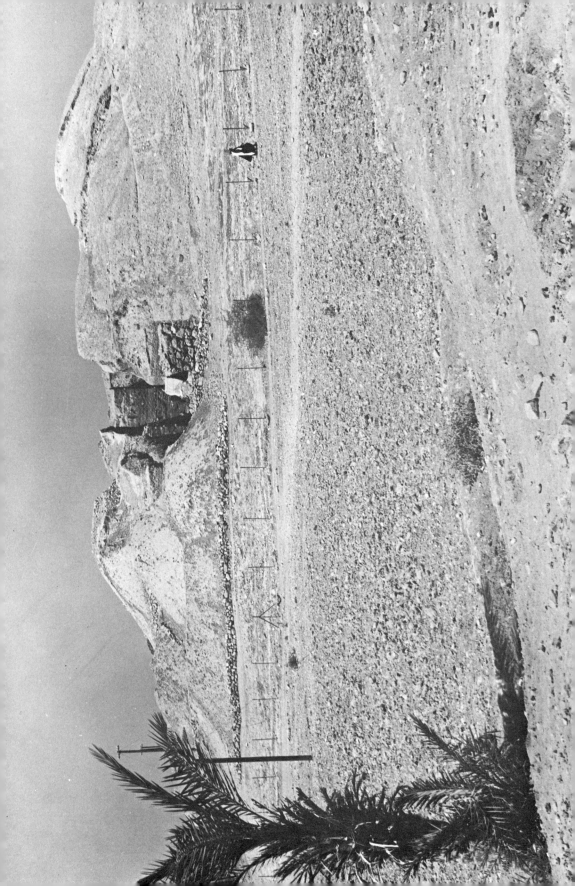

part. Now this increased attacking force is explained not only by the fact that different strategy was adopted, but the defenders themselves had been reinforced by the inhabitants of Bethel. It is clear that the people of Bethel saw in the capture of Ai a menace to their own independence. It is possible that Ai was little more than an outpost of Bethel. If, however, Joshua followed up his victory at Ai by a forward movement into the interior and destroyed Bethel, there is no reference to it in the biblical account. There is archaeological evidence, on the other hand, that Bethel did fall to the invading Israelites. The original Amorite city was called Luz, and it stood practically on the site occupied by the modern village of Beitin, ten miles north of Jerusalem.

The Hivite league.—Instead of following up the victory at Ai, there was an apparent lull in the southern campaign, during which time Israel tarried at Gilgal. The report on Jericho and Ai had come to the ears of all the neighboring peoples, especially to the Hivites, who stood next to Ai and Bethel in the line of Hebrew advance. They were quick to sense the situation and decided on a policy of deception to avoid struggle with the Hebrews. Their bold stratagem succeeded only in preserving the cities from attack. At one stroke, Israel found herself in an offensive and defensive alliance with four of the principal cities of the central plateau, that is, Gibeon, Beeroth, Kiriath-jearim and Chephirah, and in direct violation of the Mosaic commandment. There is evidence from the Amarna letters that cities in Canaan

32. The ruins of Old Testament Jericho at the edge of the Jordan Valley. The great trench excavated in the heart of the mound revealed occupation debris 70 feet deep and dating back to about 8000 B.C.

maintained such confederations for protection and economic interests.

The locations of these four cities are fairly well fixed. *Gibeon* is represented by the modern mound village of El Jib, located five miles northwest of Jerusalem. It stands at the head of the principal pass which leads from the Central Plateau by way of Beth-horon and Aijalon to the Shephelah and Maritime plains. Its elevation is 1,800 feet above the Mediterranean. The tell is located in the midst of a small plateau section and presents an attractive appearance with its well-preserved terraces rising from the plain to the village. It was a walled town, and remains of its fortifications have been uncovered. Its position was strategic. Gibeon commanded the ancient passage connecting the Jordan Valley with the coastal regions; it stood as the halfway house between the river and the sea. Gibeon is intimately associated with Israel's affairs from the beginning of the occupation.

Beeroth is tentatively identified as el-Bireh which is located just a mile east of the present town of Ramallah, eight miles north of Jerusalem. The modern Arabic name el-Bireh is certainly the equivalent for ancient Beeroth (wells), but the preservation of a name in connection with a particular site is not conclusive proof of identification.

Kiriath-jearim was located northwest of Jerusalem about eight miles, occupying a conspicuous place on the line of communication between the hill country of Judah and the maritime plains. Its modern site is marked by the village of Karyat el-Enab on the Jerusalem-Joppa highway. Kiriath-jearim was probably smaller than Gibeon, though its situation rendered it no less important in the defense of the interior plateau. During the reign of Solomon, the town was evidently converted into a fortress guarding the prin-

cipal approach to Jerusalem, and its name was changed to Baalath. In this connection it is mentioned in the same class with Megiddo, Beth-horon, Gezer, and Hazor.

The fourth Hivite town was *Chephirah*. Its position was almost five miles due west of Gibeon. The ancient name is preserved in the Arabic settlement of Kefireh which occupies the old site. The town dominated the approach to Gibeon and the interior plateau. During the period of tribal allotments, Chephirah was assigned to Benjamin, and at the return from the Babylonian captivity it was reoccupied. Chephirah was perhaps the least significant member of the confederation, although by virtue of its fine location it was strategically important.

The Amorite league.—It is evident that the adjacent cities regarded the Hivite overtures to Joshua as a breakdown in Canaanite morale under the threat of a powerful invader. The act of Gibeon and its associated cities was clearly a matter of treachery. We do not know whether there was any racial antagonism back of the movement to chastise the Hivite confederation for its defection. Still it is interesting to note that the cities which now propose to inflict the punishment are definitely characterized as Amorite, whereas the Hivites were likely a non-Semitic people of Hurrian stock.

At any rate, the Amorite league was a formidable organization, more powerful than the Hivite alliance. Its members stood in the front rank of chief cities in southern Canaan: Jerusalem, Hebron, Lachish, Jarmuth, and Eglon. The combination of such forces, bent on measures of retaliation, was clearly an ominous matter for the weaker communities; it

33. Gibeon, where the sun stood still. The ancient site is on the hill at the upper left.

had to be met with all possible speed and with adequate forces. Although not designed originally to ward off Amorite punitive expeditions, the crafty Gibeonites saw in their alliance with the Hebrews an opportunity to demand aid. Accordingly, they dispatched a messenger to Gilgal informing Joshua of the Amorite movement, and urging him to hasten to the assistance of his allies (Josh. 10:6). The summons was not unheeded. In a night march from Gilgal, covering a distance of approximately twenty-four miles, Joshua appeared at Gibeon the following morning, ready for battle.

On the other hand, the alliance worked to the advantage of the Hebrews, in that it augmented the forces of Israel in meeting an enemy whom they had to engage and under any other circumstances probably alone. An examination of these five Amorite cities will reveal, not only the elements of strength which each possessed, but will put in sharp relief their combined attack on the Hivites and the Hebrews.

The first city in order of importance was *Jerusalem*. Located in the midst of the southern highlands, 2,500 feet above the Mediterranean, it lay on the highroad between Bethel and Hebron. At the time of the Hebrew invasion Jerusalem was a dependency of Egypt, but a nonaggression treaty between Rameses II of Egypt and the Hittite king, Hattusilis, made the land a buffer zone between the great powers. Thus Jerusalem sought help against the Israelite threat in the local Amorite alliance of southern cities.

The earliest settlement at Jerusalem was located on the hill of Ophel, a spur of the temple ridge (Mount Moriah), which dips toward the southeast and is flanked on both sides by valleys—the Kedron on the east and the Tyropoeon on the west. At its southern end, Ophel stands overlooking the junction of these two ravines which are joined by a third, the Hinnom, coming down from the northwest. Although dominated by four other hills included in modern Jerusalem, Ophel was selected by the ancient settlers for the location of their city. The fortifications which they constructed for its protection were built halfway down the steep east slope of the ridge. The city embraced eight acres, a considerable area for an Amorite stronghold.

Although characterized as the head of the Amorite league, the inhabitants of Jerusalem were not of pure Amorite descent. Rather, they were an amalgamation of Hittite and Amorite peoples to whom the name Jebusites was applied (cf. Ezek. 16:3). From the Amarna letters (1400 B.C.) we know that one of their kings was Abdi-heba, that the name of the city was Urusalim, and that it was subject to the Egyptian crown. The city was certainly menaced by the Hivite defection, which threw open to the Hebrews three of the principal approaches to the plateau. It was further threatened by a possible attack from the Jordan Valley by way of Jericho.

Hebron was on the inland highway eighteen miles south of Jerusalem. It occupies a beautiful site along the edges of the vale of Hebron, and is in close proximity to "the Plains of Mamre," both of which were famed for their fertility. The original settlement was not far removed from the site of the present city, probably just above modern Hebron on the slope of the ridge to the east. Though originally occupying a more elevated position, with the establishment of a greater degree of security in Canaan the city gradually slipped towards the vale where it sprawled out to a considerable area. It is the gateway to the north and the converging point of all roads penetrating the southern highlands.

Hebron is one of the oldest existing cities in the world, perhaps as old as Damascus or Jerusalem. Its former name was Kiriath-arba (Josh. 14:15). It appears in the patriarchal narratives in connection with Abraham, Isaac, and Jacob, and maintains continuous relations with Israelitish developments thereafter, particularly during the days of Caleb, Joshua, David, Absalom, Abner, and Ishbosheth, the son of Saul. At the time of the Hebrew invasion Hebron was regarded as an Amorite city. During the patriarchal period, however, it was in the hands of Amorites and Hittites, with the latter in all probability maintaining the upper hand.

Lachish, the third Amorite city, was in all likelihood stronger than either Jerusalem or Hebron. It stood almost due west of Hebron at the edge of the foothills where the Shephelah blends with the Plain of Philistia. It is classified as an Amorite city regardless of its close proximity to the Philistine territory. The ancient city is marked by the imposing mound of Tell ed-Duweir. The first Old Testament notice regarding the city is found in the summons of Jerusalem for help against the Hivites, but Lachish had been in existence a thousand years earlier than that event.

The stronghold of *Jarmuth* was located in the Shephelah of Judah, evidently in the vicinity of Azekah, Socoh, Adullam, and Zorah (Josh. 15:35). Biblical notices define its general direction as north and northeast from Lachish, thus putting it in the heart of the Shephelah area. Jerome confirms this in a note that says Jarmuth was located about ten Roman miles northeast of Eleutheropolis (modern Beit Jibrin and ancient Mareshah), on the road to Je-

34. Ruins of Jerusalem. Excavations on Ophel, site of the Jebusite city of Jerusalem and the city of David. The city wall was found at the lower end of the trench where people are standing.

rusalem. Modern Khirbet el Yarmuk not only preserves the name but also fulfils the geographical requirements of both the Old Testament and of Jerome. It is exactly eight and a half miles northeast of Beit Jibrin, and is in the immediate vicinity of Azekah (Tell Zâkariyeh) and Socoh, overlooking the valley of Elah. It has a commanding elevation of 1,465 feet above the Mediterranean. Jarmuth, like all other Amorite fortresses, was a walled town, and its position relative to the valley of Elah made it strategic in approaches to Jerusalem.

Eglon, the fifth member of the Amorite league, was also located in the Shephelah territory on the site of modern Tell el-Hesi. This agrees with Jerome's statement that the city lay about ten miles west of Eleutheropolis, which would place it along the borders of the Philistian plain, not far from Lachish. This identification is also in line with the statement that Joshua went up from Eglon to Hebron, subsequently returning to Debir (Kiriath-sepher).

The Northern Campaign

At the end of the southern campaign, only half of the country was subdued or temporarily brought under the control of Israel. Attention was now given to the upper portion of the country centering around Galilee and the Plain of Esdraelon. An invasion of this territory, remotely separated from the base camp at Gilgal, would be attended by serious difficulties. Preparations were made, however, for the advance, and Joshua and Israel marched in battle array to the Waters of Merom.

The opposition, consisting of a Canaanite confederation under the leadership of Jabin, king of Hazor, was in many respects more formidable than the Amorite league in the south. Israel was compelled to engage for the first time in a battle where horses and horse-drawn chariots constituted the main body of the opposing army. In addition, the area of struggle was no longer in the highlands or low hills but in the open field. Finally, the forces of Joshua were at a disadvantage in being at such a considerable distance from the base of their supplies.

An examination of the background of this crucial test indicates that the Canaanite coalition was numerically very powerful, that it embraced large contingents of men from many cities, and that from a geographical standpoint it was widely distributed. *Hazor,* the chief town in the league, occupied a peculiar position in northern approaches to the land of Canaan. Situated about four miles from the southwest end of the Waters of Merom, it became the converging point for two great international highways— (1) the maritime passage, which followed the seashore from the north by way of Dog River, Beirut, Sidon, and Tyre to turn inland to the headwaters of the Waters of Merom and then to Hazor; and (2) the inland highway, which comes by way of Aleppo, Hamath, and Homs to Damascus, then from the oasis of the desert city, by way of Dan, crosses over the upper tributaries of the Jordan to Hazor.

Hazor was, accordingly, the gate city into Canaan, and it naturally became a strategic point in Canaan's defenses. Centuries after Joshua's struggle at Hazor, Solomon converted the mound into one of the principal fortified outposts guarding approaches to his dominion. It is referred to as a city of equal standing with Megiddo, Gezer, and Jerusalem. Its position carried with it a concession of leadership regarding the security of Canaan. Our narrative implies that the summons from Hazor carried recognized authority and that it was obeyed by other cities.

Among these was *Shimron,* whose location is not definitely known. Shimron was in the territory of Zebulun (Josh. 19:15), and the Jewish tradition which locates it five miles west of Nazareth and identifies it with Semuniyeh seems to be reliable. Summoned at the same time, *Madon* joined its forces with Shimron and went up to Hazor. The site of Madon is generally associated with the prominent mound of Hattin, four miles west of the Sea of Galilee. In the absence of other references, it is difficult to determine exactly its position. No more definite as regards its exact location is *Achshaph*, although referred to generally as lying within the territory of Asher along the seaboard. It was probably in the coastal Plain of Acre at modern Tell Keisan.

From the list of kings in Joshua 12:9–24, it is also inferred that the cities of Megiddo, Taanach, Jokneam, and others were involved in this struggle at Merom, but the narrative in chapter 11 does not specify them. It is probable that many cities not named here were represented in the battle. "All these kings met together; and they came and encamped together at the waters of Merom, to fight with Israel" (11:5, ASV).

The battle was fought in the vicinity of Hazor and the Waters of Merom (Lake Huleh). The contour of the land on the western side of the Huleh basin would suggest the placing of the scene of the struggle either north or south of the city. There are undulating plains to the west of the lake which gradually ascend to the low hills of the central range. Any one of these localities would have offered ample opportunity for the maneuvering of armies and the quick movement of horses and chariots. If the battle took place south of Hazor, the Canaanites fled past the city walls going to the north, with the Israelites in pursuit. The biblical account states that Joshua returned to Hazor and destroyed it by fire (11:11).

Continuing their flight, the armies of the Canaanites went up through the vales formed by the low hills of the Lebanons in the upper regions of the Jordan Valley. A portion of the routed forces followed the highway toward great Sidon on the coast, while others turned abruptly to the northeast to reach Mizpah, a commanding retreat now marked by crusader ruins high above the village of Baniyas (Dan) and the primary sources of the Jordan. With this disastrous defeat of the northern coalition, the backbone of Canaanite resistance was broken, although, according to the statement in Joshua, Israel continued to make war with native rulers for a long time.

Territory Unconquered

It is to be observed that, in summing up the results of the campaigns recorded in the book of Joshua, no claim is made that the Israelites conquered the territories of the Philistines, the Phoenicians, or people within the environs of the Lebanons proper. On the other hand, the narrative explicitly states that the land yet remaining to be subjugated included all of the maritime plain, from Shihor (the River of Egypt) on the southern border of Canaan to Gebal in the extreme north, and all the area from the entrance in at Hamath through the valley of the Lebanon and the Anti-Lebanon ranges to the shadows of Hermon (Josh. 13:2–6). A brief description of the significance of the affected areas in relation to Israel will now be given.

Foremost among these, both in the order of their importance and geographical location, are the *Philistines* who occupied the coastal plains of Canaan from the River of Egypt to the Nahr Rubin slightly south of Joppa (Jaffa). They were known as the great uncircumcised, the hereditary enemies of Israel. It is usually thought that the Philistines reached the coastal region about the same time the Hebrews entered Canaan, or later. Rameses III drove back an attempted invasion of Egypt by the Philistines about 1194 B.C., which would be near the time of their migration to the coastal areas. It is probable that they came from the region of Crete originally, with possible roots going back to Illyricum northwest of Greece. Their migration took them along the coastal region of Asia Minor and down the littoral to the fertile maritime plains of Canaan. Because of Egyptian opposition to their advance, a concentrated settlement was developed in the broad southern plains north of Gaza.

Conspicuous among their strongholds in Canaan were Gaza, Ashkelon, Ashdod, Gath, and Ekron. In Joshua 13:3 it is stated that the cities here specified were Philistine strongholds, and that they were *not* conquered at the time of the Hebrew invasion. The Amarna letters refer especially to the cities of Gath, Ashkelon, and Gaza. In the lists of cities conquered by Thutmosis III and Rameses II, others of these coastal towns are enumerated. It is evident that prior to the Philistine invasion the native population had succeeded in founding many cultural centers which were repeatedly overrun by foreign powers but, because of the strategic positions which they occupied on the great highway from Egypt to Mesopotamia, continued to survive. With the arrival of the Philistines these cities passed permanently into the hands of the invaders and became the Philistine Pentapolis, whose chief business was the preservation of Philistine culture and prestige in the maritime plain.

The second division of unconquered territory was that of the *Sidonians,* or *Phoenicians,* which stretched along the Mediterranean littoral for approximately two hundred miles. There is some ground for believing that the Phoenician area embraced the city of Dor, south of Mount Carmel, and extended north as far as the Orontes at the foot of Mount Amanus (Alma Dagh). The heart of the territory, however, lay between Acre in Canaan and Arvad, a little north of modern Tripoli. Its principal cities were Dor, Acre, Achzib, Tyre, Sidon, Berytus (Beirut), Gebal, Simyra, and Arvad. In addition to these, however, there were many other towns of some importance, especially those in the southern portion, which were assigned to the tribe of Asher.

Finally, the third district of unsubjugated territory indicated in the narrative extends from "the entering in at Hamath" down through the valley between the Lebanon and Anti-Lebanon ranges to Baal-gad under Mount Hermon. It is a marvelous strip of territory, especially in the southern portion. Along the highway which goes through the heart of the country several great cities were situated: Hamath, Homs, Kadesh, Baalbek, and Qarqar. From the middle district come the two picturesque rivers, the Orontes and the Leontes, which flow in opposite directions to their outlets into the Mediterranean. Towering ranges, rising to more than ten thousand feet at some points, shut in the area from north to south, while the valley thus enclosed constitutes an area of rare fertility and beauty. No claim is made that Joshua conquered this region, or that he even penetrated it at all, although later it became an important part of the kingdom of David and Solomon.

Allotments and Settlements

A study of the lists of tribal allotments, according to the Joshua narratives, indicates the assignment of territory as fall-

35. Ruins of Tyre, ancient coastal city of the Phoenicians.

ing within three general divisions and periods. In the first period there is found the allotment of the Transjordan section for Reuben, Gad, and East Manasseh; the second relates to the provisions made for Judah, Ephraim, and West Manasseh; the third sets forth the boundaries of the remaining seven tribes: Benjamin, Simeon, Zebulun, Issachar, Asher, Naphtali, and Dan. It will be observed that the first allocation of territory was made after the successful campaign in Transjordan; the second followed the victories of the southern campaign in Canaan; the third was the result of the defeat of the Canaanite league at the Waters of Merom. The first assignment was made by Moses in the plains of Moab, the second by Joshua at Gilgal, and the third at the sanctuary in Shiloh.

The *first allotment* concerned the whole of the East Jordan territory which fell to Israel as a prize of war. The southern portion, originally occupied by the Moabites but at the time of Israel's invasion held by the Amorite king, Sihon, was given to the tribe of *Reuben* (Josh. 13:15–23). It was bounded on the south by the river Arnon, on the east by the possessions of the Ammonites whose capital was at Rabbath-Ammon, on the west by the Jordan Valley, and on the north by the Wadi Heshbon which cuts across the hills of Moab almost due west of Heshbon. This natural break in the eastern plateau made possible the connecting highway between the Jordan and the regions of Arabia.

The area given to Reuben was, accordingly, the southernmost of Israel's inheritance in Transjordan, and it was constantly menaced by adjacent peoples. Reuben played no vital part in the history of Israel after the invasion. In all probability Reuben ceased to function as a tribe following the reigns of Omri and Ahab. The Moabites recovered their territory after the days of Ahab, according

to Mesha's record on the Moabite Stone (about 830 B.C.), and in the list of conquered peoples Reuben does not appear.

Bordering Reuben on the north was the country promised to *Gad* (vv. 24–28). It was hemmed in by the Jordan depression and the territory of the Ammonites. The narratives indicate the shore of the Sea of Chinneroth (Lake of Galilee) as the northern boundary, and the southern boundary seems to reach to Heshbon. In all probability the bulk of its territory was within Gilead, though half of the Gilead division was assigned to Manasseh, with Mahanaim on the border. It was beautiful mountain country, more rolling than either Moab or Bashan. On the whole, it was more vitally related to the west Jordan tribes. Ramoth-gilead, Jabesh-gilead, Mahanaim, Penuel, Succoth, and Tishbe (home of Elijah) are some of its outstanding cities during the Old Testament period, while later during the Roman era four of the great Decapolis cities, Gadara, Gerasa, Pella, and Dion, flourished in this region.

Finally, beginning with the Gadite tribal boundary, the territory of *Manasseh* extended north and northeast to include all of the kingdom of Og, the conquered ruler of Bashan (vv. 29–31). In general this territory lay between the foot of Hermon and the Yarmuk River, although Edrei, the mysterious underground city of the Amorites, was south of the river. It is significant that, in the matter of boundaries, the Yarmuk is altogether ignored and, furthermore, regardless of the fact that it is the most commanding stream in the East Jordan country, it is not mentioned in any biblical passage.

The *second group of tribal allotments* came at the close of the southern campaign in Canaan. The lots were apparently cast at Gilgal. These assignments were concerned with the heart of Canaan, the territory which was ultimately to witness the establishment of the two leading centers of Hebrew development —Jerusalem and Samaria. It is significant in this connection that the most prominent tribes, Judah, Ephraim, and West Manasseh, are singled out and charged with the occupation of this strategic area. The lines are fairly well fixed in the narratives and may be indicated as follows.

To *Judah* was assigned that area which was to enjoy a certain supremacy in later Hebrew development, that is, all of the territory centering around Jerusalem in the north, Hebron in the middle section, and Beer-sheba in the south (15:1–63). The southern limits of the allotment are carefully described as the borders of Edom, the wilderness of Zin, Kadesh-barnea, and the River of Egypt. The eastern border was determined by the shore line of the Salt Sea, while the northern frontier passed from the mouth of the Jordan through Jericho, Jerusalem, Jarmuth, and Makkedah to the Great Sea. The allotment evidently included the territory of the Philistines since three of the Pentapolis—Ekron, Ashdod, and Gaza—are definitely mentioned.

It should be noted that the narrative specifies Jerusalem as a city of Benjamin, though it was subsequently identified with the fortunes of Judah (18:28). The explanation probably lies in the relative strength of the two tribes, it being assumed that the men of Judah were more able to capture it. A parallel case is given in a later reference where the Canaanite strongholds of Issachar are turned over to the tribe of Manasseh for conquest (17:11–12). At any rate, it is the men of Judah who storm the city of the Jebusites, who succeed in gaining an entrance, who burn the stronghold, and who, finally subduing it under David,

converted it into the city of David, the capital of the kingdom.

Next in the order of allotments at Gilgal was the tribe of *Ephraim,* to whom was given the territory which headed up in Shechem (16:1–10). In some respects it was the most attractive part of the West Jordan country, a good land for an agricultural and pastoral people. Its southern borders lay along the edges of Benjamin and Dan. To the east was the great rift of the Jordan Valley; to the west, the coast of the Great Sea; to the north, the uneven boundary of Manasseh bent to admit Shechem into Ephraim. Within its bounds were the three great centers of Gezer, a stronghold of the Canaanites, Shiloh, the site of the first sanctuary in Canaan, and Shechem, the place where Abraham built his first altar in the Land of Promise, where Joshua delivered his farewell address, and where the division of the kingdom of David and Solomon was effected by Jeroboam. The whole area is alive with crucial events in the life of Israel and the United Kingdom. Shechem makes its appearance centuries later as the home of the bitter Samaritans who were blessed by Jesus through the woman at the well of Jacob.

The final allotment at Gilgal was made with reference to *West Manasseh* (17:1–18). The territory described has for its southern borders the tribe of Ephriam. Eastward, it is the deep Jordan gorge; to the west, the Great Sea; to the northwest, a portion of Asher under Mount Carmel; and on the north, the lower portions of the Plain of Esdraelon, where the hills of Samaria merge with the broad spaces of an open country extending from the Plain of Acre to the valley of the Jordan. Along the edges of its tribal assignment were located some of the chief Canaanite fortresses in northern Canaan, namely, Jokneam, Megiddo, Taanach, Ibleam, and Beth-

shan, the towns originally included in the inheritance of Issachar but committed to Manasseh for subjugation. It was expected that the powerful tribe of Manasseh would quickly overrun all of these strongholds, but the conquest was not completed until the reigns of David and Solomon.

The *third general division of Canaan,* made by Joshua at the sanctuary in Shiloh, came at the close of the northern campaign which witnessed the defeat of the Canaanite forces at the Waters of Merom. This division of the conquered territory was intended primarily to take care of the northern tribes of Naphtali, Zebulun, Asher, and Issachar, although the southern tribal units of Simeon, Dan, and Benjamin, which had been omitted at Gilgal, were now assigned definite areas. It will simplify our summary to take them in the order of the lots enumerated in the narrative. *First,* to *Benjamin* was given a compact region extending from the Central Plateau north of Jerusalem to the Jordan Valley (18:11–28). It was bordered on the south by Judah, and on the north by Ephraim, while its western portion merged into the territory of Dan. Originally included in Benjamin's territory were the strong centers of Jerusalem and Bethel, though both of these pivotal places were subsequently snatched from it.

Second, to *Simeon* was assigned a part of the territory of Judah, particularly the area centering around Beer-sheba (19:1–9). This was in the region of the Negeb, or South Country. Thus Simeon was compelled to face not only the certainties of desert heat, the blighting sirocco, and periods of drought but to contend with the roving tribesmen of

Amalek, and other nomads, in the great Desert et-Tih and wilderness of Shur. In all probability, it was the last factor which proved the decisive element in Simeon's withdrawal further north into closer association with Judah. To all intents their tribal territory was a common inheritance.

Third, Zebulun's lot was more favorable from a climatic standpoint, though beset by some serious factors (vv. 10–16). We know little regarding its outstanding centers during this early period, although subsequently Sepphoris was regarded as its first city in population. While Nazareth is not mentioned in contemporary records outside the Bible, it became the most famous city. The allotment consisted of the finest territory in middle Galilee—well watered, undulating, and fertile. At its foot lay the beautiful plains of lower Galilee; on the west was Asher, and on the north and east were the borders of Naphtali. Through the heart of this territory ran the great highways of the eastern world, which literally placed the region at the crossroads of the nations.

Fourth, Issachar inherited the most fertile place in all Canaan (vv. 17–23). From the point where the hills of Lower Galilee crouch down to leap over the river Kishon to Mount Carmel, Issachar looked east through the Plain of Esdraelon and the vale of Jezreel under Gilboa straight to the Jordan. It was, accordingly, coextensive with the two great areas which have played so vital a part in the affairs of Canaan since the earliest periods. The whole region throbs with historic interest from Joshua, Deborah, Barak, Gideon, Saul, Jonathan, David, and Jehu down to modern times. The territory of Issachar was converted into the battlefield of the nations, the great Armageddon. The plain is proverbially fertile, a well-watered soil which, though cultivated through thousands of years, is

36. The ruins of Shiloh, site of the first Israelite sanctuary, in the foreground, surrounded by the hill country of Ephraim.

still regarded as being practically inexhaustible.

The inheritance of Issachar was good, the most desirable in all Canaan for an agricultural people, but it was also the most precarious, both from the standpoint of its situation and its neighbors. It was dominated on the south by a line of Canaanite strongholds which successfully resisted the Hebrew occupation until the era of David and Solomon. In the clear admission of Joshua 17:11-12, Israel failed to conquer these fortresses: Jokneam, Megiddo, Taanach, Beth-shan, and others. In addition to the domination of the Canaanites, Issachar was situated at the converging point of a network of oriental highways where armies of the aliens met and battled, and where it was impossible for the tribe to survive long.

Fifth, to *Asher* was allotted a territory which was equally fraught with danger and allurements (19:24-31). In general the territory followed the topographical features of the country north of Mount Carmel, thus including all of the Plain of Acre. There is also a possibility that Asher's lot embraced a part of the land south of Carmel, particularly Dor and her towns. Assuming that the territory of Asher was coextensive with the southern part of the Phoenician kingdom, which we know included Dor, we have here indicated its boundary as reaching the Great Sea under Mount Carmel. On the east lay Issachar, Zebulun, and Naphtali, while at the north it merged with the regions of Sidon.

The lot was characterized by great fertility, especially in the interior along the foothills of Galilee, but it lay across the oriental roadways which placed it on the line of foreign invasion. Greater still, Asher was at close grips with the blandishments of a pagan civilization which caught not only its eye and heart but which later threatened the whole religious structure of Israel. The tribe quickly disappeared in a hopeless amalgamation with its overpowering neighbors.

Sixth, Naphtali was invested with the territory which, for sheer beauty, is unsurpassed in all Canaan (vv. 32-39). It was in the heart of Galilee, centering around the shores of the Sea of Chinnereth (Galilee). The whole of the region was watered from the hidden springs of Mount Hermon. Its rolling acres were compelling in their appeal to keepers of flocks and tillers of the soil. But Naphtali was also in "the circle of the nations," in the midst of an alien people whose impact was to color and largely determine its future history. Penetrated by thoroughfares from all sections of the ancient world, its contacts were varied and its population cosmopolitan. Situated thus at the entrance into northern Canaan, Naphtali became the gateway to each of the lower sections of Canaan where the distinctive features of Hebrew civilization were brought to perfection.

Seventh, to *Dan* was given a narrow strip of territory situated between Ephraim and Judah, and extending from the borders of Benjamin to the Great Sea at Joppa (Jaffa) (vv. 40-48).

The notice which we have in the book of Judges indicates that Dan was remaining in his ships as late as the period of Deborah and Barak, although it is entirely possible that the migration mentioned previous to this time was only partial. The location of the tribe during the later period was obviously under Hermon, with its center at Laish (Dan–Panias). In addition to the reasons usually assigned for the tribal migration, it is altogether probable that other factors entered into the move, especially the strong pressure of the Philistines in the south and the Canaanites immediately to the north of the Danite boundaries. Spliced in between these powerful opposing groups, there was little opportunity for tribal development; the danger was rather one of tribal extinction or certain amalgamation.

No definite allotment was made either by Moses or Joshua for the priestly tribe of Levi. Its functions as a tribe were not concerned with secular affairs but wholly with the religious life of Israel: "The offerings of Jehovah, the God of Israel, made by fire are his inheritance, as he spake unto him" (13:14, ASV). Since the tribe of Levi touched the whole of Israel at the vital point of its religious interests, it was scattered throughout the country in the special cities granted from the quota of each tribe.

From these important cities six were chosen as centers of refuge. The first three are as follows: Bezer in the wilderness in the plain country for the Reubenites, Ramoth in Gilead for the Gadites, and Golan in Bashan for the Manassites. (cf. 20:8). These points were designated by Moses in the plains of Moab, after the conquest of the East Jordan country. Subsequently, three other cities were designated in the West Jordan territory: "They set apart Kadesh in Galilee in the hill-country of Naphtali, and Shechem in the hill-country of Ephraim, and Kiriath-arba (the same is Hebron) in the hill-country of Judah" (v. 7). Finally, it is claimed that "all the cities of the Levites in the midst of the possession of the children of Israel were forty and eight cities with their suburbs" (21:41).

7
The Kingdoms

In the preceding chapter we presented the geographical backgrounds of the era of the conquest and settlement, showing particularly the tribal allotments and summing up the extensive sections of Canaan and adjacent territories which remained unconquered at the close of Joshua's campaigns. The present discussion will be chiefly concerned with a description of the geographical setting of the two succeeding periods, the judges and the kingdoms. These incorporated approximately seven and a half centuries of Israel's history.

While we will not seek to present here these far-reaching developments under the aspect of historical detail, it should be kept in mind that the whole movement, from the judges to the disruption of the kingdoms, was continuous, and that the checkered experiences of the Hebrew people were conditioned by their physical environment. This fact is readily explained on the basis, first, of Canaan's attractiveness to nomadic hordes in the early period, and second, on its inevitable relation to the military movements of the great world powers in the later period.

The Land of Israel Under the Judges

There was no organized life of the tribes during this period. In general, the various tribes were making sporadic efforts to win the whole of the territories originally assigned to them, or to entrench themselves securely in the positions already won. The narratives indicate that these efforts were only partially successful. There are frequent allusions to the inability of the tribes to dispossess the Canaanites in the regions of Esdraelon and the Shephelah, and the Philistines in the coastal plains. Furthermore, it is said that the land of Israel was repeatedly invaded by outsiders, particularly the nomadic tribesmen who pushed into Canaan from the deserts adjoining on the south and east.

An enumeration of the invasions shows a group of formidable peoples: the Sidonians from the north, the Arameans under Cushan-rishathaim of Mesopotamia, a revived coalition of Canaanites under the king of Hazor, the five lords of the Philistines, Amalekites, Moabites, Midianites, and Ammonites. Although widely distributed from a geographical standpoint, all these tribes converged on Canaan. Since a presentation of the backgrounds of some of these people has been made previously, further reference to them is omitted here. The remaining groups, however, the Amalekites, Moabites, Midianites, and Ammonites, though of less importance than the more highly organized peoples, form a definite part of biblical backgrounds and should be noted in their relation to Israel. They are presented here in the order of their occurrence in the narratives.

First are the *Amalekites* who are mentioned in connection with the Exodus of Israel from Egypt (Ex. 17:8–16). The Amalekites lived a nomadic existence in the lower portions of the great wilderness of Paran. No information is available regarding the actual territory occupied by them in this arid plateau section, but, from the account in Numbers, they are sufficiently organized to dispute the passage of the Israelites to Sinai. On the other hand, it is not necessary to think of any particular territory as their permanent habitation; like other nomadic peoples, their camps were shifted according to seasons and conditions. Life to them was a series of sojourns. At one time they are described in company with the Midianites in an invasion of Canaan from the southeast (Judg. 6:1–8), while in a southern campaign of similar nature they are allied with Moabites (3:12–30).

In other passages the Amalekites are referred to in connection with the Negeb territory and the wilderness of Shur (Num. 14:43–45). This latter area seems to have been their favorite region as late as the period of Saul and David. Here Saul met them in a disastrous battle, and David inflicted on them a defeat from which they never fully recovered (1 Sam. 30:1–20). Subsequent to these victories, the Amalekites, provoked by crop failures in the South Country, continued to annoy the more settled and prosperous communities of the interior. In general, therefore, we may regard them as marauding hordes, operating principally in the arid steppes of Paran but gradually pushing up to the Negeb territory on the borders of Canaan.

Next in order are the *Moabites* who are said to have oppressed Israel for eighteen years (Judg. 3:12–30). The account states that this oppression centered around Jericho, the city of palm trees, thus affecting primarily the tribe of Benjamin. Called descendants of Lot, the Moabites were related to Israel. Their language is preserved for us on the Moabite Stone found at Dibon, one of their chief cities. In general, their territory lay to the east of the Jordan and the Salt Sea, bounded on the north by the Jabbok, on the south by the hills of Edom, and on the east by Ammon.

With the coming of the Amorites, Moab lost the heart of its inheritance, including its agricultural lands and chief cities. Its boundary was contracted to a line south of the Arnon River. Although forbidden to invade the country now occupied by the Moabites, on the ground that it was given to the sons of Lot as a possession, the Israelites succeeded in forcing their way through the former territory of Moab, wresting it from the Amorites. This region was later given to Reuben and Gad for an inheritance. From the time of Israel's conquest there was a continual effort on the part of Moab to recover its lost dominions. They apparently succeeded at this in the period of their oppression, but during the reign of David, Moab became a tributary of the Hebrew kingdom.

The rupture of David's kingdom witnessed a rebellion of all subject states, Moab included. But with the accession of Omri and Ahab in Israel, the East Jordan country was recaptured under heavy tribute. From the records which Mesha has preserved for us on the Moabite Stone, we are informed that Moab was liberated from the power of Israel. A later account, however, indicates that this freedom was only short-lived, for Moab is assaulted by a coalition of forces from Israel, Judah, and Edom (2 Kings 3:6–27). Although appearing subsequently in the biblical narratives, Moab was ultimately swallowed up by the great world powers and the Arabians.

The oppression attributed to the *Midianites* embraced a period of seven years. Asher, Zebulun, and Naphtali were probably involved, since they are summoned by Gideon to repel the invaders. The opposing forces were massed in the valley of Jezreel, along the slopes of the hill of Moreh and Mount Gilboa. Here the hordes of Midian and Amalek were put to flight, their retreat across the Jordan following the way by which they had advanced, that is, by Succoth, Penuel, and Jogbehah, on the road to Rabbath-Ammon.

The narrative states that the Midianite invasion came from the East Jordan country, and from this we may infer the general territory occupied by them at that time. On the whole, however, we need more light regarding Midian and his people. It is claimed that they were descendants of Abraham by Keturah (Gen. 25:1–4), though subsequently there existed some connection between the Midianites and Ishmaelites. The Genesis narrative uses Midianites and Ishmaelites interchangeably.

In any treatment of nomadic peoples, however, it is very difficult to adhere rigidly to ethnographical lines; even where racial traits and descent were shared in common, the tribal distinctions tended to become obscured. Still, there is a definite body of information concerning these people. They were a pastoral folk, wandering at will in search of inviting pastures for their cattle, flocks, and camels; they engaged in caravan trade

which carried them throughout the Middle East. Our first contact with them grows out of a company of Midianite merchants who purchase Joseph at Dothan and subsequently introduce him as a slave into Egypt. Other references link them with Moses who fled to Midian from the court of Egypt, with Jethro, and probably with the Kenites in their relations to Israel. In close association with the Exodus, they are mentioned as encamped on the plains of Moab in the East Jordan territory, definitely allied with the Moabites against Israel.

During the early period, the Midianites are described as occupying the lower section of the Sinai Peninsula and the area stretching to the east. They had no permanent dwellings but moved their tents according to seasons and conditions. Nomads of the desert wastes, they roamed through an extensive territory in and adjacent to the Sinai Peninsula, at times stretching even to the northern portions of Transjordan.

The *Ammonites* occupied the region immediately bordering Moab on the east. The period of their oppression is given as eighteen years, but this is definitely stated to have included only the tribes east of the Jordan (Judg. 10:7–8). Subsequently, they passed over the river in an assault on Judah, Benjamin, and Ephraim. Although closely related, the Ammonites were hostile toward Israel from the time of the invasion. A careful study of the passages bearing on their oppression of Israel will show that it was purely a matter of aggression. The Transjordan tribes, Reuben and Gad, occupied adjacent territory, but it was an area which never belonged to Ammon. As stated in Jephthah's answer to Ammonite claims, the whole region was taken from the Amorites (Judg. 11:23).

At the time of the invasion, however, the Ammonites were located on the edge of the East Jordan country, hemmed in by the Arabian Desert. On the south they were cut off from the Moabites by the upper ravines of the Arnon Valley and the wilderness of Kedemoth. It was a contracted territory with few desirable features. It is likely that the aggressive oppression of the Transjordan tribes was part of a plan to acquire more and better land for the Ammonites themselves. Nor is it difficult to understand why Ammon coveted the possessions of Reuben and Gad; it was the best territory in all the region. Fertile acres lay west of Ammon, as they do today, while on the east the fringe of desert was unattractive and forbidding. As a consequence, the Ammonites were virtually isolated, and they maintained their tribal unity. While mostly nomadic in their habits, the Ammonites had some cities, the most

outstanding being Rabbath-Ammon, the capital.

The imposing acropolis of the ancient Ammonites dominates the modern city of Amman, the capital of Transjordan. The place is connected with numerous historical events, one of which relates to the sacrifice of Uriah the Hittite by David and Joab when they captured the city. The stronghold stands near the headwaters of the river Jabbok. The mound itself is a part of a short range of hills dominating the surrounding valleys. In later centuries Rabbath-Ammon retained something of its former importance, particularly during the Greco-Roman period when it was renamed Philadelphia and became one of the outstanding cities of the Decapolis. Ruins at the present city of Amman bear testimony to the ancient grandeur of the place. Its relation to all surrounding territory was so strategic that it naturally became the center of the Ammonite dominion and culture. Although the Ammonites are never regarded as an outstanding people, they persisted through many centuries. They made their final stand against Judas Maccabaeus during the Maccabean oppression (1 Macc. 5:6).

Extent of the Kingdom Under Saul

The position of Saul in Israel was more than that of a tribal chieftain. Unlike the Judges, who were called to meet special emergencies in the life of the people, the son of Kish was chosen to occupy a permanent office, the kingship. Samuel, the last of the Judges, witnessed the last of the oppressions, delivering Israel temporarily from the yoke of the Philistines. But it was an unfinished task which Samuel committed to the new leader. The period of the Judges, accordingly, gradually merged into that of the kingdom, running concurrently during the last days of Samuel. There is no es-

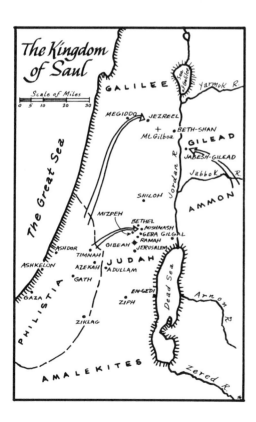

sential difference in the geographical background of these periods except that, with the accession of Saul, the era of foreign domination ended. We are no longer concerned with invasions by Ammon, Midian, Moab, and Amalek, though some of these will make their reappearance. The immediate danger confronting Israel was that of the Philistine Pentapolis in the coastal plains.

The pressure of the Philistines was a matter of grave concern to Samuel and Saul. Maintaining a co-ordinated government in the Pentapolis, the Philistines proved themselves superior to Israel in the field and succeeded in dominating the tribes for many years. Samuel's great victory at Ebenezer effectively weakened the Philistines in the interior of Canaan, but subsequent events proved that they were able to reoccupy their positions and to dominate the main approaches into the Central Plateau, particularly the passes by way of Esdraelon on the north and the Jordan Valley on the east. Their chief stronghold in the south centered around Michmash, a point on the trade route up from the Jordan, although they were also in command at Gibbethon and Gibeah. In the northern region they were definitely in alliance with the Canaanitish cities of Esdraelon and the valley of Jezreel. Their domination goaded Israel and was, in all likelihood, the chief factor in the selection of Saul as king (1 Sam. 9:16). At any rate, the main work accomplished by Saul was the breaking of the Philistine power.

The victory of Saul and Jonathan at Michmash, where the Philistines were defeated while being pursued by way of Aijalon to the maritime plains, was a crucial event in the life of Israel. Coming at the very beginning of his reign, it established Saul more securely in the thought of the people and justified loyal support. This victory, however, came subsequent to his triumph over Ammon

at Jabesh-gilead, where Saul distinguished himself in battle, and earned the hearty support of the East Jordan Israelites (1 Sam. 11:1–15). In close connection with these victories, Saul prosecuted his campaigns against Ammon, Moab, Edom, and Amalek, and in a series of engagements took vengeance on all of Israel's foes. He was evidently a man of marked generalship and unusual attractiveness.

Considering the state of affairs in Israel immediately following the chaos of the Judges, Saul accomplished a difficult thing in effecting at least a partial unification of the tribes. He demonstrated that it was possible for the East and West Jordan tribes to act in concert against a common foe. This measure of unification was not, however, the complete realization of national consciousness. The condition of affairs in Israel at this time rendered solidarity practically impossible. But Saul received representative support which came not only from Gilead but from Benjamin, Judah, Asher, Ephraim, and all sections of Israel.

In defining his kingdom, therefore, we must be careful to conceive of it in the light of the period, and not to be too exacting regarding definite boundaries and limitations. It was the first venture in kingship. The monarchy had no official palace nor capital city. At one time Saul and his men are at Bethel; at another, Gibeah stands out as the central place of influence. Gibeah seems to have enjoyed a certain preeminence as the native city of Saul (1 Sam. 10:26). It stood four miles north of Jerusalem on the highway between Jerusalem and Bethel. The ancient site is marked by the imposing mound of Tell el-Fûl. The hill dominated the surrounding country, and naturally played a leading part in the affairs of the central highlands.

Saul continued to reign at Gibeah, but

the latter part of his career was marked by a series of unfortunate circumstances growing out of his relations with David. Taking advantage of the disorders, the Philistines renewed their attack on Israel, drawing up their forces in the valley of Jezreel. The army of Israel encamped along the slopes of Mount Gilboa, the historic place occupied by Gideon and his men a century before, while the Philistines stood on the southern side of the hill of Moreh. Endor, where Saul resorted to consult the witch, was located on the north side of the same hill. The battle was waged in the vale below and proved disastrous for Saul and his army. The king and his sons were slain on Gilboa, their bodies hung on the walls of Beth-shan, and their armor placed in the temple of Ashtaroth on the acropolis.

Beth-shan was evidently occupied by the Philistines at this time or allied with them. Across the Jordan, eight miles from Beth-shan, the men of Jabesh-gilead received the news of Israel's defeat. When they learned of the disgraceful exposure of the bodies, they rescued them from the walls of the city for burial in Gilead. At this point the affairs of Israel enter an entirely new phase under the leadership of the house of Jesse and David.

The Kingdom of David and Solomon

The death of Saul and Jonathan at the battle of Gilboa not only arrested for a considerable period the movement toward tribal unification but created a number of problems which Israel was hardly prepared to meet. Chief among these was the disposition of Abner, Saul's first-line general, who was ambitious to have Ishbosheth succeed to his father's throne and to found his capital at Mahanaim in the East Jordan country. The attempt was clearly designed against David whom the tribe of Judah was de-

termined to establish in the kingship at Hebron. It was an impossible situation for Abner, however, and after two years of gradual decline the movement failed (2 Sam. 2:10).

On the other hand, emerging from the wilderness of Judea, the environs of the Philistine territory, and the South Country, David occupied Hebron and converted it into his capital. Overtures were made to all the tribes for recognition of his kingship. His manly bearing toward the house of Saul and Jonathan,

his purpose to avoid bloodshed in connection with discontented factions, finally won for David the loyal support of every tribe. For seven and a half years he reigned over Judah at Hebron, but subsequently he was acclaimed ruler over all Israel. Recognizing the need for a more central location, David planned an attack on Jerusalem, a stronghold of the Jebusites which the tribes had been unable to hold.

Although by no means a large or imposing city, Jerusalem was evidently a powerful fortress, both on account of the deep ravines which adjoined it on all sides, except the north, and the formidable walls built for its protection. From the narrative describing its capture, we may infer that the city was entered by way of a water shaft leading up from the spring of Gihon to the interior of the acropolis (1 Chron. 11:4–9; 2 Sam. 5:8). After the conquest of Jerusalem, David converted it into the capital of all Israel and called it the City of David. It became the political and religious center of Israel from the day of its capture. Here David reigned for thirty years, being succeeded by his son Solomon who, during a period of forty years, held intact the extensive kingdom of David and established a highly organized system of administration and defense. We may begin here to trace the backgrounds of this kingdom, making special note of any changes effected since the era of Judges and of Saul.

For the first time in their history, we find the Hebrews dominant in all parts of the West and East Jordan country. In quick succession the ancient enemies of Israel were brought under the yoke by the powerful armies of David. It is not necessary to present an extensive survey of these campaigns which resulted in the establishment of the kingdom of Solomon, but to point out briefly the territories affected and the order of their conquest. According to the narrative in Samuel, David's occupation of Jerusalem was immediately challenged by the Philistines (2 Sam. 5:17–25).

During the early days of Saul, Israel had successfully opposed the Philistines and, as we have seen, pushed them from the interior highlands into the maritime plains. The victory at Gilboa, however, so disastrous for Israel, resulted in the restoration of Philistine supremacy in the highlands from Jerusalem to the Plain of Esdraelon. The sphere of their influence included the interior strongholds of Jerusalem, Gibeah, and Michmash in the south, while in the northern area they were certainly allied with Bethshan, and probably with Ibleam, Taanach, Megiddo, and Jokneam.

In view of the general situation, it is likely that David's territory, centering first around Hebron, was in some measure affiliated with the Philistines. His increasing strength and, finally, the unification of the various tribes converted David into an open political enemy whom the Philistines watched with apprehension. It is clear that David's capture of Jerusalem was a direct blow to Philistine supremacy in the Central Plateau, and that it meant their ultimate withdrawal into the coastal plains. Herein lies the explanation of the counter movement to eject David from Jerusalem. Although making their greatest effort in this offensive, the Philistines were defeated on the fields of Rephaim, southwest of Jerusalem. As a result Philistia became subject to the Hebrew kingdom.

With the subjugation of the Philistines, David was left comparatively free to establish his kingdom in relation to bordering territories. There is no necessity of going into detailed statements regarding these adjacent states, particularly Moab, Ammon, Amalek, and Edom, since all have been described in former sections of this work. Our interest here is simply to classify all of this conquered area as a definite part of the enlarged Hebrew kingdom under David. In addition to these adjoining regions, the kingdom included the states of Zobah, south of Damascus, and Damascus itself. The allied kingdoms of Hamath and Phoenicia also came within the sphere of Hebrew influence.

The whole of David's kingdom fell to Solomon. It was held intact, with the exception of the Arameans who established an independent kingdom at Damascus. By aggressive policies Solomon succeeded in keeping his dependencies and in protecting his own borders from invasions. Of great interest was the system of fortresses: Hazor guarded the strategic point in northern Canaan; Megiddo stood across the open Plain of Esdraelon; Beth-horon blocked the dangerous pass to Jerusalem by way of Aijalon; Baalath stood on the connecting highway from Jerusalem to the seaport of Joppa; Gezer protected the main road and entrance to the valley of Sorek; Tamar occupied a point on the southern borders to defend caravans from the ports of Ezion-geber and Elath. It is significant that in this system of defense, no fortress was located east of Jerusalem, the valley of the Jordan being regarded as sufficient barrier.

One other aspect of the kingdom should be mentioned. The Hebrews were not men who go to sea in ships. As a consequence, Israel never attained supremacy as a maritime power. Even nature has frustrated all hope in that direction by withholding suitable harbors along the shores of Canaan. Although there were several maritime cities, none could be counted as having a real harbor. Among these, however, Joppa (Jaffa), the seaport of ancient Jerusalem, maintained its prestige through many centuries. On the southeastern borders of the kingdom,

Solomon's navy anchored in the harbor of Ezion-geber. Merchant vessels brought gold from Ophir and a variety of commodities from the Orient. These imports, in turn, passed by caravan trains through Tamar in the wilderness to Jerusalem. The Hebrew alliance with Phoenicia, the chief maritime people of the ancient world, made possible commercial contacts with all ports of the Great [Mediterranean] Sea.

This brief description of the Hebrew expansion under David and Solomon indicates a political kingdom of considerable extent, reaching from the borders of Egypt and the peninsula of Sinai to the entrance of Hamath. Its conquest, in the first instance, was due to the military genius of David, while its administration fell to Solomon who accomplished it in a most effective manner. The center of the kingdom was at Jerusalem.

The Northern Kingdom

The death of Solomon was followed by the disruption of the kingdom. The strong policies of organization and administration which Solomon put into force were effective throughout his reign. It was clearly a part of Solomon's program to submerge tribal distinctions in the interest of national unification, as evidenced by the division of his kingdom into twelve divisions, presided over by provincial governors responsible only to the king (1 Kings 4:7 ff.). But the tribal jealousies persisted, particularly those of the northern and East Jordan tribes, waiting only favorable opportunity to be asserted. The outward expression of this situation came to the front at the Shechem gathering, when Rehoboam was rejected because of his unfortunate decision regarding the continuation of state policies (1 Kings 12:1–20).

As a consequence, there was an open rupture between the southern and northern peoples which was never healed.

From this date the history of the Hebrews actually centers around two kingdoms, Judah and Israel, with affairs of state heading up in the capital cities, Jerusalem in the south, Shechem and Samaria in the north. In describing each of these kingdoms, the first matter of importance is to determine the territories comprising the various divisions, and then to show their relations to the neighboring states which finally conquered them.

Israel, or the Northern Kingdom, embraced in its territory the West Jordan tribes of Ephraim, Manasseh, Issachar, Zebulun, Naphtali, and Asher; on the east side of Jordan were Reuben, Gad, and Manasseh. Dan, whose original settlement in southern Canaan was abandoned because of the pressure of Philistines and Canaanites, stood at the upper reaches of the Jordan Valley. Enumerated in this manner, ten tribes constituted the Northern Kingdom. The tribe of Levi, having no territorial allotment, is not reckoned in this geographical division. The area represented by these tribes was considerably larger than the rival kingdom on the south, and included regions on both sides of the Jordan Valley. This fact, however, in the long run, proved to be one of its weaknesses, particularly with reference to the East Jordan tribes and the border territories of Dan, Naphtali, and Asher. The pressure of alien peoples in each case almost cut off distinctive Israelite survival. As a consequence, the heart of the Northern Kingdom was found in the interior tribes of Ephraim and West Manasseh.

Geographically it was a disjointed territory; its many natural barriers, chief among which was the Jordan Valley, affected every degree of tribal cooperation. Close union between the peoples dwelling on opposite sides of the ravine was practically impossible. The

East Jordan Israelites were a valiant people and gave to the kingdom some of its outstanding leaders, but the detached nature of their territory invited invasions and continued struggles. In all probability, Jeroboam of Israel sensed the situation and tried to counteract the disadvantage by building Penuel, an East Jordan city near the Jabbok River, at the same time he built the capital at Shechem. The exact location of Penuel is not known, but from the biblical references it probably stood south of the Jabbok.

Shechem (Nablus) was situated in the Ebal-Gerizim Valley, through which ran an ancient trade route. It occupied the mound on which is located the village of Balata at the embouchure of the valley, looking east into the Plain of Moreh. Called the Queen City of the land of Canaan during the period of the patriarchs, Shechem was the most important political and religious center in the hill country at the time of the conquest. A massive temple-fortress with walls seventeen feet thick has been uncovered on the acropolis of the city. This is probably the Tower of Shechem (Judg. 9:47), or the house of El-berith (v. 46), where Abimelech destroyed the rebels who opposed his rule, and where he was fatally injured by a millstone hurled from the tower by a woman. Shechem became the first capital of the Northern Kingdom, with a thousand years of tradition as a capital city behind it.

In view of the rival sanctuaries of calf worship established at Bethel and Dan, Shechem lost its religious leadership. As a consequence, the center of government was transferred to Tirzah, where it remained from the latter days of Jeroboam to the accession of Omri. Situated on the Wadi Farah northeast of Shechem, Tirzah faced toward the Jordan Valley. Its location suggests the provincial nature of the Northern Kingdom when its interests

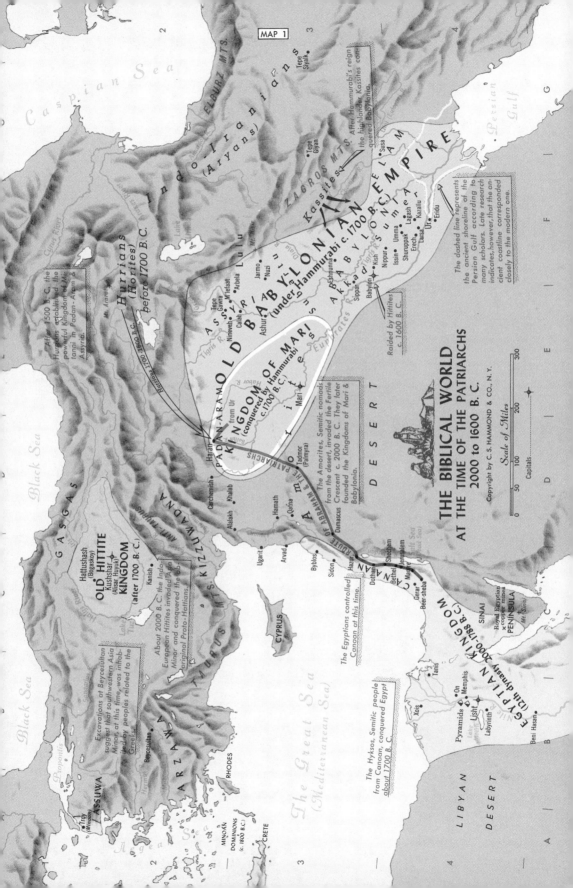

THE BIBLICAL WORLD AT THE TIME OF THE PATRIARCHS 2000 to 1600 B.C.

MAP 2

CANAAN BEFORE THE CONQUEST

Copyright by C. S. Hammond & Co., N. Y.

Scale of Miles

0 5 10   20   30   40

Perennial Rivers ────────
Seasonal Rivers & Streams ────────
Capitals .... ✦

The Great Sea

(Mediterranean Sea)

Phoenicians from
the cities of Sidon and
Tyre traded throughout
the Mediterranean.

Canaan at this time was
an Egyptian province organized on a city-state system.
The local kings were only
required to pay tribute and
to furnish labor for Egyptian
royal projects.

The 13th and 12th
century kingdoms of
Bashan, Ammon, Moab
and Edom displaced the
Rephaim, Zuzim, Emim
and Horites respectively.

The destroyed cities of
Sodom and Gomorrah are believed to be beneath the shallow waters of the Dead Sea
which now cover the Vale of
Siddim (shaded portion).

HITTITE
EMPIRE
Ubi
Damascus

Sidon
Zarephath
Tyre
Kanah
Misrephoth-maim
Achzib
Accho
Achshaph
Shimron
Jokneam
Dor
Megiddo
Taanach
Ibleam
Dothan
Sochoh
Tirzah
Shechem
Jacob's Well
Aphek
Tappuah
Joppa
Ono
Lod
Bethel
Beeroth
Ai
Gezer
Chephirah
Gibeon
Jericho
Gilgal
Ekron
Kirjath-jearim
Jerusalem
(Jebus, Salem)
Ashdod
Beth-shemesh
Makkedah
Jarmuth
Libnah
Bethlehem
Ashkelon
Adullam
Gath
Mamre
Lachish
Kirjath-arba
(Hebron)
Gaza
(Azzah)
Eglon
Kirjath-sepher
(Debir)
Hazeon-tamar
(En-gedi)
Gerar
Raphia
Sharuhen
Beer-sheba
Arad
Hormah

Kedesh
Hazor
Merom
Chinnereth
Madon
Mt. Tabor
Mt. Ebal
Mt. Gerizim

MT. CARMEL
Kishon R.
Plain of Sharon
Canaanites
Hittites
Jebusites
Hittites
Kenites
Amalekites

Sidonians
(Phoenicians)
MOUNT LEBANON
MT. HERMON

Laish
(Dan)

BASHAN
(KINGDOM OF OG)

Karnaim
Ashtaroth
Yarmuk R.
Edrei
Ramoth-gilead

Beth-shan
Pella
Jabesh-gilead
Mahanaim
Ham
Succoth
Penuel
(Peniel)
Adam
Jazer
Rabbath-ammon
Plains of Moab
Heshbon
Mt. Nebo
(Pisgah)
Medeba
Jahaz
Kiriathaim
Dibon
Aroer
Ar
Kir-moab
(Kir-haresheth)
Bozrah
Oboth
Punon
Zoar

River Jordan
Jabbok R.
Salt Sea
(Dead Sea)
Arnon R.

KINGDOM OF SIHON
Amorites

AMMON

MOAB

EDOM
MT. SEIR

Rehoboth
Ascent of
Akrabbim
Wilderness of Zin
River of Egypt
Besor R.
Gerar R.
Arabah
Kadesh-barnea
(En-mishpat)

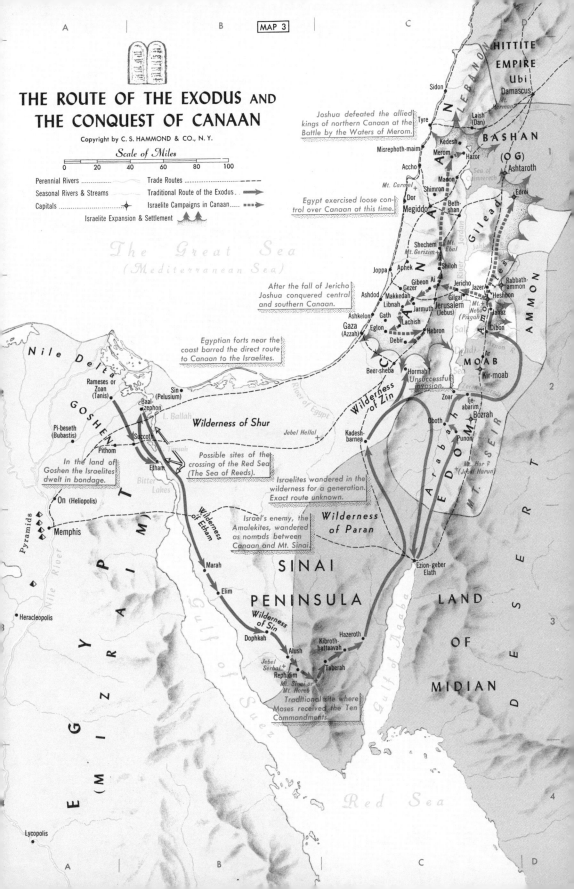

MAP 3

THE ROUTE OF THE EXODUS AND
THE CONQUEST OF CANAAN

Copyright by C. S. HAMMOND & CO., N.Y.

Scale of Miles

0   20   40   60   80   100

Perennial Rivers ....   Trade Routes ....
Seasonal Rivers & Streams   Traditional Route of the Exodus ..→
Capitals ....✛   Israelite Campaigns in Canaan ..... ┅┅►
Israelite Expansion & Settlement ⌃⌃

The Great Sea
(Mediterranean Sea)

Joshua defeated the allied
kings of northern Canaan at the
Battle by the Waters of Merom.

Egypt exercised loose control over Canaan at this time.

After the fall of Jericho
Joshua conquered central
and southern Canaan.

Egyptian forts near the
coast barred the direct route
to Canaan to the Israelites.

Nile Delta

In the land of
Goshen the Israelites
dwelt in bondage.

Wilderness of Shur

Possible sites of the
crossing of the Red Sea
(The Sea of Reeds).

Israelites wandered in the
wilderness for a generation.
Exact route unknown.

Israel's enemy, the
Amalekites, wandered
as nomads between
Canaan and Mt. Sinai.

Wilderness
of Paran

Unsuccessful
invasion

SINAI
PENINSULA

Wilderness
of Sin

LAND

OF

MIDIAN

Traditional site where
Moses received the Ten
Commandments.

Red Sea

Place names

HITTITE
EMPIRE
Ubi
Damascus
Sidon
Tyre
Laish
(Dan)
Kedesh
BASHAN
Merom
Hazor
(OG)
Misrephoth-maim
Ashtaroth
Accho
Madon
Shimron
Edrei
Mt. Carmel
Megiddo
Beth-shan
Gilead
Shechem   Mt. Ebal
Mt. Gerizim
Shiloh
Joppa   Aphek
Rabbath-
ammon
Gibeon Ai
Gezer
Ashdod Makkedah
Jericho Jazer
AMMON
Libnah   Gilgal Heshbon
Ashkelon Gath Jarmuth Jerusalem Mt.
(Jebus) Nebo
Gaza   Eglon Lachish   (Pisgah)
(Azzah)   Debir   Hebron Jahaz
Dibon
Beer-sheba   Hormah
MOAB
Ar Kir-moab
Wilderness
of Zin Zoar
Ije-
abarim
Oboth Bozrah
Kadesh-
barnea   Punon
EDOM

Rameses or
Zoan
(Tanis) Sin
(Pelusium)
GOSHEN
Baal-
zephon
L. Ballah
Pi-beseth
(Bubastis)
Succoth
Pithom
Etham
Bitter
Lakes
On (Heliopolis)
Pyramids
Memphis
Nile River
Heracleopolis
Marah
Elim
Wilderness
of Etham
Dophkah
Alush
Kibroth-
hattaavah
Hazeroth
Rephidim
Taberah
Jebel
Serbal
Mt. Sinai or
Mt. Horeb
Gulf of Suez
Gulf of Aqaba
Ezion-geber
Elath
Lycopolis

E G Y P T (M I Z R A I M)

Mt. Hor?
(Jebel Harun)

Sea of
Chinnereth

River of Egypt

Jebel Hellal

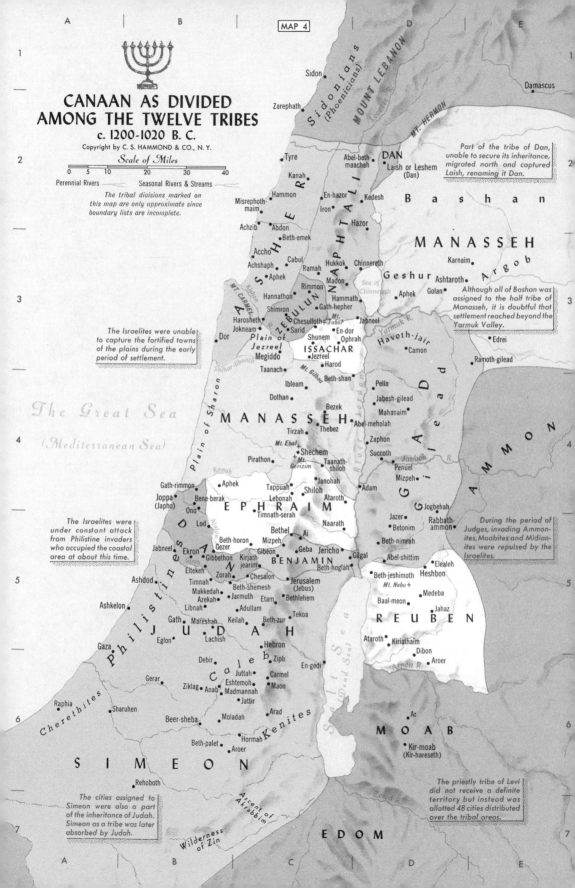

MAP 4

CANAAN AS DIVIDED AMONG THE TWELVE TRIBES
c. 1200-1020 B.C.

Copyright by C. S. HAMMOND & CO., N.Y.

Scale of Miles

0   5 10   20   30   40

Perennial Rivers   Seasonal Rivers & Streams

The tribal divisions marked on
this map are only approximate since
boundary lists are incomplete.

Part of the tribe of Dan,
unable to secure its inheritance,
migrated north and captured
Laish, renaming it Dan.

The Israelites were unable
to capture the fortified towns
of the plains during the early
period of settlement.

Although all of Bashan was
assigned to the half tribe of
Manasseh, it is doubtful that
settlement reached beyond the
Yarmuk Valley.

The Israelites were
under constant attack
from Philistine invaders
who occupied the coastal
area at about this time.

During the period of
Judges, invading Ammon-
ites, Moabites and Midianites were repulsed by the
Israelites.

The cities assigned to
Simeon were also a part
of the inheritance of Judah.
Simeon as a tribe was later
absorbed by Judah.

The priestly tribe of Levi
did not receive a definite
territory but instead was
allotted 48 cities distributed
over the tribal areas.

The Great Sea
(Mediterranean Sea)

Damascus

MOUNT LEBANON

Sidonians
(Phoenicians)

Sidon
Zarephath
Tyre
Kanah
Hammon
Misrephoth-maim
Achzib
Abdon
Beth-emek
Accho
Achshaph
Cabul
Aphek

MT. HERMON
MT. CARMEL

A S H E R

Z E B U L U N

N A P H T A L I

DAN
Abel-beth-maachah
Laish or Leshem
(Dan)
En-hazor
Kedesh
Iron
Hazor
Hukkok
Chinnereth

Bashan

MANASSEH

Karnaim
Geshur   Ashtaroth
Aphek   Golan
Edrei
Ramoth-gilead

Ramah
Madon
Rimmon
Hammath
Gath-hepher
Hannathon
Shimron
Harosheth
Jokneam
Dor

Sea of
Chinnereth

Havoth-jair

Chesulloth
Sarid
Shunem
Jabneel
En-dor
Ophrah
Camon

Plain of
Jezreel
Megiddo
Taanach
Ibleam
Dothan

ISSACHAR
Jezreel
Harod
Beth-shan

Pella
Jabesh-gilead
Mahanaim
Abel-meholah

G I L E A D

A M M O N

Bezek
Thebez

M A N A S S E H
Tirzah

Zaphon
Succoth
Penuel
Mizpeh

Jabbok R.

Jogbehah
Jazer
Betonim
Rabbath-ammon

Mt. Ebal
Shechem
Mt. Gerizim
Taanath-shiloh
Janoah
Adam

Gath-rimmon
Joppa
(Japho)
Ono
Lod
Aphek
Bene-berak

Tappuah
Lebonah
Shiloh
Ataroth
Timnath-serah

E P H R A I M

Naarath

Beth-nimrah

Abel-shittim

Beth-jeshimoth
Mt. Nebo
Baal-meon

Elealeh
Heshbon
Medeba
Jahaz

Jabneel
Ekron
Gibbethon
Eltekeh
Zorah

Beth-horon
Gezer
Mizpeh
Gibeon
Chesalon

Bethel
Ai
Geba
Jericho
Gilgal

B E N J A M I N
Beth-hoglah

R E U B E N

Ashdod
Timnah
Makkedah
Azekah
Libnah

Beth-shemesh
Jarmuth
Etam

Jerusalem
(Jebus)
Bethlehem

Kirjath-jearim

Ataroth
Kiriathaim
Dibon
Aroer

Ashkelon

Gath
Mareshah
Keilah
Eglon
Lachish

Adullam
Beth-zur
Tekoa
Hebron
Ziph

En-gedi

Ar

P h i l i s t i n e s

D A N

J U D A H

C a l e b

Gaza
Debir
Juttah
Carmel
Ziklag
Anab
Eshtemoh
Madmannah
Maon
Jattir
Arad

M O A B

Kir-moab
(Kir-haresheth)

Raphia
Sharuhen

Beer-sheba
Moladah
Hormah
Beth-palet
Aroer

K e n i t e s

Gerar

Cherethites

S I M E O N
Rehoboth

E D O M

Salt Sea
(Dead Sea)

Ascent of
Akrabbim

Wilderness
of Zin

Arnon R.

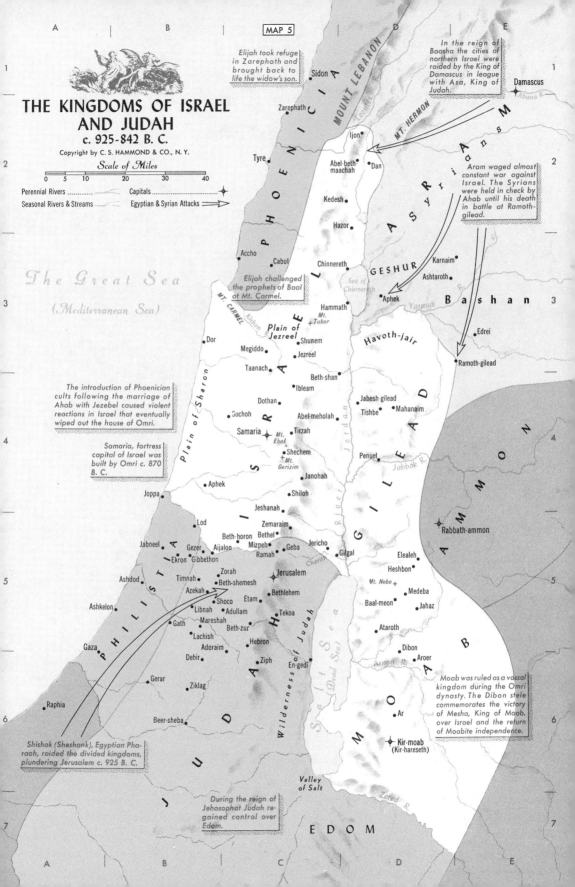

MAP 5

THE KINGDOMS OF ISRAEL AND JUDAH
c. 925-842 B.C.

Copyright by C. S. HAMMOND & CO., N.Y.

Scale of Miles

0   5   10   20   30   40

Perennial Rivers ....
Seasonal Rivers & Streams
Capitals .... ✦
Egyptian & Syrian Attacks ⟶

Elijah took refuge in Zarephath and brought back to life the widow's son.

In the reign of Baasha the cities of northern Israel were raided by the King of Damascus in league with Asa, King of Judah.

Aram waged almost constant war against Israel. The Syrians were held in check by Ahab until his death in battle at Ramoth-gilead.

Elijah challenged the prophets of Baal at Mt. Carmel.

The introduction of Phoenician cults following the marriage of Ahab with Jezebel caused violent reactions in Israel that eventually wiped out the house of Omri.

Samaria, fortress capital of Israel was built by Omri c. 870 B.C.

Moab was ruled as a vassal kingdom during the Omri dynasty. The Dibon stele commemorates the victory of Mesha, King of Moab, over Israel and the return of Moabite independence.

Shishak (Sheshonk), Egyptian Pharaoh, raided the divided kingdoms, plundering Jerusalem c. 925 B.C.

During the reign of Jehosophat Judah regained control over Edom.

The Great Sea (Mediterranean Sea)

PHOENICIA · MOUNT LEBANON · MT. HERMON · Syrians · ASSYRIA · GESHUR · Bashan · ISRAEL · Havoth-jair · GILEAD · AMMON · MT. CARMEL · Plain of Jezreel · Plain of Sharon · River Jordan · JUDAH · Wilderness of Judah · Salt Sea (Dead Sea) · MOAB · EDOM · PHILISTIA

Sidon · Zarephath · Tyre · Ijon · Abel-beth-maachah · Dan · Damascus · Abana R. · Kedesh · Hazor · Accho · Cabul · Chinnereth · Karnaim · Ashtaroth · Sea of Chinnereth · Aphek · Yarmuk R. · Edrei · Hammath · Mt. Tabor · Dor · Megiddo · Shunem · Jezreel · Taanach · Beth-shan · Ibleam · Ramoth-gilead · Dothan · Abel-meholah · Jabesh-gilead · Tishbe · Mahanaim · Sochoh · Samaria · Tirzah · Mt. Ebal · Shechem · Mt. Gerizim · Penuel · Jabbok R. · Aphek · Janohah · Shiloh · Joppa · Jeshanah · Zemaraim · Rabbath-ammon · Lod · Bethel · Beth-horon · Mizpeh · Geba · Jericho · Jabneel · Ramah · Gilgal · Elealeh · Gezer · Aijalon · Heshbon · Ekron · Gibbethon · Zorah · Jerusalem · Mt. Nebo · Medeba · Ashdod · Timnah · Beth-shemesh · Baal-meon · Jahaz · Azekah · Bethlehem · Shoco · Etam · Ashkelon · Libnah · Adullam · Tekoa · Gath · Mareshah · Beth-zur · Ataroth · Lachish · Hebron · Dibon · Adoraim · Aroer · Debir · Ziph · En-gedi · Amon R. · Gerar · Gaza · Ziklag · Ar · Raphia · Beer-sheba · Kir-moab (Kir-haresheth) · Valley of Salt · Zered R.

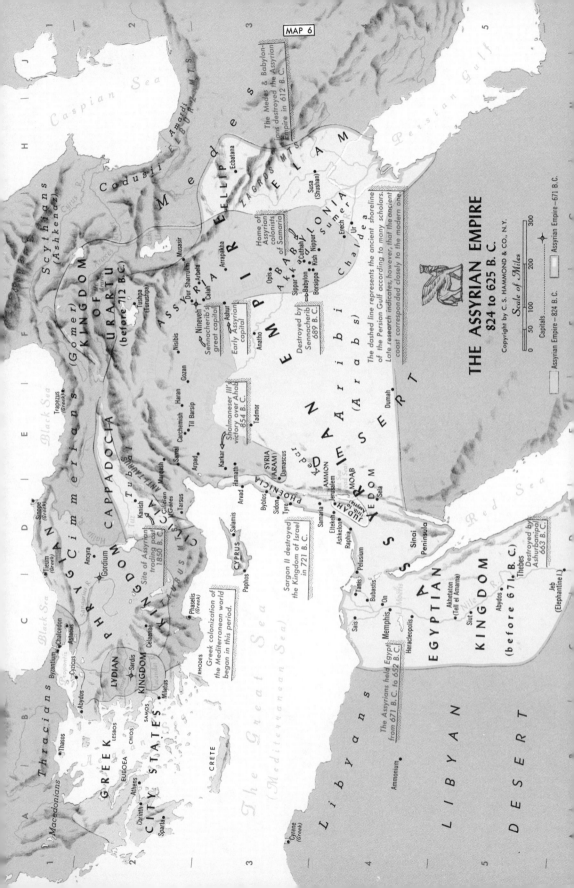

MAP 6

THE ASSYRIAN EMPIRE
824 to 625 B.C.

Copyright by C. S. HAMMOND & CO., N.Y.

Scale of Miles

0   50   100   200   300

Assyrian Empire–824 B.C.   Assyrian Empire–671 B.C.

Capitals

Assyrian Empire–671 B.C.

The dashed line represents the ancient shoreline of the Persian Gulf according to many scholars. Late research indicates, however, that the ancient coast corresponded closely to the modern one.

The Medes & Babylon-ians destroyed the Assyrian Empire in 612 B.C.

Home of Assyrian colonists of Samaria

Destroyed by Sennacherib 689 B.C.

Sennacherib's great capital

Early Assyrian capital

Shalmaneser III's victory over Ahab 854 B.C.

Sargon II destroyed the Kingdom of Israel in 721 B.C.

Greek colonization of the Mediterranean world began in this period.

Site of Assyrian trading post 1850 B.C.

The Assyrians held Egypt from 671 B.C. to 652 B.C.

Destroyed by Ashurbanipal 663 B.C.

Regions and Seas

Caspian Sea

Black Sea

The Great Sea (Mediterranean Sea)

Red Sea

Persian Gulf

S c y t h i a n s (Ashkenaz)

C i m m e r i a n s (Gomer)

T h r a c i a n s

Cadusii

M e d e s

ELLIPI

ELAM

KINGDOM OF URARTU (before 712 B.C.)

A S S Y R I A

E M P I R E

BABYLONIA

Sumer

Akkad

Chaldea

A r i b i (A r a b s)

S Y R I A N   D E S E R T

CAPPADOCIA

PHRYGIAN KINGDOM

LYDIAN KINGDOM

CILICIA

PHOENICIA

SYRIA (ARAM)

JUDAH (Assyria)

EDOM

MOAB

AMMON

EGYPTIAN KINGDOM (before 671 B.C.)

L i b y a n s

L I B Y A N   D E S E R T

GREEK CITY STATES

Mountains

BURNUZ MTS.

ZAGROS MTS.

ANTI-TAURUS MTS.

TAURUS MTS.

Cities and Places

Sinope (Greek)
Trapezus (Greek)
Tieium (Greek)
Byzantium
Chalcedon
Astacus
Cyzicus
Abydos
Ancyra
Gordium
Celaenae
Sardis
Miletus
Phaselis (Greek)
Paphos
Salamis
CYPRUS
RHODES
CRETE
SAMOS
CHIOS
LESBOS
EUBOEA
Athens
Corinth
Sparta
Thasos
Macedonians
Cyrene (Greek)
Kanish
Mazaka
Tarsus
Cilician Gates
Gozne
Arad
Byblos
Sidon
Tyre
Samaria
Jerusalem
Eltekeh
Ashkelon
Raphia
Pelusium
Tanis
Bubastis
On
Memphis
Heracleopolis
Sais
Siut
Akhetaton (Tell el Amarna)
Abydos
Thebes
Jeb (Elephantine I.)
Ammonium
Sela
Dumah
Sinai Peninsula
Tadmor
Hamath
Karkar
Arpad
Samal
Maqash
Til Barsip
Carchemish
Haran
Nisibis
Musasir
Tushpa (Turushpa)
Nineveh
Calah
Arbela
Dur Sharrukin
Ashur
Anatho
Arrapkha
Opis
Sippar
Cuthah
Babylon
Borsippa
Kish
Nippur
Erech
Ur
Susa (Shushan)
Echatana
Damascus

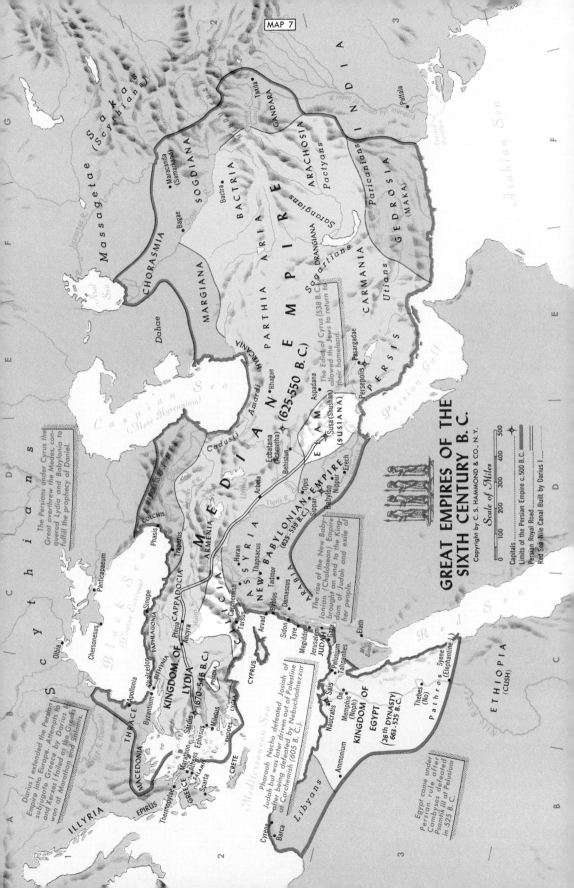

MAP 7

GREAT EMPIRES OF THE SIXTH CENTURY B.C.

Copyright by C. S. HAMMOND & CO., N.Y.

Scale of Miles

0 100 200 300 400 500

Capitals ▲
Limits of the Persian Empire c. 500 B.C.
Persian Royal Road
Red Sea-Nile Canal Built by Darius I

The Persians under Cyrus the Great overthrew the Medes, conquered Lydia and Babylonia to fulfill the prophecy of Daniel.

Darius I extended the Persian Empire into Europe. Attempts to subjugate Greece by Darius and Xerxes I failed as the Greeks won at Marathon and Salamis.

The Edict of Cyrus (538 B.C.) allowed the Jews to return to their homeland.

The rise of the New Babylonian (Chaldaean) Empire brought an end to the Kingdom of Judah and exile of her people.

Pharaoh Necho defeated Josiah of Judah but was later driven out of Palestine after being defeated at Carchemish (605 B.C.).

Egypt came under Cambyses' rule after Psamtik III defeated in 525 B.C. at Pelusium.

MEDIAN EMPIRE (625-550 B.C.)

NEW BABYLONIAN EMPIRE (625-539 B.C.)

KINGDOM OF LYDIA (670-546 B.C.)

KINGDOM OF EGYPT (26th DYNASTY 663-525 B.C.)

MASSAGETAE (Sakā Scythians)

Saka (Scythians)

I N D I A

Arabian Sea

CHORASMIA
SOGDIANA
MARGIANA
BACTRIA
GANDARA
ARIA
PARTHIA
ARACHOSIA
HYRCANIA
DRANGIANA
GEDROSIA (MAKA)
CARMANIA
PERSIS
ELAM (SUSIANA)
ASSYRIA
ARMENIA
CAPPADOCIA
PAPHLAGONIA
BITHYNIA
PISIDIA
LYCIA
CYPRUS
JUDAH
ARABIA
ETHIOPIA (CUSH)
Pathros
Libyans
Utians
Sagartians
Sarangians
Pactyans
Paricanians
Dahae
Amardi
Cadusii
Mardi

Maracanda (Samarkand)
Bagae
Bactra
Taxila
Pattala
Aspadana
Pasargadae
Persepolis
Susa (Shushan)
Ecbatana (Achmetha)
Behistun
Rhagae
Arbela
Haran
Thapsacus
Carchemish
Opis
Sippar
Babylon
Nippur
Erech
Erech
Tadmor
Damascus
Byblos
Sidon
Tyre
Arvad
Tarsus
Ancyra
Pteria
Sinope
Trapezus
Phasis
Colchis
Panticapaeum
Chersonesus
Olbia
Apollonia
Byzantium
Chalcedon
Sardis
Ephesus
Miletus
Rhodes
Crete
Megiddo
Jerusalem
Gaza
Elath
Pelusium
Tahpanhes
Sais
On
Memphis (Noph)
Naucratis
Ammonium
Thebes (No)
Syene (Elephantine)
Cyrene
Barca
Marathon
Athens
Sparta
Thermopylae

THRACE
MACEDONIA
GREECE
EPIRUS
ILLYRIA
CILICIA

Caspian Sea (Mare Hyrcanium)
Black Sea (Pontus Euxinus)
Mediterranean Sea
Aral Sea
Persian Gulf
Red Sea
Nile R.
Tigris R.
Euphrates R.
Indus R.
Jaxartes R.
Oxus R.

Present shoreline

SCYTHIANS

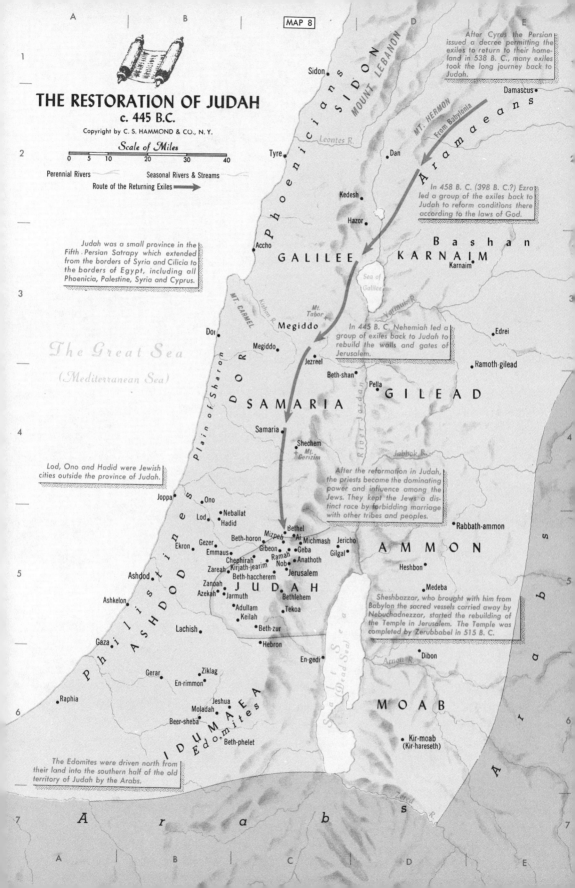

MAP 8

THE RESTORATION OF JUDAH
c. 445 B.C.

Copyright by C. S. HAMMOND & CO., N. Y.

Scale of Miles

0 5 10   20   30   40

Perennial Rivers ⟶

Seasonal Rivers & Streams ⟶

Route of the Returning Exiles ⟶

After Cyrus the Persian issued a decree permitting the exiles to return to their homeland in 538 B. C., many exiles took the long journey back to Judah.

In 458 B. C. (398 B. C.?) Ezra led a group of the exiles back to Judah to reform conditions there according to the laws of God.

Judah was a small province in the Fifth Persian Satrapy which extended from the borders of Syria and Cilicia to the borders of Egypt, including all Phoenicia, Palestine, Syria and Cyprus.

In 445 B. C. Nehemiah led a group of exiles back to Judah to rebuild the walls and gates of Jerusalem.

Lod, Ono and Hadid were Jewish cities outside the province of Judah.

After the reformation in Judah, the priests became the dominating power and influence among the Jews. They kept the Jews a distinct race by forbidding marriage with other tribes and peoples.

Sheshbazzar, who brought with him from Babylon the sacred vessels carried away by Nebuchadnezzar, started the rebuilding of the Temple in Jerusalem. The Temple was completed by Zerubbabel in 515 B. C.

The Edomites were driven north from their land into the southern half of the old territory of Judah by the Arabs.

The Great Sea
(Mediterranean Sea)

Sidon

Tyre

Leontes R.

Damascus

MOUNT LEBANON

MT. HERMON

From Babylonia

Phoenicians · SIDON

Aramaeans

Dan

Kedesh

Hazor

Accho

GALILEE

KARNAIM

Bashan

Karnaim

Sea of Galilee

MT. CARMEL

Kishon R.

Mt. Tabor

Megiddo

Dor

Megiddo

Jezreel

Yarmuk R.

Edrei

Ramoth-gilead

Beth-shan

Pella

DOR

SAMARIA

GILEAD

River Jordan

Samaria

Shechem

Mt. Gerizim

Plain of Sharon

Jabbok R.

Joppa

Ono

Neballat

Lod

Hadid

Bethel

Mizpeh

Ai

Michmash

Jericho

Rabbath-ammon

Beth-horon

Gibeon

Geba

Gilgal

AMMON

Ekron

Gezer

Emmaus

Chephirah

Ramah

Anathoth

Zareah

Kirjath-jearim

Nob

Heshbon

Ashdod

Zanoah

JUDAH

Jerusalem

Medeba

Ashkelon

Azekah

Jarmuth

Bethlehem

Adullam

Keilah

Tekoa

Lachish

Beth-zur

Gaza

Hebron

En-gedi

Dibon

Arnon R.

Philistines

ASHDOD

Gerar

Ziklag

En-rimmon

MOAB

Raphia

Jeshua

Moladah

Beer-sheba

Beth-phelet

IDUMAEA

Edomites

Kir-moab
(Kir-haresheth)

A r a b i a

Salt Sea (Dead Sea)

Zered R.

A r a b a h

MAP 9

THE EMPIRE OF ALEXANDER THE GREAT 323 B.C.
AND THE KINGDOMS OF ALEXANDER'S SUCCESSORS
c. 305 B.C.

Copyright by C. S. HAMMOND & CO., N.Y.

Scale of Miles

0 100 200 300 400 500

Alexander's Route
Nearchus' Voyage
Major Battles Fought by Alexander ✕
Limits of Alexander's Empire 323 B.C.

Prior to the Battle
of Ipsus 301 B.C.

Kingdom of Antigonus Cyclops
Kingdom of Seleucus
Kingdom of Ptolemy
Kingdom of Lysimachus
Kingdom of Cassander

Alexander, after succeeding
his murdered father, strengthened
his kingdom in Macedonia and in
334 B.C. crossed the Hellespont
with an army of about 35,000 men.

Alexander defeated the western satraps
of Darius III at the Granicus R. near Zelea.

After defeat-
ing Darius at
Issus Alexander
occupied Phoe-
nicia, Judaea
and Egypt.

Alexander founded
the city of Alexandria
in 332 B.C. He visited
the oracle of Ammon
and was told of his
divine origin.

At Gaugamela in 331 B.C. Alexander
defeated the reorganized Persian army.
Darius fled to Media and was later
slain by his own men.

Persepolis
was looted
and burned
by Alexander
in 331 B.C.

Alexander died
at Babylon, June 13,
323 B.C., after a
short illness.

Seleucus ceded
Alexander's east-
ern provinces
to Sandrocottus
of India for 500
war elephants
(307 B.C.).

While Nearchus
explored the Arabian
Sea, Alexander made
the difficult overland
march to return to
Babylon.

Alexander
army refused to
go beyond the
Hyphasis R.

Alexander subdued the eastern
satrapies after a long and
difficult campaign. At Maracanda,
Persian satraps were murdered.
Alexander killed his friend Cleitus.

ILLYRIA
MACEDONIA
Pella
Thessalonica
EPIRUS
HELLAS
Athens
Sparta
CRETE
THRACE
Byzantium
BITHYNIA
Heraclea
PAPHLAGONIA
PONTUS
Sinope
Trapezus
COLCHIS
Get ae
Olbia
Panticapaeum
SCYTHIANS
Black Sea
Tanais R. (Don)
Borysthenes R.
Caucasus
Caspian Sea
(Mare Hyrcanium)
Chorasmii
Dahae
Aral Sea
Jaxartes R.
Massagetae
Sakas
Oxus R.
SOGDIANA
Maracanda (Samarkand)
Bactra
BACTRIA
Alexandria Eschate
ARIA
PARTHIA
HYRCANIA
Hecatompylus
Rhagae
Caspian Gates
MEDIA
Ecbatana
Ninus
Gaugamela
Arbela
ARMENIA
Nisibis
MESOPOTAMIA
Euphrates R.
Tigris R.
Thapsacus
SYRIA
Damascus
Antioch (300 B.C.)
Issus
CILICIA
Tarsus
Cilician Gates
TAURUS MTS.
CAPPADOCIA
Mazaca
Ancyra
PHRYGIA
PISIDIA
Ipsus
MYSIA
Ilium
Sardis
LYDIA
Ephesus
CARIA
LYCIA
RHODES
CYPRUS
PHOENICIA
Tyre
Jerusalem
JUDAEA
Gaza
Petra
Pelusium
Nabataeans
Memphis
EGYPT
Alexandria
Ammonium
LIBYA
CYRENAICA
Cyrene
LIBYAN DESERT
Mediterranean Sea
Aegean Sea
Mt. Sinai
Red Sea
Nile River
Thebes
Syene
Ptolemais
Seleucia (Opis)
Babylon
BABYLONIA
Susa
SUSIANA
PERSIS
Persepolis
331
324
Persian Gulf
Harmozia
CARMANIA
Carmana
Pura
GEDROSIA
DRANGIANA
Prophthasia
Alexandria Arion (Herat)
Alexandria Arachosiorum
ARACHOSIA
HINDU KUSH
Alexandria
Bucephala
Nicaea
Taxila
INDIA
Indus R.
Hydaspes R.
Patala
Arabian Sea
Pattala Islands
Present shoreline

MAP 10

ABILENE

· Abila

Damascus ○

SYRIA

PHOENICIA

MOUNT LEBANON

Orontes R.

MT. HERMON

ITURAEA

Sidon

Tyre

PANIAS

Panias ·

Ulatha and Panias were placed under Herod's control in 20 B.C.

ULATHA

TRACHONITIS

Cadasa
(Kedesh)

Ecdippa

Gischala ·

L. Semechonitis

GAULANITIS

BATANAEA

Raphana ◎

Herod's first territory was Galilee, given to him by his father, Antipater.

Ptolemaïs

GALILEE

Taricha (Magdala)

Arbela

Sea of Galilee

Gamala ·

Dion ·

AURANITIS

Kanatha ◎

Sepphoris ·

· Gaba

Nazareth ·

Philoteria ·

Hippos ◎

Yarmuk R.

Abila ·

Gadara ·

· Edrei

Dora ·

MT. CARMEL

Plain of Esdraelon

Hippos and Gadara were cities of the Decapolis given to Herod by Augustus.

Bostra ·

Caesarea
(Strato's Tower)

City and port were rebuilt by Herod.

Scythopolis □

Pella □

DECAPOLIS

Plain of Sharon

SAMARIA

Herod rebuilt Samaria, giving it the new name of Sebaste.

River Jordan

Gerasa □

The Decapolis was a league of neighboring city districts united for mutual protection against marauding tribes. It was not a compact geographical or political unit with definite boundaries.

Apollonia ·

Sebaste
(Samaria) ·

Sychem ·

Mt. Gerizim

Amathus ·

NABATAEA

Antipatris ·

Alexandrium ·

Jabbok R.

Joppa ·

Thamna ·

Phasaelis ·

Gophna ·

Philadelphia □

Lydda ·

Modin ·

Bethel ·

Beth-nimrah ·

AMMON

Jamnia ·

Ekron ·

Gazara ·

Emmaus ·

Beth-horon ·

Jericho ·

Heshbon ·

Ascalon

Herod gained control of Jerusalem in 37 B.C., defeating Antigonus, and became King of Judaea.

Jerusalem

Mt. of Olives

Khirbet Qumrân ×

Livias
(Beth-haram) ·

PERAEA

Azotus ·

Hyrcanium ·

Ascalon

Birthplace of Herod.

Bethlehem ·

Herodium ·

Callirhoë ·

Anthedon
(Agrippium) ·

Beth-gubrin ·

Marisa ·

Beth-zur ·

Machaerus ·

Gaza ·

JUDAEA

Hebron ·

En-gedi ·

Dibon ·

Salt Sea
(Dead Sea)

THE DOMINIONS OF
HEROD THE GREAT
37 to 4 B.C.

Copyright by C. S. HAMMOND & CO., N.Y.

IDUMAEA

Bersabee ·

Masada ·

Kir-moab
(Kir-hareseth) ·

Arnon R.

Scale of Miles

0   5   10   20   30   40

Perennial Rivers .... Capitals ....
Seasonal Rivers & Streams   Cities of the Decapolis □

Kingdom of Herod the Great–4 B.C.

Decapolis

Autonomous city state of Ascalon

Roman province of Syria

Kingdom of Lysanias

NABATAEANS

MAP 11

PALESTINE IN THE TIME OF CHRIST

Copyright by C. S. HAMMOND & CO., N. Y.

Scale of Miles

0   5   10   20   30   40

Perennial Rivers ....
Seasonal Rivers & Streams

Capitals ....
Roads & Trade Routes ------

Tetrarchy of Lysanias
Tetrarchy of Philip
Tetrarchy of Herod Antipas
Territory under Roman procurator

Areas tributary to Salome
Decapolis *
Independent *
Roman province of Syria

Cities of the Decapolis........□

* The Decapolis and Ascalon retained their independence under the Roman governor of the province of Syria.

Archelaus, upon Herod's death, became ruler of Judaea, Samaria and northern Idumaea. His reign lasted until 6 A.D. when he was removed and exiled. His territory then was placed under a Roman procurator.

Salome, Herod's sister, was given Jamnia, Azotus, Phasaelis and Archelais. They in turn passed to Livia, wife of Augustus, and then to the emperor Tiberius.

The Great Sea

(Mediterranean Sea)

ABILENE
Abila

Sidon

Sarepta (Zarephath)

MOUNT LEBANON

MT. HERMON

Damascus

I T U R A E A

PHOENICIA

Tyre

Cadasa (Kedesh)

Gischala

PANIAS
Dan Caesarea Philippi

ULATHA
Lake Semechonitis

Seleucia

TRACHONITIS

BATANAEA

BASHAN

Raphana

Ptolemais (Accho)

MT. CARMEL

Jotapata
Cana
Sepphoris
Nazareth

Chorazin Bethsaida
Magdala (Dalmanutha) Capernaum Julias
Tabigha Gergesa?
Horns of Hattin Sea of Galilee
Tiberias Hippos
Philoteria
Mt. Tabor
Plain of Esdraelon Nain

GALILEE

Gamala

Dion

AURANITIS

Edrei

GAULANITIS

Abila
Gadara
Capitolias

Dora

Caesarea
Residence of Roman procurator.

Ginaea Scythopolis

Pella

DECAPOLIS

Salim?

Gerasa

SAMARIA

Sebaste (Samaria)
Mt. Ebal
Sychem (Sychar?)
Mt. Gerizim Jacob's Well
Salim?

Amathus

G I L E A D

Jabbok R.

Apollonia

Antipatris

Arimathaea
Lydda (Diospolis)
Gophna
Gazara (Gezer)
Bethel
Ramah

Joppa

Jamnia

Ekron
Nicopolis (Emmaus)

Azotus

Emmaus
Jerusalem
Bethany
Bethlehem

Ascalon

Gaza

JUDAEA

Marisa
Bethsura
Hebron
Ziph
Juttah
Carmel

Raphia

Bersabee

Elusa

Alexandrium

Phasaelis

Archelais
Ephraim
Jericho

PERAEA

Bethennabris

Julias (Livias, Beth-haran)

Philadelphia (Rabbath-ammon)

Essebon

AMMON

Mt. of Olives
Herodium

Khirbet Qumrân

Ruins of Essene community found here; also Dead Sea Scrolls in caves nearby.

Callirhoe

Machaerus

Dibon

Wilderness of Judaea

Salt or Dead Sea (L. Asphaltitis)

En-gedi

Masada

MOABITIS

Kir-moab

IDUMAEA

N A B A T A E A N S

A R A B I A

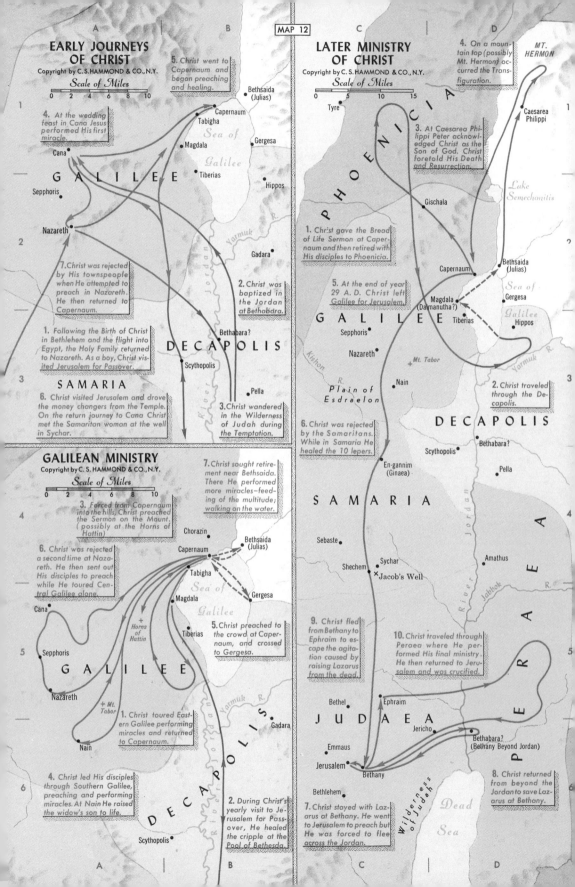

MAP 12

EARLY JOURNEYS OF CHRIST

Copyright by C.S. HAMMOND & CO., N.Y.

Scale of Miles

0 2 4 6 8 10

4. At the wedding feast in Cana Jesus performed His first miracle.

5. Christ went to Capernaum and began preaching and healing.

7. Christ was rejected by His townspeople when He attempted to preach in Nazareth. He then returned to Capernaum.

1. Following the Birth of Christ in Bethlehem and the flight into Egypt, the Holy Family returned to Nazareth. As a boy, Christ visited Jerusalem for Passover.

6. Christ visited Jerusalem and drove the money changers from the Temple. On the return journey to Cana Christ met the Samaritan woman at the well in Sychar.

2. Christ was baptized in the Jordan at Bethabara.

3. Christ wandered in the Wilderness of Judah during the Temptation.

GALILEE
SAMARIA
DECAPOLIS

Cana · Sepphoris · Nazareth · Magdala · Tiberias · Capernaum · Tabigha · Bethsaida (Julias) · Sea of Galilee · Gergesa · Hippos · Gadara · Bethabara? · Scythopolis · Pella

Jordan River · Yarmuk R.

LATER MINISTRY OF CHRIST

Copyright by C.S. HAMMOND & CO., N.Y.

Scale of Miles

0 5 10 15

4. On a mountain top (possibly Mt. Hermon) occurred the Transfiguration.

3. At Caesarea Philippi Peter acknowledged Christ as the Son of God. Christ foretold His Death and Resurrection.

1. Christ gave the Bread of Life Sermon at Capernaum and then retired with His disciples to Phoenicia.

5. At the end of year 29 A.D. Christ left Galilee for Jerusalem.

2. Christ traveled through the Decapolis.

6. Christ was rejected by the Samaritans. While in Samaria He healed the 10 lepers.

9. Christ fled from Bethany to Ephraim to escape the agitation caused by raising Lazarus from the dead.

10. Christ traveled through Peraea where He performed His final ministry. He then returned to Jerusalem and was crucified.

8. Christ returned from beyond the Jordan to save Lazarus at Bethany.

7. Christ stayed with Lazarus at Bethany. He went to Jerusalem to preach but He was forced to flee across the Jordan.

MT. HERMON · Caesarea Philippi · Lake Semechonitis · Tyre · Gischala · Capernaum · Bethsaida (Julias) · Magdala (Dalmanutha?) · Tiberias · Gergesa · Hippos · Sea of Galilee

PHOENICIA · GALILEE · Sepphoris · Nazareth · Mt. Tabor · Nain · DECAPOLIS · Scythopolis · Bethabara? · Pella · Plain of Esdraelon · Kishon R. · Yarmuk R.

SAMARIA · En-gannim (Ginaea) · Sebaste · Shechem · Sychar · ×Jacob's Well · Amathus · River Jabbok · PERAEA

JUDAEA · Bethel · Ephraim · Jericho · Emmaus · Jerusalem · Bethany · Bethlehem · Bethabara? (Bethany Beyond Jordan) · Wilderness of Judah · Dead Sea

GALILEAN MINISTRY

Copyright by C.S. HAMMOND & CO., N.Y.

Scale of Miles

0 2 4 6 8 10

3. Forced from Capernaum into the hills, Christ preached the Sermon on the Mount. (possibly at the Horns of Hattin)

7. Christ sought retirement near Bethsaida. There He performed more miracles—feeding of the multitude; walking on the water.

6. Christ was rejected a second time at Nazareth. He then sent out His disciples to preach while He toured Central Galilee alone.

5. Christ preached to the crowd at Capernaum, and crossed to Gergesa.

1. Christ toured Eastern Galilee performing miracles and returned to Capernaum.

4. Christ led His disciples through Southern Galilee, preaching and performing miracles. At Nain He raised the widow's son to life.

2. During Christ's yearly visit to Jerusalem for Passover, He healed the cripple at the Pool of Bethesda.

GALILEE · DECAPOLIS · Cana · Sepphoris · Nazareth · Chorazin · Capernaum · Bethsaida (Julias) · Tabigha · Magdala · Tiberias · Gergesa · Sea of Galilee · Horns of Hattin · +Mt. Tabor · Nain · Gadara · Scythopolis · Yarmuk R.

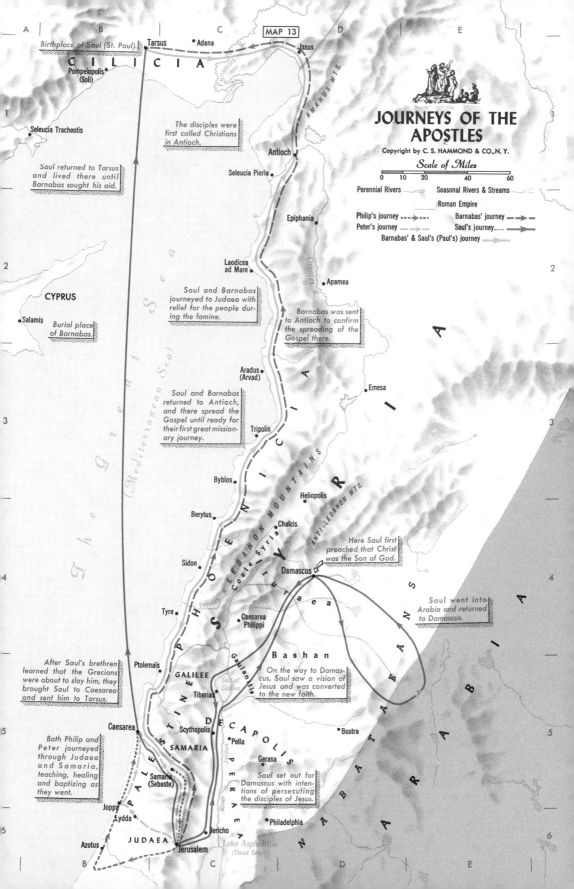

A | B | C | D | E

Birthplace of Saul (St. Paul). **Tarsus** • Adana

MAP 13

Issus

CILICIA

Pompeiopolis (Soli)

Seleucia Tracheotis

The disciples were first called Christians in Antioch.

Saul returned to Tarsus and lived there until Barnabas sought his aid.

Antioch

Seleucia Pieria

JOURNEYS OF THE APOSTLES

Copyright by C. S. HAMMOND & CO., N.Y.

Scale of Miles

0 — 10 — 20 — 40 — 60

Perennial Rivers — Seasonal Rivers & Streams

Roman Empire

Philip's journey — — — — Barnabas' journey — — →

Peter's journey — — → Saul's journey . . . . .

Barnabas' & Saul's (Paul's) journey →

Epiphania

CYPRUS

• Salamis

Burial place of Barnabas.

Laodicea ad Mare

Saul and Barnabas journeyed to Judaea with relief for the people during the famine.

• Apamea

Barnabas was sent to Antioch to confirm the spreading of the Gospel there.

• Emesa

Aradus (Arvad)

Saul and Barnabas returned to Antioch, and there spread the Gospel until ready for their first great missionary journey.

Tripolis

Byblos •

Heliopolis •

Berytus •

Chalcis •

Here Saul first preached that Christ was the Son of God.

Sidon •

Damascus

Saul went into Arabia and returned to Damascus.

Tyre •

Caesarea Philippi •

B a s h a n

On the way to Damascus, Saul saw a vision of Jesus and was converted to the new faith.

After Saul's brethren learned that the Grecians were about to slay him, they brought Saul to Caesarea and sent him to Tarsus.

Ptolemaïs •

GALILEE

Tiberias •

Caesarea

Both Philip and Peter journeyed through Judaea and Samaria, teaching, healing and baptizing as they went.

Scythopolis •

• Pella

SAMARIA

DECAPOLIS

• Bostra

Samaria (Sebaste) •

Gerasa •

Saul set out for Damascus with intentions of persecuting the disciples of Jesus.

Joppa •

Lydda •

Philadelphia •

Azotus •

JUDAEA

Jerusalem

Jericho •

Lake Asphaltitis (Dead Sea)

PHOENICIA

LEBANON MOUNTAINS

Coele-Syria

ANTI-LEBANON MTS.

S Y R I A

Ituraea

Leontes R.

PALESTINE

Gaulanitis

Sea of Galilee

Jordan River

PERAEA

N A B A T A E A N S

A R A B I A

The Great Sea (Mediterranean Sea)

Orontes R.

Pyramus R.

AMANUS MTS.

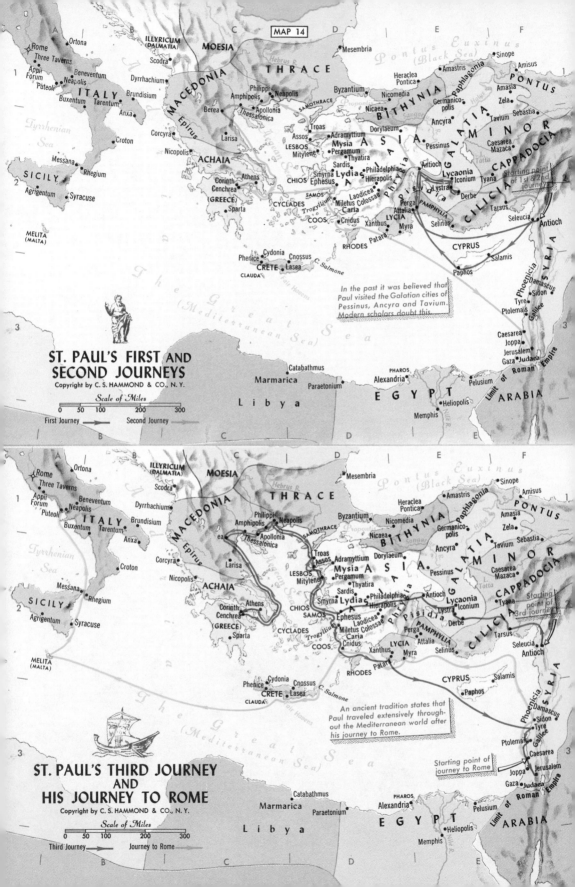

MAP 14

ST. PAUL'S FIRST AND SECOND JOURNEYS
Copyright by C. S. HAMMOND & CO., N.Y.

Scale of Miles

0   50   100   200   300

First Journey ⟶   Second Journey ⟶

In the past it was believed that Paul visited the Galatian cities of Pessinus, Ancyra and Tavium. Modern scholars doubt this.

ST. PAUL'S THIRD JOURNEY AND HIS JOURNEY TO ROME
Copyright by C. S. HAMMOND & CO., N.Y.

Scale of Miles

0   50   100   200   300

Third Journey ⟶   Journey to Rome ⟶

An ancient tradition states that Paul traveled extensively throughout the Mediterranean world after his journey to Rome.

Starting point of journey to Rome

MAP 15

THE SPREAD OF CHRISTIANITY
Copyright by C. S. HAMMOND & CO., N.Y.

Scale of Miles

0   100   200   400   600

INTRODUCTION OF CHRISTIANITY

Areas known to contain Christians
at the time of Irenaeus, c. 185

185-325
(by the time of Constantine)

325-600
(by the time of Gregory I)

600-800
(by the time of Charlemagne)

800-1300

Northern limit of area permanently lost to Mohammedanism. ---------

During the 7th cent. the
Nestorian Christian Church
introduced Christianity into
Central Asia.

The Christian Coptic Church
was introduced on the Upper Nile
and in Ethiopia in the 4th cent.

Christianity in Roman
Britain was wiped out
by the Anglo-Saxon inva-
sion. The faith was rees-
tablished in the 7th cent.
by Irish missionaries.

Caspian Sea
Black Sea
Mediterranean Sea
Red Sea
Baltic Sea
North Sea
Atlantic Ocean

IRELAND
Clonard

BRITAIN
York
Lincoln
London
Canterbury
Caerleon

Lithuanians (13th Cent.)
Riga

Prussians (13th Cent.)
Marienburg
Pomeranians (1122-1130)
Gnesen
Poles (962-1025)

Russians (989-1015)
Kiev

Magdeburg
Bremen
Utrecht
Cologne
Trier
Fulda
Mainz
Reims
Paris
Rouen
Tours
Bourges
Luxeuil

Magyars (950-1050)

Czechs (c. 1000)
Regensburg
Augsburg
Esztergom
Sirmium
Siscia

Thuringians (8th Cent.)
Saxons (785-805)
Alamanni (7th Cent.)

GAUL
Lyons
Vienne
Arles
Narbonne
Toulouse
Nantes
Bordeaux

SPAIN
Leon
Astorga
Toledo
Merida
Evora
Faro
Cadiz
Seville
Cordova
Malaca
Valencia
Cartagena
Saragossa
Tarragona

BALEARIC IS.

CORSICA
SARDINIA

ITALY
Milan
Genoa
Pisa
Florence
Verona
Aquileia
Ravenna
Ancona
Rome
Puteoli
Naples
Beneventum
Messina

SICILY
Syracuse

Tingis
Caesarea
Cirta
Lambaesis
Hippo Regius
Madaura
Carthage
Hadrumetum
Lepis Magna

Salona
Durazzo
Sardica
Singidunum
Preslav
Nicopolis
Beroea
Philippi
Thessalonica
Larissa
Corinth
Athens
Sparta
CRETE
Gortyna
Cnossus

Chersonesus
Tomi
Anchialus
Develtum
Constantinople
Chalcedon
Nicomedia
Nicaea
Pergamum
Thyatira
Sardis
Smyrna
Ephesus
Laodicea
Tralles
Myra
Perga
RHODES

Sinope
Amastris
Ancyra
Antioch
Iconium
Tarsus
CYPRUS
Salamis
Paphos
Caesarea

Cyrene
Berenice

Pityus
Vagarshapat
ARMENIA
Melitene
Edessa
Nisibis
Abela
Ctesiphon
Seleucia
Palmyra
Damascus
Tyre
Jerusalem

EGYPT
Alexandria
Memphis
Oxyrhynchus
Hermopolis
Ptolemais
Thebes

Volga R.
Don R.
Dnieper R.
Dniester R.
Dnjestr R.
Danube R.
Euphrates R.
Tigris R.
Sea of Azov

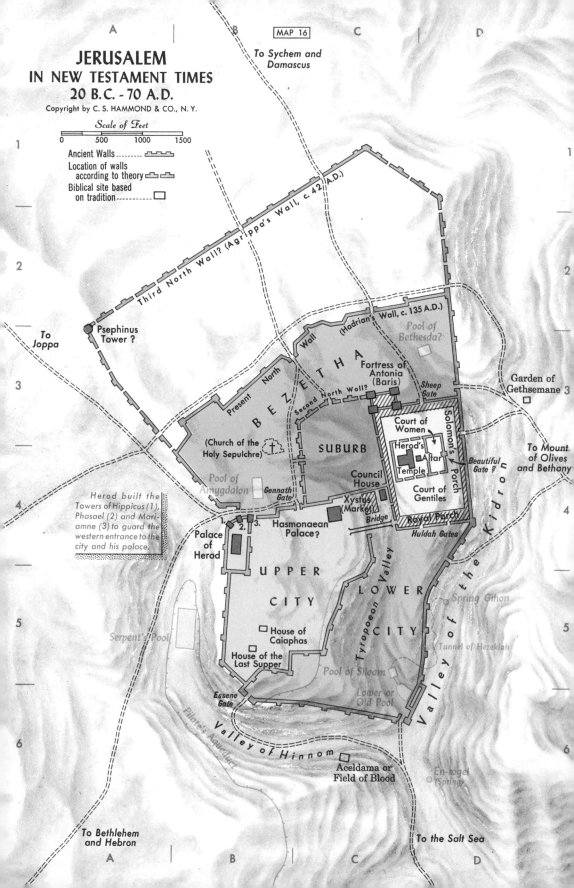

JERUSALEM
IN NEW TESTAMENT TIMES
20 B.C. - 70 A.D.

Copyright by C. S. HAMMOND & CO., N.Y.

MAP 16

Scale of Feet

0   500   1000   1500

Ancient Walls ·········
Location of walls
according to theory
Biblical site based
on tradition ----------

To Sychem and
Damascus

To Joppa

Third North Wall? (Agrippa's Wall, c. 42 A.D.)

Psephinus
Tower ?

(Hadrian's Wall, c. 135 A.D.)

Pool of
Bethesda?

Present North

BEZETHA

Wall

Fortress of
Antonia
(Baris)

Sheep
Gate

Garden of
Gethsemane

Second North Wall?

SUBURB

Court of
Women

Herod's

Solomon's Porch

To Mount
of Olives
and Bethany

(Church of the
Holy Sepulchre)

Altar

Temple

Beautiful
Gate ?

Pool of
Amygdalon

Gennath
Gate

Council
House

Court of
Gentiles

Herod built the
Towers of Hippicus (1),
Phasael (2) and Mari-
amne (3) to guard the
western entrance to the
city and his palace.

Xystus
(Market)

Bridge

Royal Porch

1. 2. 3.   Hasmonaean
Palace?

Huldah Gates

Palace
of Herod

UPPER

CITY

LOWER

Tyropoeon Valley

Kidron

Valley of the

Spring Gihon

Serpent's Pool

House of
Caiaphas

CITY

Tunnel of Hezekiah

House of the
Last Supper

Pool of Siloam

Essene
Gate

Lower or
Old Pool

Pilate's Aqueduct

Valley of Hinnom

Aceldama or
Field of Blood

En-rogel
(spring)

To Bethlehem
and Hebron

To the Salt Sea

were localized in the hill country away from the great trade routes along the coastal region. For almost forty years Tirzah maintained its leadership in Israel but was finally superseded by Samaria, an entirely new stronghold, which was destined to become "the head of Ephraim."

The founding of the new capital is attributed to Omri whose dynasty was the most conspicuous, politically and religiously, in the whole course of the Northern Kingdom (1 Kings 16:23–24). His wisdom was fully justified in selecting the hill of Shemer for the chief city in Israel, and in building on its summit a capital of considerable proportions and strength. Omri called the new city Samaria, after the name of its original owner. The term means "watchtower," and the idea suggested finds complete justification in the nature of the location. The elevation of the hill ranges from three to four hundred feet above the surrounding plains. It is practically impregnable on all sides, except the northeast, where the mound is approached by slow ascent.

The summit of the hill accommodated the royal palaces, particularly the quarters of Omri, and the "Ivory Palace" whose ruins have been exposed by excavation. From the top of the hill, one looks around on a scene of beauty, especially toward the west, where the sand dunes of the Mediterranean coast appear twenty-three miles away. Secure in its position, the great city successfully resisted all assaults, except that of Shalmaneser who besieged it for three years (2 Kings 17:5 ff.). His death, which occurred while the town was being surrounded, was followed by the accession of Sargon, to whom Samaria surrendered in 722 B.C. In his court annals, Sargon claims the capture of Samaria and the consequent exile of the inhabitants.

The deportation will be presented in the next chapter, but it is of interest to note here that numerous peoples were imported from the Assyrian kingdom and established in the heart of Israel. From these people, according to the biblical narratives, we derive the Samaritans whose bitterness toward the Southern Kingdom persisted until the days of Jesus. The fall of Samaria marked the end of the Northern Kingdom whose checkered course extended through a period of almost 209 years.

The Southern Kingdom

The open breach at Shechem did not affect the succession of David's house, since the southern tribesmen openly rallied to the standard of Rehoboam and proclaimed him king over Judah. We are not to infer from this that no other parts of Israel joined Judah in the movement. Apart from Levi, to whom no tribal allotment was made, there are two tribal groups, Simeon and Benjamin, which need to be considered in connection with the division. There is no difficulty regarding Simeon whose interests, from the days of the conquest and settlement, coincided with those of Judah. The two tribes were accordingly functioning as a unit.

On the other hand, there is a clear statement that no other followed the house of David but the tribe of Judah only, which, if rigidly pressed, would exclude Benjamin from the southern alliance (1 Kings 12:20). That such is not the meaning is clearly shown in the verses following where Benjamin is mentioned in connection with Judah. All that the statement implies is that to Judah fell the responsibility of assuming the leadership in championing the cause of Rehoboam. It would be remembered also that Benjamin and Judah were almost as closely identified as Simeon and Judah. Regarded in this manner, therefore, the tribal units constituting the Southern Kingdom were Judah and Benjamin. The capital city of the Southern Kingdom continued at Jerusalem.

The territory of Judah differed in two important respects from Israel, its rival kingdom on the north. The first of these was its unitary nature. It was a compact area with no artificial barriers, such as the Jordan Valley, to affect its solidarity. Judah had its weaknesses, but its geographical characteristics were wholly favorable. In the second place, the region was comparatively isolated, or at least rendered inaccessible to marauding hordes. It was a highland kingdom, with difficult mountain passes constituting its first line of natural defense. Armies pressed on to Judah but not by chance. Israel, on the contrary, lay across the path of the world conquerors from the time they entered into the northern boundaries until, through Esdraelon or Sharon, they passed on to Egypt. With many accessible valleys leading into Samaria, with low-lying hills not difficult to ascend, the interior was constantly exposed to alien powers. Israel's variegated history, its sorrows and total collapse, have a profound connection with its openness to foreign influence.

None of this was true of Judah, however, for not one acre of its rugged soil, not one hill in its massive range was exposed to passing armies, inviting attack. No army ever approached Jerusalem without provocation or serious purpose. The extreme width of Judah exceeded not more than forty miles, while its length was hardly more than seventy. Surrounded by hostile peoples—Edom on the south, Philistia on the west, Israel on the north—and the Jordan Valley on the east, Judah was practically isolated from world contacts. Its position would have assured security had it not been for certain state policies which resulted in foreign entanglements.

A brief summary of these contacts shows that the first invasion of Judah was made by the Egyptian Shishak, who captured Jerusalem and pillaged its treasures (1 Kings 14:25). This campaign, in all likelihood, began as a punitive measure in behalf of Jeroboam who had been banished to Egypt by Solomon, although 155 other towns in Canaan, including some in the Northern Kingdom, are named on the temple walls at Karnak as paying tribute to the Pharaoh. This invasion occurred five years after the division of the kingdom. Shishak, the founder of the Twenty-Second Dynasty, was probably a Libyan. Either he or his predecessor gave a daughter to Solomon and, as a part of her marriage dowry, the captured city of Gezer (9:16). It is clear, therefore, that Egypt was closely connected with the affairs of Canaan, and that Judah, particularly, was inclined to lean on the Nile kingdom.

But other movements were just as foreboding of evil. When Baasha, king of Israel, undertook to fortify Ramah, in order to strengthen his borders against Judah, Asa made an appeal to the Syrians, and with their aid expelled Baasha from the strategic point (15:16–22). Although the alliance was successful in this case, in the long run it proved disastrous. Jehoshaphat allowed Judah to be drawn into a struggle which concerned primarily the Syrians and Israel, when Ahab was killed at the battle of Ramoth-gilead. An aftermath of the alliance is witnessed during the reign of Ahaz when, confronted by a coalition of Israel and Syria, Ahaz appealed to Tiglath-pileser, king of Assyria. The full fruit of it is seen during the days of Hezekiah, when Sennacherib of Assyria overran Judah, pillaging forty-six of its cities.

Hezekiah also introduces us to the Babylonians who were finally to disperse Judah and despoil the Temple. All these contacts illustrate how closely Judah became involved with alien peoples whom the prophet Isaiah describes as "firebrands burning at both ends," and how they finally accomplished its destruction. Secure in its own mountain fortresses, Judah might have continued, but in its atheism of force and fear it leaned on bruised reeds which offered no effective assistance.

Although the Southern Kingdom consisted of only a small territory, within its boundaries were some of the choicest cities in Canaan. No mention is made here of the Pentapolis in the Philistine plains which, after the death of Solomon, reverted to a measure of independence. We name only the outstanding centers of Judah. Beginning from Beer-sheba in the south, one passes through the strongholds of Kiriath-sepher, Lachish, Hebron, Mareshah, Keilah, Adullam, Bethlehem, Beth-shemesh, Kiriath-jearim, Gezer, Beeroth, Gibeon, Gibeah, Jericho, and Jerusalem. This is an imposing list of populous and fortified cities, but the full significance is seen when to each city are added its towns, villages, and the rural sections regarded as dependent. Among these daughters of Judah, however, none was compared with Jerusalem, the daughter of Zion. Because of its surpassing importance in the affairs of the Southern Kingdom throughout its history, attention must be given to a closer description of the city, including its site, fortifications, and general characteristics, from the time of its founding until the destruction by Nebuchadnezzar in 587 B.C.

Jerusalem

Writers in the Old Testament, particularly in the Psalms, vie with one another in their efforts to describe the features of Jerusalem, the city of the Great King. "Beautiful for situation, the joy of the whole earth, is mount Zion" (Psalm 48:2). "Jerusalem is builded as a city that is compact together"; "in the mountain of his holiness" (122:3; 48:1). "For the Lord hath chosen Zion; he hath desired it for his habitation" (132:13). "Walk about Zion, and go round about her: tell the towers thereof. Mark ye well her bulwarks, consider her palaces" (48:12–13). Of special interest is the topographical reference which the psalmist gives regarding the general location of Jerusalem, that is, as nestling in the mountains round about her.

This description is literally true. Bethel, the Mount of Olives, and Bethlehem are all parts of the same great range, but these and other points are superior in elevation to the City of David. While this is also applicable to the several hills of Jerusalem, it is especially true regarding the city of the psalmist which was located on Ophel at the southern end of the eastern ridge. This was the original fortress of the Jebusites, the boasted impregnable city which David conquered and converted into his capital.

The wedge-shaped city occupied the slopes of the eastern ridge, considerably elevated above the beds of three great valleys bordering it on the east, the south, and the west. The Kidron Valley, now partially filled in with debris of the ages, was probably between 150 and 200 feet below the city, while the Tyropoeon on the west was perhaps shallower. The two depressions converged on the south to form another valley, subsequently known as the Gehenna or Topheth (Hinnom). On the other hand, the northern portion of the city gradually ascended with the slopes of Mount Moriah, having at the foot of Mount Moriah a small natural valley intervening. Cut off on all sides, the city was then encompassed with a stone wall which provided additional protection. Portions of this wall, now standing, are found halfway down the east slope toward Gihon Spring, and its foundation is dated to about 1800 B.C.

In time of siege the Jebusites had access to the Gihon Spring by a subterranean passage which led from the interior of the city. It was on the order of a horizontal shaft to which was joined a vertical passage at the lower end connecting with the water supply. The secret passage reflects real initiative on the part of the Jebusites regarding measures of protection. The passage here referred to, in all probability, gave Joab the opportunity to capture the city by surprise attack (2 Sam. 5:8; 1 Chron. 11:6). Furthermore, the manner in which the Jebusites gained access to their water supply might have suggested to Hezekiah in 701 B.C. the improved arrangement whereby the Gihon water was tunneled under Ophel, through what is now known as the Siloam Tunnel, to be stored in the pool of Siloam just inside the city wall at the southwest. The tunnel is still in existence.

After the conquest of Jebus, it was named the City of David and converted into the capital of the United Kingdom. The conquerors proceeded to repair all damage caused by the siege and capture, improving at the same time the city's fortifications. Chief among these defenses was the Millo, which stood near the water gate issuing into the Kidron Valley. The statement that David repaired the Millo suggests that it was in existence previously. Recent evidence indicates that the great fill, or Millo, on the east crest of Ophel above Gihon Spring was first built by the Jebusites to extend the top of the ridge eastward some sixty feet. The magnitude of the project suggests that it was for royal buildings and not private houses.

The Jerusalem of Solomon was considerably larger than the old City of David. In addition to the original city, Mount Moriah to the north with its bulging southern connection with Zion was added. A new palace and temple complex was constructed, and Jerusalem doubled its fortified area. There is insufficient evidence to claim that the western hill was included in the enlarged city.

Ancient Jerusalem was to the Israelite a beautiful city. The policy of Solomon to make the capital the outstanding religious, cultural, and political center was followed by his successors. It was the eye of the Southern Kingdom, the pride of every Israelite. Jerusalem was the central place to which all the tribes went up. Its capture by Nebuchadnezzar in 587 B.C., together with its complete destruction by Nebuzaradan, was a tragedy, perhaps the greatest suffered by Israelites since the bondage in Egypt. The city fell after a determined siege. Walls uncovered on the east slope of Ophel measure sixteen feet in thickness, founded on bedrock. Their destruction is mute testimony to the overwhelming force of Nebuchadnezzar's army. The duration of the siege was remarkable, but even Jerusalem could not hold out indefinitely.

With its fall, the Temple was totally destroyed, the walls demolished, and the Israelites deported to Babylonia as slaves. But, according to Jeremiah, this was not the end of Jerusalem, nor of the people of his choice: "Behold, I will bring again the captivity of Jacob's tents, and have mercy on his dwellingplaces; and the city shall be builded upon her own heap" (Jer. 30:18).

8
The Scattered Nation Restored

The captives of Israel and Judah, deported to countries beyond the great Euphrates, were carried back to practically the same sections which Abraham left in search of a promised land. In many respects the northern and southern exiles were retracing the steps of the patriarchs. In view of the fact that a general description of the Mesopotamian sector has been given in the early chapters of this work, we may confine our discussion to the two principal countries affected by the enforced exile of the Hebrew people, namely, Assyria and Babylonia. As will be seen later, the Egyptian phase of the Hebrew dispersion and the remnant left in Palestine had significant features, and for this reason are included in the following survey. As a final consideration we shall trace also the main outlines of the Persian Empire which was instrumental in the restoration.

The Assyrian Deportations

In the procession of ancient kingdoms, the appearance of the Assyrian Empire was relatively late. It stood intermediate between the kingdom of the Arameans and the new Babylonian Empire. The principal portion of the early Assyrian kingdom lay in the northeastern section of Mesopotamia and the area east of the Tigris to the Zagros mountains. The heart of the territory, determined mainly by the watercourse of the great Tigris, consisted of long stretches of agricultural lands which the Assyrians cultivated with a high degree of efficiency, while the uplands on both sides of the river provided extensive pastoral sections. The nature of the country suggests, accordingly, the two main divisions of Assyria's population, that is, the agricultural and the pastoral, which in turn formed the chief support for an urban element dwelling in the great centers of Asshur, Nimrud, Nineveh, and Khorsabad.

Although dominated by the early Babylonian Empire, the Assyrians engaged continually in a struggle for their independence. It was natural that their decisive victory over the Babylonians should have been followed by an attempt at empire on the part of the Assyrians themselves. In point of time, this expansion began under the leadership of Tiglath-pileser I whose dominions included not only the northwestern sections of Mesopotamia but spread beyond to the Taurus mountain area, Syria, and to the Phoenician littoral. With the Egyptian encroachments under Thutmosis I and Rameses II, however, neither Babylonia nor Assyria was able to maintain supremacy in the western countries. But following the rapid decline of Egypt and Babylonia, Assyria asserted itself about 900 B.C., and continued its empire for three hundred years. The dominion eventually included the whole great area which stretches from the Nile Basin through the Fertile Crescent to the headwaters of the Persian Gulf.

The captivity of Israel falls within this period of Assyrian supremacy. It was preceded by a ferocious assault on the western lands by Tiglath-pileser III, who was probably the ablest of Assyrian rulers, the author of several distinctive policies which characterized the empire. These policies included radical measures of deportation and administration. Native rulers of conquered states were usually succeeded by Assyrian administrators around whom was thrown a network of checks and balances, while the prominent classes of the native population were deported to other lands. Invariably these deportations were followed by importations of foreign elements. It was a drastic policy, called forth by generally unsettled conditions. As a precautionary measure, it was designed to avert sedition in dependent states and to assure nonresistance. The Northern Kingdom of Israel was one of the outstanding victims of this oriental program in its rigid operation, when Sargon, the conqueror of Samaria, carried 27,290 of the Israelites into various parts of Assyria.

The direction of Israel's dispersion is clearly stated, though there is some uncertainty regarding the places named. "The king of Assyria took Samaria, and carried Israel away into Assyria, and

placed them in Halah and in Habor by the river of Gozan, and in the cities of the Medes" (2 Kings 17:6). In the earlier deportation of the Transjordan tribes under Tiglath-pileser the same cities are mentioned with the addition of Hara (1 Chron. 5:26). A geographical survey of these localities shows that the general section affected by the northern captivity was the region centering around Haran, the early home of the Arameans.

Several place-names are mentioned, but there is no uniformity of opinion regarding definite locations. Strictly regarded, this region is in the heart of Aram-Naharaim of the patriarchal period. The city of Halah is provisionally placed on the western bank of the Khabur which is not to be confused with the Chebar, or Kabari, southeast of Babylon. This would fix its position almost in the center of the upper Mesopotamian country. It is equally clear that the term Gozan, or Assyrian Guzana, probably refers to a provincial area which, during the Seleucid period, bore the name Gauzanitis.

While these general divisions are specified in connection with the dispersion of the Northern Kingdom, it is not improbable that the Israelites were brought into other large Assyrian cities. Nineveh, the capital of the empire, stood on the east bank of the Tigris opposite the modern town of Mosul. Two mounds in the limits of the capital, Quyunjiq and Nebi Yunus, have been excavated, the former disclosing the palace of Sennacherib and Asshurbanipal, and the latter the royal residence of Sennacherib and Esarhaddon.

When P. E. Botta excavated the ruins of Khorsabad, twelve miles to the north,

37. The Dog River Inscriptions in Lebanon, where Rameses the Great and Tiglath-pileser left records of their campaigns.

he found the remains of the royal palace of Sargon, the conqueror of Samaria. The palace area consisted of more than twenty-five acres. Excavations by A. H. Layard at Calah or Nimrud, twenty miles south, revealed the imperial residences of Ashurnasirpal and Sargon. In addition to these metropolitan centers, other cities were not far distant, especially Arbela (Erbil) which was east of Nineveh, and Asshur on the southwest by the Tigris. It is not claimed here that Israel was scattered throughout these communities, but the Assyrian policy of deportation was so thorough that such a diffusion was altogether likely.

The second phase of the northern captivity relates to the imported peoples who replaced the expelled population in the cities of Israel. It is a striking fact that these foreign elements were introduced from regions not affected by the northern exiles. The biblical account specifies the cities of Babylon, Cuthah, Avva, and Sepharvaim, all of which were located in the middle section of the Tigris-Euphrates Valley. The introduction of these foreign elements is regarded by the biblical writer as the explanation of two additional apostasies on the part of the Northern Kingdom: (1) it was the productive cause of a racial amalgamation which issued in the hybrid Samaritans; and (2) this was the occasion for the religious innovations which further corrupted their worship.

The Babylonian Captivity

Great Nineveh, "the besieger of men," was itself surrounded by a coalition of Medes, Scythians, and Babylonians under Nabopolassar in 612 B.C. and completely destroyed. The center of imperialism shifted accordingly to Babylon on the Euphrates. The new Babylonian Empire, founded by Nebuchadnezzar (605–561 B.C.), represented a powerful organization, both politically and cultur-

ally. In the latter phases of this new Babylonian development there was an introduction of two new elements, the Medes and Persians, whose cultural contribution was no small factor in the civilization which finally blended with the Hellenistic culture under Alexander the Great and the Macedonians. The introduction of the Medo-Persian leaven witnessed not only a modified racial background in Mesopotamia but a marked improvement in government policies of which the Jews were the first beneficiaries. In any case, the era of the new Babylonian Empire was short, its beginning being assigned to Nebuchadnezzar in 605 B.C. and its close marked by the capture of Babylon in 539 B.C. under Cyrus. Though of brief duration, this period embraces the two most outstanding events in the affairs of southern Palestine, namely, the exile of Judah and the restoration.

Our description of the Babylonian captivity will be based, not only on the references in the historical and prophetic portions of the Old Testament, but on a mass of extrabiblical material provided by investigations in the middle and lower regions of Mesopotamia. Unfortunately, we do not have detailed information regarding the whole movement, but a relatively accurate picture may be drawn concerning two important points: (1) the approximate line of advance from Judah into Babylonia, and (2) the Babylonian territory affected by the exile.

Regarding the first point, we have the statement that Nebuchadnezzar made his headquarters at Riblah, a city described as a dependency of Hamath (2 Kings 25:6). It was located on the Orontes River in the upper regions of the

38. Nineveh. Ancient ruins of the Assyrian capital of Sennacherib and Sargon II.

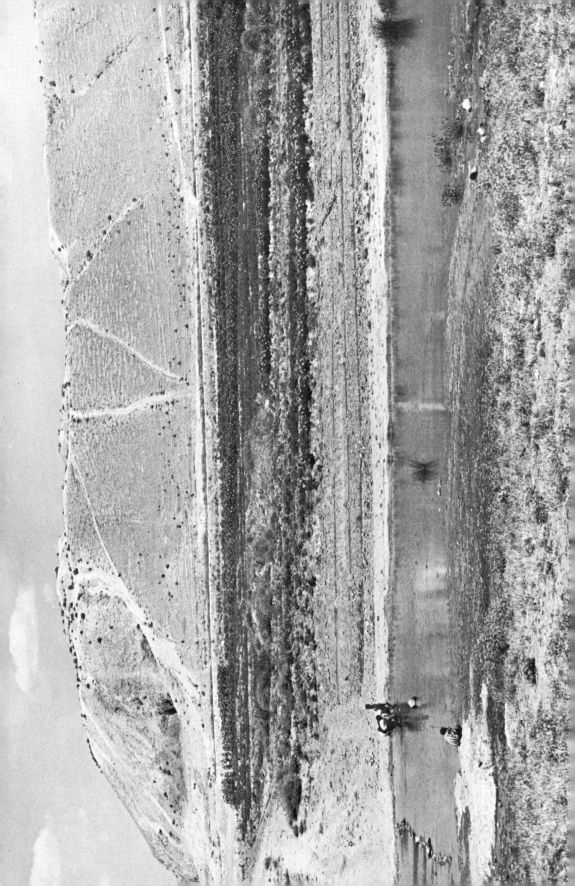

Lebanon Valley, thirty-five miles north-east of Baalbek. The site is marked by the modern settlement of Riblah in the vicinity of Hamath. The city occupied a strategic position intermediate between the southern and northern divisions of the broad valley, and was capable of sustaining a large body of men for an indefinite period. It was a recognized camping place for all invading armies whether proceeding east or west (cf. 2 Kings 23:33).

The exact situation of Riblah in the Lebanon area makes it altogether likely that the captive bands were led out of Palestine by the connecting highway to Damascus, Homs, Hamath, Aleppo, and Carchemish on the Euphrates, and then down the river country to Babylon. This was certainly the route followed by armies and caravans in normal times. The alternative way which ran along the Mediterranean seaboard from Mount Carmel, through the Phoenician lowlands, was more difficult, and would have been followed only under special conditions.

Turning now to the Babylonian area affected by the southern exile, we must depend mainly on prophetic and poetic passages for facts regarding the location and circumstances of the captives. The psalmist complains that "by the rivers of Babylon, there we sat down, yea, we wept, when we remembered Zion" (Psalm 137:1). This reference indicates that the center of the dispersion is probably to be sought either in or near Babylon, the capital city. Another geographical note is given in the introductory statement of Ezekiel: "I was among the captives by the river of Chebar" (1:1). Several notations in Daniel suggest the land of Shinar as the home of the early

39. Winged bull guarding an entrance at Calah (Nimrud), a royal city of the Assyrians.

captivity under Nebuchadnezzar, and the city of Babylon as the scene of Daniel's remarkable career. From these and other biblical references, it is clear that the exiles were located in the heart of Babylonia, probably in the metropolitan area of Babylon.

While it is likely that many of the ten thousand captives were settled in Babylon, the reference to the river Chebar shows that a larger area was affected. There is reason to believe that the Chebar was one of the principal canals designed by early Babylonians for irrigation purposes, but subsequently converted into navigable streams.

The Chebar flowed in a southeasterly direction from Babylon, close by the city of Nippur. It was part of a great inland waterway project which was originally about 150 miles long, receiving its waters from the Euphrates 40 miles above Babylon but returning to the main stream in the vicinity of Ur. Nippur, the chief city on its banks, was located 60 miles southeast of Babylon. It was one of the earliest settlements in Lower Mesopotamia, its antiquity dating from the Sumerian era. Excavations at Nippur indicate not only an extremely early settlement but, through the recovery of a large number of contract tablets with Jewish names, show the site to have been occupied by a considerable colony of Israelites during the exilic period.

On the other hand, it is reasonable to suppose that Babylon received many of the deported captives, and that their intimate connection with the capital city determined in large measure the state policies affecting them. Babylon is one of the pivotal points of biblical interest. The city stood on the east bank of the Euphrates in the middle Mesopotamian section. It was in the heart of the great Plain of Shinar, famed for its beauty and fertility.

Although the time of the earliest

settlement at Babylon is uncertain, the importance of the city dates from the reign of Hammurabi who adopted it as his capital instead of Nippur, situated to the southeast. It was embellished by that illustrious ruler and converted into the religious, political, and commercial center of the early Babylonian Empire. The city attained renewed glory under Nebuchadnezzar, the second of its two outstanding rulers, who boasted of its beauty and greatness.

During the new Babylonian era, the area covered by Babylon was greatly expanded to include territory on the western bank of the Euphrates, although the principal part of the city was always east of the river. Babylon consisted of considerable acreage enclosed by formidable walls. The defenses represented by these walls show a strongly fortified place, particularly on the eastern side, where there was an outer wall of huge dimensions supported by an inner one. Between these walls there was a spacious moat providing additional protection. Although the river constituted a natural defense on the west side, there were mural fortifications in the vicinity of the palace area and temples. It is likely that these served not only against assault but acted as levees in the time of flood.

The metropolis was planned in an orderly manner as indicated by the direction of the main streets which ran at right angles. There was a canal which ran through the midst of the city, providing not only sanitation facilities but making possible extensive irrigation projects. Within the confines of this urban center public buildings, including temples and palaces, were erected and adorned in the manner of oriental elegance. Babylon became the metropolis of

40. Excavated ruins of the "hanging gardens" of Babylon, dating from the time of Nebuchadnezzar.

Asia, a city of such attractive features that the Persians adopted it as one of the capitals of their vast domains.

Alexander the Great also held the city in high esteem. From the city on the Euphrates the Macedonian conqueror was ruling the world at the time of his death in 323 B.C. During subsequent phases of the Greek period, Babylon was superseded by Antioch as the political center of the Near and Middle East. At the dawn of the Christian era it had ceased to exist. Its destruction was so complete that only three small mounds marked the site of the ancient metropolis, but these held securely the treasures of Babylonian life and history until they could be recovered through excavation.

Life in Babylon was on the whole not unfavorable to the dispersion. The destruction of the Temple at Jerusalem created the greatest problem for the exiles, who were thus not only deprived of a central sanctuary but completely cut off from the ritual and the sacrifice. The problem was partly solved, however, by the organization of a place of meeting which gradually developed into the most outstanding and potent expression of Jewish life whether in the dispersion or, subsequently, in Palestine, that is, the synagogue, the house of study and of prayer. It is fairly certain that the synagogue was the product of the Babylonian captivity. Around this central organization were grouped all of the social and religious activities of dispersed Judah; it was their unifying bond in a strange country.

Other interests, however, were seen coming to the fore, particularly the commercial. This development was obviously inevitable, since their new location in Babylon brought the exiles immediately into contact with business relations involving East and West. Babylon was astride the roads of world trade and communication. An international highway crawled through the midst of the city toward the borderland of the Orient.

The remarkable business genius, which has so definitely characterized the Jews through the centuries, received perhaps its first great impulse in Babylon, and has remained to the present. The result of this development was that, when the restoration took place, only a small number of the dispersion were willing to face the austerites and uncertainties of a return to Palestine. The picture, however, is not completely darkened, though its background be composed of these shadows. Light is found in the earnest decision of those who did care for the land of their fathers and its hallowed associations. When the opportunity came, this remnant proceeded again along the trail of Abraham to fulfil his mission.

Egypt and the Refugees

The eastern dispersion, embracing both the Assyrian and Babylonian phases, has hitherto loomed so large and determinative in the biblical backgrounds that little attention has been given to the third part of the scattered nation, the refugees in Egypt. The explanation is found in the fact that, until recently, no information was in hand to justify our looking for a western dispersion on any extended scale until the period of Alexander the Great.

The biblical narratives indicate that centuries before the Macedonian conquests Jewish nationals were found in many parts of the West, having emigrated not only because of oppression by foreign powers in the land of Palestine but because of adverse economic conditions following in the wake of the Assyrians and Babylonians. While there was no general exodus prior to the captivities, with the fall of Jerusalem in 587 B.C. we observe a definite movement toward

Egypt. In close connection with the insurrection of Ishmael at Mizpah, the narrative states that "all the people, both small and great, and the captains of the armies, arose, and came to Egypt" (2 Kings 25:26).

The notice given in Jeremiah indicates that these refugees fled to *Tahpanhes,* a town located close to the border between Egypt and Palestine, establishing there a large Jewish settlement (Jer. 43:6-7). Tahpanhes, the modern Tell Defenneh, was also known as Daphnae during the Greek period. At the time of the dispersion there was in the town a considerable colony of Phoenician and Aramean fugitives. The city of *Migdol,* situated on the border of Goshen, received its quota of refugees, while *Noph* (Memphis) was probably the goal of a larger contingent (Jer. 44:1). In addition to these specific places, a more general movement is indicated in the phrase "and in the country of Pathros" (i.e., the land of the south, or Upper Egypt), which appears in the same passage.

But there were other Jewish communities in Egypt not mentioned in any biblical sources. Among these the settlement at *Elephantine* is the most important. Information regarding the colony is obtained from the recovery (1904, 1907) of a collection of papyri documents giving details concerning Jewish life in Elephantine, a garrison town located on an island opposite Syene (modern Aswân). Ezekiel refers to "the tower of Syene" in a passage of denunciation, but this probably has no connection with the Jews in Elephantine. These papyri are written in the Aramaic language, thus showing the wide prevalence of the tongue which

41. The tomb of Cyrus the Great, in whose reign the Israelites returned from exile in 537 B.C. under the leadership of Zerubbabel.

finally superseded Hebrew in the land of Palestine.

Information contained in these ancient records refers to legal documents, temple accounts, and petitions, all pertaining to the activities of this upper Nile community between the years 471–410 B.C. The item that has caused greatest surprise, however, is the implication that the Jews had already been in Egypt for more than a century. They had a temple at Elephantine which was in existence during the Persian period; we are told that Cambyses (525 B.C.) spared the edifice on his invasion of Egypt. This temple was not an ordinary meeting place, a synagogue, but a real place of sacrifice; its altar and sacred vessels were similar to those prescribed for the Temple services at Jerusalem. While this reflects the attitude of the colonists toward the Jerusalem sanctuary, it likewise suggests their persistence in carrying out at least a part of the religious customs of their fathers in this far-off outpost. Here they were living their own life separate from the rest of the population, observing the Passover and keeping in communication with the national center in Palestine.

But we are shocked to find among these refugees a certain amount of religious syncretism, which shows the worship of Yahweh (Yahu) in a strange setting with pagan deities. This latter state of affairs might have a partial explanation in the retort of the refugees in Upper Egypt when denounced by the prophet Jeremiah for continuing to follow pagan beliefs and practices in Egypt (cf. Jer. 44:15–19). In this connection, it is noteworthy that the Elephantine petition addressed to Bagoas, the Persian

42. Ancient mound of Ecbatana in Persia, where Cyrus issued his decree allowing the Israelites to return to Jerusalem.

governor of Judea, is accompanied by an urgent appeal to the sons of Sanballat of Samaria to intercede in their behalf. Evidently the remnant at Jerusalem looked with disfavor on the syncretistic worship associated with the temple at Elephantine or, as suggested by the appeal to Sanballat, there was some connection between the Elephantine colony and the Samaritans.

Obviously there were other settlements of the refugees in Egypt not here enumerated. Isaiah speaks of the dispersion in the Nile area under three aspects: *Egypt, Cush,* and *Pathros.* It is not clear just what distinction is intended here, but probably Egypt points to the northern or delta territory, Cush refers to the border country of Ethiopia in the extreme south, and Pathros has to do with the land of the South in the vicinity of Thebes. The settlements mentioned above fall within the general period of the dispersion commencing with Nebuchadnezzar. Thousands of Jewish refugees will be found coming into Egypt during the other periods, particularly the era of Alexander the Great and the disruption in Palestine under the Seleucid-Maccabean struggles, but these will be discussed in their proper connection.

The Situation in Palestine

Palestine was completely devastated by the Assyrian and Babylonian incursions. In the former territory of the Northern Kingdom, the struggling city of Samaria appears at the head of a foreign toparchy, administered by representatives of oriental despots. Israelite stock, already enfeebled by foreign admixtures from Phoenicia and surrounding countries, unable to maintain its identity, was finally absorbed into a racial amalgamation which produced the Samaritans. Determinative in this new race was the Mesopotamian element introduced by the Assyrians. According to their policy of deportation, the best people had been carried into the East, while alien races were brought into the conquered territory as permanent residents. Deported Israel was ultimately absorbed by the peoples among whom they dwelt. Thus for the Northern Kingdom there was no sequel of a restoration, except in the attachment of elements of the northern tribes to those who returned with Zerubbabel.

In the Southern Kingdom, on the other hand, while the exilic experience was in some respects similar, there were fundamental differences. The inhabitants of the tribes of Judah and Benjamin were deported at intervals, beginning as early as 605 B.C., although the majority were carried away after the destruction of Jerusalem in 587 B.C. While the principal people of Judah were taken as captives, the number was probably not as large as that which marked the northern dispersion. We are told, however, that "the captain of the guard left of the poor of the land to be vinedressers and husbandmen" (2 Kings 25:12). The wholesale destruction of property by the Babylonians no doubt rendered livelihood very precarious in Judah. We may believe that life in the struggling community was only a bare existence, aggravated by continuous demands for tribute both of money and products of the soil. It was perhaps this latter phase of the situation that influenced thousands of the people to seek refuge in Egypt, where there was not only grain but relative freedom.

On the other hand, unlike the experience of the Northern Kingdom, when the captives of Judah were deported to Babylonia, there was no corresponding influx of alien peoples to take their places, thus assuring that the racial stock of the Southern Kingdom would remain comparatively pure. It is known that there was some intermingling with foreign strains, particularly the intermarriages singled out by Ezra and Nehemiah at a later date, but Israelite blood remained at its best in the southern tribes.

The existence of the little community at Jerusalem, though in dire proverty, implied not only a survival of distinctive Hebrew life and traditions in Palestine, but contributed greatly to the preservation of the hope of a return from Babylonia by the captives. There was certainly uninterrupted communication between these two segments of the scattered nation; the story of Jerusalem never lost its charm, nor her restoration its appeal. Fortunately for the exiles by the waters of Babylon, the prophetic vision survived in Ezekiel, Haggai, and Zechariah. The prophetic outlook of a restored nation gripped the heart of the people and pointed to Canaan as still the Land of Promise.

Restoration Under Persia

The majority of the scattered nation remained in the east beyond the Euphrates River, refusing permission of the Persian king, Cyrus, to return to the land of their fathers. The decision to remain in Babylonia set in sharp relief the attitude of these exiles to the future of Israel. To them the captivity meant the extinction of the prophetic outlook which envisaged a restoration and continued mission of the Chosen People. The glories of a promised restoration, portrayed so fervently by the prophets, made no great appeal; the whole experience of the captivity ran counter to all their expectations. Jerusalem rehabilitated was to them the supreme delusion.

43. The ruins of Persepolis, capital of the Persians during the time of Nehemiah.

On the other hand, there were some who dared to hope for better things. A remnant, cherishing the hope of a national restoration, resisted the temptations of their environment and, when the opportunity came, returned to Palestine to re-establish the faith of their fathers. According to the enumeration in the historical narratives, a few more than 42,000 accepted the decree of Cyrus in 537 B.C. and under the leadership of Zerubbabel returned to Judea (Ezra 2:64). The number involved in this movement, plus the great majority who remained in Babylonia, suggests that the original contingent of captives, instead of being approximately 10,000, was probably much larger. It should be remembered, however, that there were three deportations, the last occurring when Jerusalem was totally destroyed.

In the immediate background of the restoration stands the Persian Empire whose continental organization included the territories of preceding world powers —Babylonian, Egyptian, Hittite, Aramean, and Assyrian. To this vast area it was now in the process of adding bits in the north Aegean sector beyond the Hellespont. In point of time, the Persian Empire succeeded the new Babylonian. To the east, Persia touched India almost as far as the Indus River; to the north, its possessions bordered the coasts of the Caspian and Euxine [Black] Seas. To the west, its outposts included not only the coasts of Asia Minor but reached over the Aegean into Macedonia; the whole of the Mediterranean littoral, in the region of Syria, Palestine, and Egypt, acknowledged Persian rule. To the south, its boundaries reached from the peninsula of Sinai across the Arabian desert to the Persian Gulf. It was a vast empire, more expansive than any that had yet flourished. The biblical narrative suggests the extremes of this kingdom when it describes the Persian monarch, Ahasuerus, as one who "reigned, from India even unto Ethiopia, over an hundred and seven and twenty provinces" (Esther 1:1).

These provincial units are not to be regarded as simply partitions of various states; in most cases they were large territories, embracing many nationalities. Each province was governed by an adminstrative official called the satrap, or commander, whose duties were both civil and military. The satrap, charged with the maintenance of order and the wellbeing of his people, was the personal representative of the king, from whom his powers were derived and to whom he was responsible. So close were these relations that in process of time the satraps came to be regarded as princes of the royal line, and thus dictated policies of state. On the whole, the system was a great improvement over the ancient Babylonian and Assyrian, in that it gave not only closer contacts with governing officials but promoted a fair degree of local self-government.

The earliest capital of the Persian Empire was Babylon, the metropolis of Asia, although previously the Medes centered at Ecbatana, and the Persians at Persepolis. From the accession of Cyrus to the reign of Cambyses, Babylon was the recognized cultural, commercial, and political center of the world, a position which it maintained through several centuries in spite of its rivals. In continuing Babylon as one of their chief cities, the Persians displayed not only respect for the prestige of the former world power but recognized its strategic place in the imperial system. A description of the metropolis has already been given in the preceding section. Cambyses, however,

44. Tombs of the Persian kings who ruled during the Post-Exilic period. On the right is the tomb of Darius I (522–486 B.C.).

ambitious to found a new capital, and having selected a site northeast of the gulf headwaters, commenced to build at Susa one of the most pretentious cities of the ancient world. The place is mentioned in connection with the exile and the restoration, being referred to both as the capital city and the site of the royal palace.

Susa was situated on the left bank of the Choaspes [Karkheh] River (called the Ulai in Dan. 8:2,16), in a valley of marvelous fertility. In all probability the valley has been formed by alluvia brought down from the hills, the Choaspes and other neighboring waterways entering the Persian Gulf much above their present mouths. The nature of the country proved a great attraction, and favorable climatic conditions invited settlements. The period of its greatest importance was reached when Cambyses undertook to supplant Babylon as the capital of the empire by building a new Susa. In this project he showed rare insight, since the place selected had practically all of the advantages of Babylon minus some of its disadvantages.

The city was situated in a fertile region through which ran the great highway to the Indus Valley; it was not exposed to any neighboring world powers, and was more nearly located at the heart of the empire. The glory of Susa finds expression in the Old Testament phrase "Shushan the palace" (Esther 3:15; 8:14). It is stated that many Jews lived in the city and that they were important factors in its commercial, cultural, and political affairs. One recalls the story of Esther, the Jewess, who became Queen of the Persians. From this capital Nehemiah, the loyal Jew, set out on his perilous undertaking to revisit Jerusalem and to rebuild the walls of the city.

Finally, from this Persian capital comes the great stela [code] of Hammurabi containing the codified laws of Su-

merians and Babylonians prior to 1700 B.C. Directly north of Susa stands another very interesting monument, the Behistun rock, rising more than 1,700 feet from the surrounding plain. Here Henry Rawlinson risked his life to copy the trilingual inscription of the Persian king Darius. His marvelous success in that undertaking placed in the hands of scholars the key to the ancient Sumerian, Babylonian, and Assyrian cuneiform writings. The record here preserved sets forth the power of the Great King who dominated not only Persia but the world.

With a splendid system of provincial government heading up in the monarch at Susa, affairs of state were carried on efficiently and, on the whole, humanely. The restored community in Palestine came under the head of these provincial interests. The country fell within the zone of the fifth Persian satrapy with its capital either at Damascus or Samaria. It is remarkable, however, that the Jews, though occupying only a mere patch of territory in the Persian continental organization, were made the objects of several unusually favorable state policies. There is evidence that the Persian government actually gave the remnant financial help.

Indeed, it was inevitable that all the activities of the returning captives should have been carried on under the auspices of the empire. Even so, there is no suggestion that the Jews were sorely oppressed by the Persians; on the contrary, they had fared unusually well as compared with their experience under former masters. The relations between the Jews and Persians here described were continued from the era of Cyrus (539 B.C.) to Alexander the Great (331 B.C.). Thus for two centuries the Jews both in Palestine and Babylonia remained under the Persian yoke, receiving in turn not only imperial protection but encouragement in the re-establishment of the national home in Palestine.

The geographical backgrounds of the re-established community, dominated by the vast empire of the Persians, are accordingly very significant. In the center of the Palestinian province is Judah, and at the heart of Judah, Jerusalem. While the actual area occupied by the remnant, including rural and urban settlements, was restricted to the hills around Jerusalem, no territory in the land was more strategic. It was the sole possession of the restored captives, and at every point vitally related to the future of the Jewish people.

The city of Jerusalem whose walls were rebuilt by Nehemiah "in fifty and two days" (Neh. 6:15) was about half the size of preexilic Jerusalem. Excavations indicate that the walls of Nehemiah were built upon the ruins of structures at the crest of the hill of Ophel, while the preexilic city walls extended halfway down the slope toward Gihon. No occupation evidence after the fall of Jerusalem to Nebuchadnezzar in 587 B.C. is found on the slopes. Thus the postexilic city was only a shadow of its former glory in size and magnificence, which probably encouraged the nuisance tactics of the Samaritans and Ammonites who sought to obstruct the work of Nehemiah.

In the absence of any other world power to dispute the claim, Judea was nominally held by the Persians, but it had many neighbors, especially the Samaritans, Arabians, Ammonites, and Ashdodites, who were constantly opposing its interests. The incursions of these hostile peoples enfeebled the Judean settlement in its efforts to maintain existence under the most adverse circumstances. The city of Jerusalem still lay in ruins, while the whole of the surrounding territory had been ravaged by invading hordes. The economic situation was distressing. In spite of these difficulties, however, the remnant persisted, greatly improving its situation by the construction of the Temple and the city walls, until a more orderly state of affairs was effected by the arrival of Alexander the Great.

Subsequently, the territory of Judea was enlarged to include a compact area centering around Jerusalem, and embracing the Shephelah region to the northwest and portions of the Plain of Sharon in the vicinity of Modin and Joppa. Its northern boundary ran close to Bethel, while the eastern frontier was determined by the Jordan River and the Dead Sea. On the south, Judea reached almost to Hebron, being strongly entrenched at the fortress of Beth-zur.

The restored community maintained its identity until the advent of Alexander the Great. It was the area that had to bear the brunt of the Greek invasion represented by Alexander and continued by his successors, the Seleucids in Syria and the Ptolemies in Egypt. Having discussed the geographical backgrounds of the remnant in relation to Palestine and to Persia, we now turn to one of the most far-reaching movements in world affairs, whereby the Judean commonwealth was severed from the Persians and thrown into the main current of Greek influence.

9
The Hellenistic East

Alexander the Great followed on the heels of the Persians from whom he inherited an imperial organization of continental proportions. In point of time he stands practically midway between the restoration and the Christian era. The accession of Alexander, his vital relation to disordered Greece, and his fiery bitterness against the Persians constitute pivotal points in the world course. His passage of the Hellespont was the initial step in an expanding movement destined to affect all the borderlands of the Mediterranean. Alexander introduced on the widest scale the Greek language, art, and polity, which brought in their train the supremacy of western culture to the Near East.

The imperial organization which followed in the wake of his unprecedented conquests included all of the territories embraced by former world powers. A survey of the empire, beginning with Macedonia, shows Greece and Thrace as important parts of the new kingdom, Asia Minor, Syria, Palestine, Egypt, the Mesopotamian sector from the Persian Gulf to the Armenian Taurus mountains, Media, Persia, Parthia, and lower and upper

India beyond the Indus Valley. With the exception of the Far East division and the western Mediterranean borderlands, the Alexandrian conquests struck at the heart of the biblical backgrounds. The capital of this vast territory was located at Babylon on the Euphrates, almost halfway between Macedonia and the Indus River.

Disintegration of the Persian Empire

The main obstacle that lay across the path of Alexander was the shell of empire dominated by the Persians. The gateway to Persia was Asia Minor. Darius the Great understood the serious nature of the Macedonian threat from its inception, although he probably underestimated the skill of the son of Philip. Alexander's advance was disputed by the Persians, who massed their forces on the banks of the Granicus River in the vicinity of ancient Troy (Ilium). The ill-disciplined and discontented troops of Darius, though practically on the same numerical footing as the Greeks, were no match for the latter. Nor was the stratagem of the Persians able to counteract the new form of phalanx attack em-

ployed by Alexander. The battle resulted in an overwhelming defeat of the
Persians. Alexander was in no haste to
pursue the fleeing enemy into the interior, but he did linger in the vicinity of
his victory to consolidate the newly ac-
quired territory. He overran the whole
Aegean coast before turning into the plateau region.

After a slow advance of about twelve
months, Alexander passed through the
Taurus Cilician Gates to meet the Persians on the Plains of Issus. Although
confronted by a greatly superior force
occupying a strong position, Alexander
won a decisive victory. As a consequence
of this battle the Persian king offered to
compromise with Alexander by sur-
rendering the whole of the Asia Minor
territory west of the Euphrates River,
but the proffer was instantly rejected.
The Persians again retreated eastward to
make their final stand at Arbela (Erbil)
beyond the Tigris.

The coastal area of the Mediterranean
was accordingly thrown open to the advance of Alexander. There was a ready
decision to subdue all of the region as a
base of supplies and operations before
following up the flight of the Persians
into Mesopotamia. The decision issued
in an immediate offensive against the
coastal cities, particularly Sidon and
Tyre, and ultimately against Palestine
and Egypt. Sidon offered no serious opposition to Alexander's advance, but
Tyre was more obstinate, prolonging the
campaign by successfully resisting a siege
of seven months.

It was with the siege of Tyre that the
Jews became definitely involved in Alexander's campaign. Scattered along the
eastern Mediterranean littoral were
settled communities of dispersed Jews
who still regarded themselves as subjects
of Darius and professed loyalty to the
Persian cause, though after the Battle of
Issus there was a general disposition to

surrender to the Macedonians, and even
to participate in the progress of the invasion. Josephus says that the Samaritans
rushed forward under Sanballat to assist
Alexander in the siege of Tyre, and that
their share in the victory over the Tyrian
stronghold resulted in certain concessions to the auxiliaries of Sanballat. It is
stated that Alexander colonized Samaria.
The displaced Samaritans fled to the site
of ancient Shechem where they established a refugee village. Meanwhile,
Alexander contributed to the re-establishment of worship on Mount Gerizim. It is with the restored Jewish community at Jerusalem, however, that we
are chiefly concerned, since their contact
with Alexander determined in large
measure the whole course of subsequent
developments.

After the fall of Tyre, Alexander proceeded along the Mediterranean coast
through the Plain of Acre, then by way
of Esdraelon to one of the southern
routes leading into Sharon and the cities
of the Philistine area. It is highly probable that the expedition of Alexander to
Jerusalem took place while his two-
month siege of Gaza was in progress, or
immediately at its close. From the account of Josephus, who stands alone in
describing this movement to the Judean
highlands, we may approximate both the
time and the general direction of the
offensive.

It was during the high priesthood of
Jaddua. This priest, who is the last one
listed in Old Testament chronology, refused to comply with Alexander's demands for food and auxiliaries on the
ground that the Jews were still under
oath to Darius, and that a transfer of
allegiance would be an act of treason.
The same passage recites how greatly in-
censed Alexander was at this reply, and
how he determined to deal decisively
with Jerusalem and Judea. In addition
to this note of time, we may also approxi-

mate the direction followed by Alexander in his approach to Jerusalem. The notice that the Macedonians appeared before Jerusalem from the northwest indicates the valley of Aijalon by way of Beth-horon and Gibeon as the route adopted. As pointed out in another section, this was the most direct approach to the Judean plateau, the one generally followed by all attacking forces. The surrender of Jerusalem to Alexander definitely marked the close of Persian domination in Palestine.

After the conquest of Palestine, Alexander pressed his campaign against the remaining strongholds of the Persians. His descent into Egypt, where the enfeebled foreign dynasties were nominally ruling, was hailed with delight. The country surrendered without a battle. Alexander's memorable visit to the temple of Jupiter-Ammon, where he was proclaimed son of the Egyptian god, reacted favorably on the conqueror and probably won for him the loyal support of the whole people. Of prime importance was the founding of Alexandria at the Canopic branch of the Nile.

Egypt subjugated, the Macedonian army retraced its steps along the Palestinian coasts to follow up the Persians into Mesopotamia. The approach to the Tigris-Euphrates region was by way of the Plain of Esdraelon to Homs, Hamath, and Aleppo. Almost due east of Aleppo, Alexander crossed the Euphrates at Thapsacus, proceeding to Nisibis (Nusaybin), then across the Tigris River, turning south by way of ancient Nineveh to meet Darius in a final engagement at Arbela (Erbil). Defeating the Persian hosts in a decisive encounter, the Macedonians continued their advance to Babylon, following the trail which Xenophon and the ten thousand Greeks had made three quarters of a century before. The great city on the Euphrates surrendered without a struggle.

Its strategic position was acknowledged by Alexander who converted it into the capital of the empire.

Turning eastward, the invaders stormed the ancient capitals and treasure cities of Susa and Persepolis. The final stages of Alexander's campaign witnessed the overrunning of all the Median territory, Parthia, and on through lower and upper India across the heart of the Indus Valley. The advance would have been carried to the Ganges area, but Alexander's soldiers refused to follow. The conqueror, having completely subdued the kingdom of the Persians, returned to Babylon to organize the new empire along the line of his own imperial ideas and the Greek spirit. His death in 323 B.C. made it impossible for the world kingdom of Alexander to reach its mature expression, but the contributions which flowed from the genius remained as distinctive and permanent factors in all the territory that had acknowledged his mastery. One of the important phases of Alexander's work will now be briefly described.

It was a definite part of Alexander's constructive program to establish great centers of culture throughout the empire. In this policy he differed widely from all those who had preceded him, especially the Egyptians, Assyrians, Babylonians, and Persians, whose chronicles, recovered from temples, mountains, stelae, and official correspondence, recount the desolation following their advancing armies. The chief glory of conquest, if we may accept the records, was the degree of destruction wrought on men and property. But the accounts of Alexander's triumphs are different.

Except in isolated cases where drastic action was demanded, every one of his victories was also a triumph for the local community. Instead of wreaking vengeance by indiscriminate acts of violence, he engaged in programs of constructive service. Where formerly the hostile stronghold was brought to the dust and curses pronounced against its reconstruction, under Alexander it was rebuilt, its walls strengthened, and the city embellished with magnificent public works. In the wake of his armies new cities came into existence. It is estimated that he founded more than seventy centers, sixteen of which are called after his own name. These cities were not built at random; they were designed for strategic and cultural ends and usually located on the great commercial highways. They became outstanding centers of Greek life, thought, and speech. So brilliant was the foresight shown in the selection of locations that some of these cities have continued to flourish even down to modern times.

Era of the Ptolemies and the Seleucids

Following the death of Alexander in 323 B.C., his kingdom was divided among his generals, the strongest of whom were Ptolemy Lagos and Seleucus Nicator. These men became the founders of the Ptolemaic and Seleucid dynasties respectively, the seat of the former being at Alexandria in Egypt, and of the latter at Antioch in Syria. We are not concerned here with the political fortunes of the two dynasties, characterized by Josephus as "princes ambitiously striving one against another, every one of his own principality," nor with the consequent impoverishment of their kingdoms and all bordering territory. Our interest is to show the geographical backgrounds, particularly the outstanding centers where the new civilization became dominant and determinative in the life of Palestine.

As a buffer state between the two kingdoms, Palestine was subjected to all the hardships of a dependency, being repeatedly overrun and despoiled. In point of

time the Ptolemies had the first opportunity to launch their Hellenistic offensive in Palestine and, as will be shown, were probably more successful than the Seleucids who appear subsequently. The movement, however, is regarded here as a whole, as a continuous effort of the Hellenized courts of Alexandria and Antioch to introduce the new culture into Palestine.

In the forcible settlement of the Alexandrian territory, Palestine fell to Ptolemy Lagos as a spoil of war, remaining under the domination of his dynasty, practically without interruption, during the period 315–198 B.C. Within this century and a quarter of rule and misrule are thrown together the various attempts of Egypt to convert Palestine to the civilization of the Greeks. The chief agent in this sustained effort was Ptolemy Philadelphus (285–247 B.C.). His reign introduced the first offensive at Hellenization in Palestine. The methods employed were not based on force but took more the form of permeative and fusive attempts.

Philadelphus inaugurated his plan of Hellenization on the tracks of commerce by establishing an intricate system of new caravan routes, supplementing arteries of trade which had been in existence since earliest times. While serving the purposes of commerce between Egypt and Palestine, these routes also provided lines of communication for a throng of government officials who traveled constantly in the interest of provincial affairs. Thus business was promoted, and through frequent contacts there was ample opportunity for exchange of ideas.

More important than government business, however, was the privilege of unhampered movement from one country to another, the mingling of the common people. Between the valleys of the Nile and the Jordan there was uninterrupted communication. Mixed multitudes came up from Egypt as in the days of the Exodus. They were found not only in Jerusalem but in all parts of Palestine. It was inevitable that the religious concepts which these Greco-Egyptians held should have been transplanted to this new environment.

The most effective aspect of the Ptolemaic scheme of Hellenization was the establishment of great centers of culture. Philadelphus was outstanding in his building enterprises. An exhaustive treatment of this aspect of his reign cannot be given here, but it will be in order to mention some of the Hellenistic cities which were built or rebuilt during his rule. To these were assigned the chief role in the establishment of Greek culture in Palestine. In the Maritime Plain and in the Shephelah the new Greco-Egyptian civilization was completely identified with the surviving strongholds of the ancient Philistines, the hereditary enemies of Israel. Ashdod and Ashkelon were rehabilitated and converted into strong centers, where the religions of Greece and Egypt were fused together in a sordid amalgam. Gaza and Joppa (Jaffa) were conspicuous for their royal connections, possessing government mints from which Ptolemaic coins were distributed throughout the country, and harboring garrisons of Egyptian troops. Gezer, overlooking the plains from the Shephelah of Judea, was an ally of the Ptolemies. Strato's Tower, subsequently called Caesarea, was a center of Ptolemaic supremacy, a fact which was unknown until the discovery of an Egyptian obelisk there by Schick in 1889. Mejdel, two miles from Ashkelon, made its appearance during the reign of Philadelphus.

Of special importance are the painted tombs of Marisa (ancient Mareshah) and a large number of *kokhim* in the vicinity of Tell Sandahannah. These wonderful rock-cut tombs, explored by Peters and Thiersch in 1902, contained more than thirty Greek inscriptions, giving various details concerning the occupants of the *kokhim,* while the sculpture indicated a fusion of Greco-Egyptian conceptions such as the griffin, man-headed lion, Cerberus, ibex, and panther. Sidon on the coast also exerted a great influence in Palestine under the Ptolemies. Accho, under the shadows of Mount Carmel, was rebuilt and renamed Ptolemais, later to be visited by the apostle Paul. In the more central section of Palestine, Samaria and Neapolis were predominantly Greek in population, while Scythopolis (ancient Beth-shan) in the valley of Jezreel retained its old prestige, now reinforced by the new culture of the Greeks.

Rabbath-Ammon, ancient capital of the Ammonites and the scene of the Uriah's sacrifice by David and Joab, was restored under the name of Philadelphia and converted into a magnificent city. In later centuries it was to be one of the most important members of the Greek Decapolis. Scattered here and there were eighteen cities which Philadelphus (Ptolemy II) founded in honor of his wife Arsinoë. Not much actual building occurred in Jerusalem under the Ptolemies.

From this geographical survey of Hellenistic centers in Palestine under the Ptolemies, it is clear that the new culture was beginning to fulfil in large measure the mission which Alexander assigned to it. It should be noted, however, that this steady progress was accomplished quietly and peaceably. Had the Ptolemies continued masters of the country, the story of the Jews might have been considerably modified. But Palestine was snatched from Egypt in 198 B.C. by a coalition of forces under Antiochus III of Syria and Philip V of Macedonia. It was converted into a Syrian dependency, a relationship which continued until independence was won by the Maccabees. A brief description will now be given of the advance of Syrian Hellenism in Palestine during the period 198–67 B.C.

Josephus informs us that the Jews were not averse to a change of their political allegiance from the Ptolemies to the Seleucids. In fact, they welcomed Antiochus III as a deliverer. They assisted him with auxiliaries and provisions in the last phases of the conflict when Scopas, Ptolemy's general, was the adversary. Nor were they unjustified in expecting improved conditions under the new conquerors. Seleucus Nicator, founder of the Syrian dynasty, adhered strictly to the liberal policies of Alexander the Great. He accorded unusual treatment to the Jews in Antioch, giving "them privileges equal to those of Macedonians and Greeks." In like manner he extended favors to Jews residing in other cities of Asia. The immediate successors of Seleucus followed him in this liberal policy, at times even surpassing him in their bestowal of favor on the Jewish dependency.

Antiochus the Great made partial restoration to the Jews for losses suffered during the Seleucid-Ptolemaic struggle, and he repatriated a number of dispersed Jews, made repairs about the Temple in Jerusalem, granted remission of crown taxes for a period of three years and a reduction in amount of all taxes for future years. Other concessions of no less importance are described, particularly that all the nation should be allowed "to live according to the laws of their own country." We do not know exactly the extent of Antiochus the Great's building program in Palestine, but Josephus states that, after the king had defeated Scopas at Baniyas, he seized Samaria, Batanaea, Abila (Jebel Musa), and Gadara. In the case of every one of these cities or districts we must understand the whole region as included and made subject to Syrian Hellenism under Antiochus. There is no suggestion of maladministration of any Jewish territory, nor of any repressive measures directed against the Palestinian dependency by the early Seleucid rulers. Under his favorable patronage of the Jews and Jewish institutions Antiochus probably conserved all the values of Hellenism inherited from the Ptolemaic successes in Palestine, and to those he added contributions of his own.

The net result of this Hellenistic invasion of Palestine under the Seleucid and Ptolemaic rulers shows that Palestine was not in a backwater but rather in the mainstream of Greek culture as it flowed north and south, east and west. Within the little kingdom of the Jews are found numerous ruins of Greek walled towns. Suggestive as such ruins are, however, they should not be regarded as mere archaeological monuments of a bygone civilization but as historical remains reflecting a steady expansion of alien culture in a hostile territory. Everywhere, both in cities and rural sections, Greek ideas and customs were promoted.

Josephus calls attention to "the neighboring cities of the heathen" in the bounds of Judea. On each side of the Jordan was a fringe of centers from which emanated the culture of the stranger. In the north, Tyre, strengthened and embellished by Alexander after its fall, continued as an outstanding factor in the Hellenistic movement, being assisted by Sidon whose sympathies were clearly on the side of the Greeks. It is obvious that Jewish life and culture, thus exposed to the liberal influence at work within and without its borders, must have felt the effects of the new civilization and have been colored thereby. The situation in Palestine during the early Christian era, when Greco-Roman life became most strongly entrenched, reflects an openness and a cosmopolitanism hardly surpassed in any other section of the Near East.

The introduction of the Greek way of life, its secure establishment in many influential centers in Palestine, was the immediate occasion of the stirring epoch of the Maccabean rebellion which constituted the greatest crisis in the history of the Jews subsequent to the time of the restoration. In this uprising the Jewish community emerged from religious seclusion and registered its protest against the stream of Hellenism which threatened to dissipate its traditions and aspirations. Possibly the Maccabean successes preserved an environment of Hebrew life and thought until the seeds of Christianity could be effectively germinated in their native soil.

10
Herodian Palestine

The appearance of Rome at the cross-currents of Greco-Jewish affairs was perhaps the most important political event growing out of the Maccabean revolt. While it is true that there had been indications of Roman interest in eastern affairs prior to the Maccabean uprising, apart from the defeat of Antiochus the Great by Scipio in Asia Minor (189 B.C.), and the expulsion of Epiphanes from Egypt (167 B.C.), it was hardly more than a passive interest based on a policy of watchful waiting. With the progress of Ptolemaic-Seleucid struggles in Palestine, particularly the unequal combat of the Jews with the Seleucid rulers, Rome's interest in Near East affairs increased. Judas Maccabeus, sensing clearly the main direction of the political winds, dispatched a deputation of Jews to "the justice-loving Romans" to request assistance on the ground that "the kingdom of the Grecians did oppress Israel with servitude."

In responding favorably to the request of Judas, the Roman Senate negotiated a lopsided treaty with the Jews, the main item being to guarantee Roman prestige in the East. From that time the Jewish commonwealth was placed in the main current of world movements from which it never extricated itself. In 63 B.C., Rome stepped in to assume full responsibility for the territory of Syria and Palestine, a relationship which was sustained until the destruction of Jerusalem in A.D. 70. Since this period is practically coextensive with the Herodian dynasty in Palestine, and since the Herods themselves were hardly more than Roman officials, the backgrounds here described will be considered from the standpoint of Rome and the Herods. It follows, of course, that we are dealing with the immediate environment of Jesus and the disciples.

Palestine, a Greco-Roman State

Located at the gateway of Rome's eastern possessions, the strategic position of Palestine was never affected by the passing of time or of empires. It was still the causeway of the nations, offering to the Romans the same approach to territorial extremes as to the Assyrians, Babylonians, Persians, and Greeks. Across its borders were the highways to everywhere. In the hands of Rome, Palestine

provided the master key to the Middle East. Beyond Palestine lay Egypt; beyond its northern borders were Syria and Mesopotamia. Its gateways opened in all directions, while within its confines was the perennial problem of the Jews. The steps of Rome were, therefore, guarded in dealing with this new territory. It is significant that, while Roman supremacy was unquestioned, when Pompey assumed control of the Syrian littoral in 63 B.C., the arrangements with the Jews left Judea subject to the general control of the proconsul of Syria, but with freedom of religion and of internal administration.

Politically, therefore, Palestine was an important part of the Roman Empire, though its status as a dependency frequently changed. Within a period of approximately half a century the territory witnessed five distinct phases of government, but the hand of Rome was always at the helm. From the time of Pompey to Herod, the administration of the country was committed to the proconsul of Syria, with numerous subordinate officials charged with local affairs in Idumea, Judea, Samaria, Galilee, and Transjordan. Under Herod the Great, however, the whole of this disjointed area was unified to constitute the kingdom of the Jews. As will be seen later, though the kingdom of Herod was divided among the surviving members of his family, Rome viewed with interest every phase of the development. Finally, because of the inefficiency of native princes, Rome was compelled to establish her own officials throughout the land.

On the other hand, the political domination by Rome safeguarded the entrenchment of Greco-Roman civilization, thus determining the immediate

45. Synagogue ruins at Capernaum, in Galilee, which may be on the same site as the synagogue where Jesus taught.

cultural backgrounds of Palestine during the days of Jesus and the early disciples. While the most powerful agent in this movement was the Philhellene, Herod the Great, the work was carried forward throughout under the auspices of Rome. Every part of Palestine and Transjordan was affected. In the following survey, disregarding for the time being the political subdivisions of the country, the student will see at a glance the general sweep of the Greco-Roman life and thought from the slopes of Mount Hermon in the north to Mount Seir in the south, from the Mediterranean seaboard to the borders of the Arabian Desert. While nothing more than a geographical summary is here attempted, the evidences of the alien culture can be seen on every hand. Any locality in Palestine or in Transjordan, west or east of the Jordan Valley, could be used to illustrate the thoroughness of the invasion. With the progress of excavations, deserted mounds are providing convincing proof of the Greco-Roman transformation and its permanent results.

Apart from the area of the Decapolis, where a few of the cities were self-governing, Herodian Palestine embraced all of the West Jordan territory from Dan to the river of Egypt, Transjordan (including Perea), and the adjacent regions of Ituraea, Trachonitis, Auranitis, and Batanaea. Greco-Roman remains have come to the surface in all of these districts.

Geographical Survey of Herodian Kingdoms

Herod the Great, though proclaimed king of the Jews by the Roman Senate in 40 B.C., did not come into full possession of his kingdom until 37 B.C., after the defeat of Antigonus and the Parthians east of Bethlehem. The territory finally embraced in his kingdom included all the area west of the Jordan Valley to the

Mediterranean, that is, *Judea, Samaria,* and *Galilee*. Immediately south of the Judean borders, beginning in the vicinity of Beth-zur and including Hebron, Eleutheropolis (Beit Jibrin), Ashkelon, and Beer-sheba, was the postexilic kingdom of the Idumeans which fell to Herod both by virtue of his Jewish-Idumean descent and by the political successes of his father Antipater.

The northern and southern boundaries of this West Jordan area, consisting of the Leontes and the river of Egypt respectively, were practically the same as in the early Hebrew period. On the eastern side of the Jordan, the kingdom of Herod included the borders of the Jordan Valley and the Dead Sea to the river Arnon, but it did not extend south of the Arnon, nor into the Desert of Arabia,

which was a part of the Arabian kingdom of Aretas whose capital was at Petra. The technical name applied to this fringe of land along the Jordan was *Perea*. The territory immediately east of this Perean district was largely under the control of the self-governing cities which ultimately united to form the Decapolis, although Gadara and Hippos belonged to Herod.

In the northern Transjordan section east and northeast of the Sea of Galilee, that is, the area represented by Bashan of the Old Testament, were five distinct districts belonging to Herod's kingdom. All of these districts lay between the Yarmuk River valley and the slopes of Mount Hermon. *Gaulanitis* may be described as the border area extending along the river Jordan from the Yarmuk and the Sea of Galilee to the foothills of Mount Hermon. Within this district fell Paneas, or Caesarea Philippi. *Auranitis* lay directly east of the Gaulanitis section, being practically coextensive with the modern plains of Hauran, a volcanic area famed for its great fertility. *Batanaea* is more difficult to define. It was apparently a general designation applied to the ancient territory of Bashan. It should be observed, however, that Batanaea is distinguished from Auranitis (and Trachonitis) as an integral part of a later Herodian kingdom. *Trachonitis* extended in a southeasterly direction from Damascus to Jebel Hauran, its borders reaching to Gaulanitis in the vicinity of Caesarea Philippi. Finally, *Ituraea*, though a definite part of Herod's kingdom, is not certainly located. It is not known whether Ituraea and Trachonitis are to be regarded as a unified area, as some interpret the passage in Luke 3:1. The Ituraeans, being of Arabian descent,

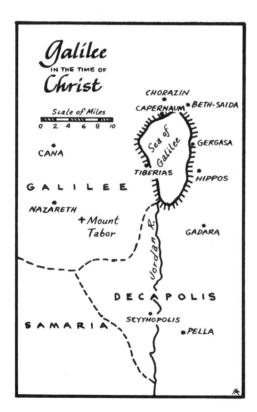

46. The south end of the Sea of Galilee where the Jordan River begins its sixty-mile rush toward the Dead Sea.

were probably nomadic in habit, wandering throughout these fertile steppes with no settled habitation.

Under the terms of Herod's will, the whole of this territory was subdivided among his successors, all of whom, with the exception of Salome, his sister, are mentioned in the New Testament. To Salome was given an inheritance of three revenue-producing cities, namely, the old Philistine strongholds of *Ashdod* and *Jamnia* (Jabneel), in the Plain of Philistia, and the Herodian fortress-city of *Phasaelis*, in the Jordan Valley above Jericho. To Herod Archelaus was bequeathed all of middle and southern Palestine, that is, *Samaria, Judea,* and *Idumea.* It was Herod the Great's desire that Archelaus should become king, but the Roman Senate accepted him only in the capacity of an Ethnarch.

With his capital at Jerusalem, Archelaus ruled over three distinct peoples— the Jews, Idumeans, and Samaritans— until his deposition in A.D. 6. After the banishment of Archelaus, the provinces of Idumea, Judea, and Samaria were taken over by a line of Roman officials, the procurators, and included in the general Province of Syria. They retained this status until the territory reverted to Herod Agippa I in A.D. 40. The whole of the Galilean area, plus the Perean district, was inherited by Herod Antipas, whose official title was tetrarch. It was apparently an unwieldly and disjointed territory but characterized in the main by a predominantly Jewish population.

The capital city of Galilee and Perea was Tiberias, founded by Antipas in A.D. 26 and named in honor of Tiberius Caesar. Of the nine flourishing cities which Josephus locates along the shores of the Sea of Galilee during the days of Jesus, only Tiberias remains. But there is no

47. The Jordan River at the traditional site of the baptism of Jesus.

record that Jesus ever visited the capital of Herod Antipas. The Perean territory extended from the Yarmuk River to the Arnon. Through this strip of land ran the pilgrim highway from Galilee to Jerusalem, entering Perea by way of Scythopolis (Beisan), at the opening of the valley of Jezreel, and again across Jordan opposite Jericho. By traveling this highway, Jewish pilgrims avoided passing through Samaria. At the southern end of the Perean district stood Machaerus, the Maccabee-Herodian fortress, where John the Baptist was beheaded.

Finally, to Herod Philip was given the ancient region of Bashan, now divided into five districts: Gaulanitis, Batanaea, Auranitis, Ituraea, and Trachonitis. Ruins of Greco-Roman towns may be found throughout the region—more than one hundred in Gaulanitis alone. Probably the most outstanding was Caesarea Philippi (Paneas), located at one of the principal sources of the Jordan, the most northerly point visited by Jesus. Modern ruins of Paneas indicate a city of considerable importance; in the vicinity are evidences of the pagan worship conducted here from a very early period. Bethsaida Julias, on the east bank of the Jordan at the head of the Sea of Galilee, was also an important city, having been embellished by Herod Philip and named in honor of Julia, the daughter of Augustus Caesar. On the whole, the tetrarchy of Philip was one of the most desirable of the geographical divisions specified in the will of Herod the Great.

To the above mentioned Herods must be added two others, Agrippa I and Agrippa II. While both are described as kings, there is no little difficulty in determining their kingdoms, due probably to the fact that as dependencies there was necessarily some overlapping in administration on the part of the native rulers and the dominant Roman power represented by proconsuls, governors, and procurators.

To Agrippa I the Emperor Caligula gave the tetrarchies of Herod Philip and of Lysanias, the latter being located in the Lebanon—Anti-Lebanon area. After the death of Herod Antipas, Agrippa came into possession of Galilee and Perea. Samaria and Judea (regarded as including Idumea also) were added in A.D. 40, thus making his kingdom practically coextensive with the kingdom of his grandfather, Herod the Great. Agrippa was evidently a vigorous ruler. To him has been attributed the great third wall recently unearthed on the north side of Jerusalem, although it may be a later construction. The south wall of the western hill, which enclosed the Tyropoeon at the pool of Siloam, was first built by Agrippa I. He appears in the Acts in connection with the death of James and the deliverance of Peter. His horrible death is referred to in the same context.

Herod Agrippa II, a youth of seventeen years, stood in the line of succession to his father, but the Romans hesitated to entrust him with the affairs of such a difficult kingdom as Palestine. As a consequence Agrippa was given a subordinate position, while the actual administration of the territory was in the hands of the Roman procurator with headquarters at Caesarea. Later, however, Claudius Caesar granted the kingdom of Herod of Chalcis to Agrippa (A.D. 48), to which were added subsequently the old tetrarchies of Herod Philip and Lysanias. In addition to the foregoing, Nero gave to Agrippa some scattered cities in Galilee and Perea. After the destruction of Jerusalem in A.D. 70 and the end of the Jewish state, Agrippa moved to Rome. He died about A.D. 100, the last of the Herodian rulers. He is referred to in the Acts in connection with Paul's imprisonment (Acts 25:13; 26:32).

The Decapolis

The term "Decapolis," occurring only three times in the New Testament, means the region or league of ten cities. While the area designated may be regarded as a working unit, being closely connected in military, commercial, social, religious, and political matters, it is unlikely that it ever formed a geographical unit. This seems obvious when the locations of these widely separated cities are taken into consideration. Two were situated on the borders of the great Syro-Arabian Desert; one was west of the Jordan at the mouth of the valley of Jezreel; one was located in the area of Gaulanitis; another was situated in the region of ancient Bashan; three huddled together in the northern portion of the Perean-Gilead district; there was one in the territory of the old Amorites and one in the heart of Gilead.

The generally accepted list of the cities included in the Decapolis names the following: *Damascus, Kanatha, Scythopolis, Hippos, Raphana, Gadara, Pella, Dion, Philadelphia,* and *Gerasa.* It will be observed at once that among these cultural centers are some of the most ancient foundations mentioned in the Old Testament, particularly Damascus, Scythopolis (Beth-shan), and Philadelphia (Rabbath-Ammon). However, while these Decapolis cities (Damascus excepted) all fall within the general territory of Herodian Palestine, not a single one is named in the Gospels; Damascus is found within the writings of the New Testament only in connection with the career of Saul of Tarsus. There is, of course, a very probable reference to one member of the Decapolis in the Gospels where we have "the country of the Gadarenes" (Matt. 8:28, RSV) or "of the Gerasenes" (Mark 5:1, RSV).

48. Cana in Galilee, north of Nazareth.

But too much emphasis is not to be placed on the absence of definite citations to these cities in the New Testament, for though we do not know the exact part which they played in the ministry of Jesus and of the disciples, it is entirely probable that it was far more important than is usually thought. Fuller records might disclose a more extended ministry of Jesus, touching some of the chief cities of the Decapolis, or an enlarged territory traversed when passing "through the midst of the borders of Decapolis." It is definitely stated that among the multitudes following Jesus some were from the Decapolis (Matt. 4:25). We may have reasons to believe also that the Greeks who visited him in Jerusalem were from beyond the Jordan (John 12:20).

Historically, the Decapolis is a definite product of the contacts of Alexander the Great with Palestine. While many of the cites were in existence prior to the Macedonian conquest, it may fairly be said that they received their distinctive Greek mold as new foundations during the Alexandrian and Roman periods. As Greek cities in foreign territory they were founded and developed by those who were sympathetic with Greek culture. It is certain that these sympathizers and promoters came largely from the armies of Alexander, since it was his regular policy to allow all veterans liberal land grants and other rewards in making new settlements. The large number of men taking advantage of this liberality gave rise to numerous Greek cities in the Near East, especially those beyond the Jordan. Two of these cities, Pella and Dion, were actually named for Macedonian towns. In general we may say that the Greek role assumed by these new and old foundations dates from about 300 B.C., continuing almost uninterruptedly through A.D. 300. We turn now to a brief description of the Decapolis centers from

the standpoint of both their geography and outstanding characteristics.

Damascus, one of the oldest existing cities in the world, stood on the northeastern edge of the Decapolis region, on the route of highways and movements affecting East and West. It is not clear whether Damascus was an active or honorary member of the league, but any confederacy involving commercial and military aspects, such as those characterizing the Decapolis, must necessarily have taken into consideration this pivotal city of the Near East. It was the great halfway house to every quarter of the biblical world. Situated at the foothills of the Anti-Lebanon mountains, sprawling eastward into the great Syro-Arabian Desert, it was the thriving emporium between the extremes of Asia and Africa. From time immemorial its streets have hummed with strange tongues and wares.

As a cosmopolitan city Damascus was at the center of everything. It is probable that the relation which it sustained to the Decapolis was more beneficial to the effectiveness of the confederacy than that of any other city. Definitely linked up with the Roman Empire, Damascus reflected the finest characteristics of the Greco-Roman civilization. Frequently appearing in the backgrounds of the Old Testament, the city is more retiring in the New Testament, coming to the fore only in connection with the career of Saul of Tarsus.

Kanatha was one of the frontier cities of the league, its situation being almost due south of Damascus in the region of Jebel Hauran. It stood on the edge of the desert. The present village of Kanawat marks the old site. Its position as a junction point for the network of caravan

49. Jacob's Well, where Jesus met the woman of Samaria. The well is inside the walled enclosure with the trees.

routes rendered Kanatha of extreme importance to the Decapolis. Some of the best preserved ruins of the Greco-Roman period are found here. The city was certainly older than the Greek era, and is frequently identified with Kenath of the Old Testament.

The oldest city of the Decapolis was probably *Scythopolis,* which stood at the mouth of the valley of Jezreel overlooking the Jordan. Its distance from the Jordan River was about four miles, while from the Sea of Galilee it was only fourteen miles. Its name during the Old Testament period was Beth-shan. In the early narratives of Israel's conquest of Canaan, Beth-shan appears as an impregnable fortress of the Canaanites. At the death of Saul it was in alliance with the Philistines. It was not until the reign of David that the city was brought under the control of Israel.

The old city is represented by modern Beisan which is located opposite the precipitous mound. The strategic position of Scythopolis in relation to the Jordan Valley, the valley of Jezreel, and the Plain of Esdraelon, rendered it necessary that the town should assume all the aspects of a strongly fortified place. It commanded not only all highways into Perea and the Hauran but was the outlet to the Mediterranean seaboard. By its portals passed caravans and armies from East and West. These physical characteristics converted it into the most important city of the Decapolis. Josephus regarded Scythopolis as the capital of the confederacy. Although the pilgrim highway from Galilee to Jerusalem led by its gates to cross the Jordan into Perea, we have no record that Jesus or the disciples ever visited the town.

50. Wadi Qumran, with Cave IV in the right center. Many fragments of scrolls were found in these caves overlooking the Dead Sea.

Hippos was in the southern portion of Gaulanitis on the headland overlooking the Sea of Galilee. Tiberias stood opposite on the western side of the lake. While an important city, it is likely that Hippos was overshadowed by Gadara which was in the immediate vicinity. The modern settlement of Qal'at el-Husn represents the old town, the name itself being the Arabic equivalent of the Greek word meaning "horse." Hippos was relatively a frontier city. In this respect it was doubtless charged with protective duties concerning the Decapolis members which lay to the south.

Raphana, modern er-Rafeh, stood on the main highway between Gadara and Damascus, about thirty miles east of the Sea of Galilee. Josephus refers to a Raphon in the vicinity of Carnaim, meaning perhaps Ashteroth-Karnaim of the Old Testament. Thus Raphana was north of the valley of the Yarmuk River in Batanaea, on the fringes of the eastern desert.

Gadara was situated on the northern border of the Perean district a little south of the Yarmuk River, the site being marked by Umm Qeis, or Muqeis, six miles from the Sea of Galilee. The city makes its first appearance as a Greek center in 218 B.C. when it was a powerful fortress. Later, during the reign of Alexander Jannaeus, when it was conquered and brought under the Jewish yoke, it appears again. Its independence was restored in 63 B.C. by Pompey who placed it, with other free cities in the region, under the Roman Province of Syria. During the rule of Herod the Great, Gadara was given to the king by Augustus Caesar. After the death of Herod, Gadara became a member of the Decapolis.

Many coins of the city have been recovered. Suggestive is the fact that Gadara chose for its insignia or seal a trireme, thus indicating naval interests in connection with this city of the interior. This of course throws considerable light on the disputed phrase "the country of the Gadarenes" (Matt. 8:28, RSV; elsewhere Gerasenes or Gergesenes) in the Gospel records. The modern village of Kursi or Gergesa on the eastern shore of the Sea of Galilee indicates, in all likelihood, the existence at this place of an old town by the name of Gerasa. The Arabic Kursi is clearly a corruption of Gergesa or Gerasa. The country of the Gerasenes would then refer to the immediate territory of this town, not to the Decapolis Gerasa located in the heart of Gilead thirty-five miles away. The reference in Matthew could then be explained on the basis of an enlarged territory which, in the Greek fashion, was regarded as dependent on a mother "polis," that is, the country belonging to Gadara. We know that it was the common practice for each city of the league to take full responsibility for neighboring communities under its care. If this is correct, the region of Gadara included the southern and eastern borders of the Sea of Galilee, where were located the naval interests suggested by the coins.

Pella was situated in the Perean district slightly southeast of Scythopolis. It stood on the border of the Jordan Valley, opposite one of the principal fords of the Jordan River. Extensive ruins at Khirbet Fahil, the site of ancient Pella, indicate a city of considerable importance. While the founding of the Greek Pella is attributed to Alexander the Great, the Amorite town was much older, appearing first in the lists of cities conquered by the Egyptian kings, Thutmose and Seti. Through it ran the Roman highway connecting oriental trade routes with the Mediterranean seaboard. It was also on the pilgrim road from Galilee to Jerusalem. The Hebrew Christians fled to Pella at the destruction of Jerusalem under Titus in A.D. 70.

Dion is usually identified with Tell el-'Ash'ari, northeast of Pella. This would place it across the Yarmuk from Abila (Jebel Musa), an important Greco-Roman foundation now marked by Irbid.

Philadelphia is to be classified with Damascus and Scythopolis as one of the oldest cities in the league. It appears in Old Testament narratives as Rabbath-Ammon. Situated in the heart of the ancient Ammonite kingdom, Rabbath flourished as their capital through many centuries. Its importance was recognized by Ptolemy Philadelphus who rebuilt the city in Greco-Egyptian fashion and called it in honor of himself. Its greatness continued through the Roman period. The acropolis at Philadelphia is literally covered with imposing ruins, while in the surrounding valley there are the remains of colonnaded streets, theaters, Roman baths, and so on, which speak of the great significance of Philadelphia as a member of the Decapolis. It stood at the southernmost end of the Decapolis territory, hence a strong outpost against marauding desert tribes and the powerful kingdom of the Arabians. The old city of Philadelphia is now represented by Amman, the largest town in the region and the capital of Transjordan.

Gerasa stood in a rolling section of the old Gilead territory midway between Pella and Philadelphia. The Roman highway connecting these cities had important branches reaching to other members of the Decapolis. Gerasa was situated thirty-five miles from the Sea of Galilee and about twenty-five miles from the Jordan Valley. The city must not be confused with the lakeside town which was probably a dependency of Gadara. The Greek city of Gerasa came into ex-

51. Ruins of the harbor of ancient Caesarea, constructed by Herod the Great.

istence immediately after the Macedonian invasion. The earliest reference to it occurs in connection with Alexander Jannaeus who brought it under the domination of the Jewish kingdom.

It is of interest to note here that the conquest of Gerasa was the result of a punitive expedition to terminate its powerful influence in behalf of Hellenistic civilization in Transjordan. After the invasion of Pompey, Gerasa and other cities of the later Decapolis were released from the Jewish bondage, being vested with self-governing privileges and subject only to the legate of Syria. The expansion of the city was very rapid during the early part of the Christian era, its highest stage of development coming between A.D. 100–200. Out of this period are the recovered evidences of Greco-Roman civilization which shows Gerasa to be a city of extraordinary strength and beauty. In view of the fact that we have here the best preserved ruins of any Greco-Roman town in the Near East, and considering Gerasa as typical of the other Decapolis cities, we present below a brief description of the plan of the town, together with a summary of its temples, theaters, baths, and streets.

As one enters Gerasa from the south, two characteristic features of Greco-Roman cities appear. There is first the triumphal arch, usually erected as part of the wall, or within the forum area as at Rome, or at some other conspicuous place in the city as at Paris and Berlin. In the case of Gerasa there was a slight departure in that the arch, though on the principal approach to the city, was located about five city blocks or fifteen hundred feet from the wall. Immediately to the left of this arch was the second feature, the hippodrome, which was pri-

marily designed for races and gladiatorial combats.

Approaching the city proper we observe that the town was completely surrounded by a wall two and a half miles in circumference, fortified by towers at each break or turn in its course and penetrated by eight gates. The area enclosed was capable of sustaining a population of sixty thousand people. Through the heart of Gerasa ran the colonnaded way, the main street of the town. This Gerasene boulevard is the finest example of the extensiveness and beauty of such avenues that we have. It ran north and south for almost a mile and was paved throughout with large limestone blocks which show the ruts or grooves made by chariots nearly two thousand years ago. On both sides of the street there was a continuous row of beautiful Doric and Corinthian columns joined with heavy entablatures. Two other streets crossed this colonnaded broadway at right angles, showing purpose in city planning and adornment.

The temples of the Greco-Roman cities were, of course, dedicated to the various deities of the pagan pantheon, two of whom were especially prominent at Gerasa. Here we have a temple to Jupiter or Zeus, the chief of all Greco-Roman gods, and to Diana or Artemis whose temple at Ephesus was one of the seven wonders of the ancient world. It is obvious that Artemis was the principal deity at Gerasa. Her temple stood in the most prominent position in the city, being approached from the main street by the wonderful Propylaea now in the process of reconstruction. During the early Christian centuries these temples were superseded by Christian churches, five of which have been found, the most important being the church of Theodore (ca. A.D. 492).

In addition to the temples which adorned every city of the Decapolis,

52. Roman amphitheatre at Caesarea, where Pilate had his official residence.

there were the theaters. The Gerasenes provided themselves with two places of assembly and amusement within the city, the North Theatre and the South, both of which are in a fine state of preservation. They were, of course, open to the skies with some arrangement made for protection from rain and sunshine when necessary. The thermae or baths, a definite characteristic of every city founded by the Romans, were in the northeastern part of the city by the watercourse. Finally, the forum, the central meeting place for business and pleasure, was located at the entrance to Gerasa. In form it was semicircular, adorned with fifty-six columns of the Ionic pattern and paved throughout.

In concluding this survey of the Decapolis cities we summarize seven other distinct features. In the *first* place, the Decapolis did not come into existence as a working organization until after the death of Herod the Great. It was in full force, however, during the ministry of Jesus. Fundamentally it was an anti-Semitic league, designed to maintain Greco-Roman life and institutions on foreign soil. Its power was brought to bear not only against the Jew across the Jordan but against Semites from any quarter. Exposed to the incursions of Arabian hordes from the desert, from north and south, the Decapolis was the answer of Greco-Roman civilization in the interest of survival.

Second, from a political standpoint these cities were regarded as self-governing and independent, but the privileges thus granted were not absolute; they were answerable in the last analysis to the governor or legate of Syria. Still they possessed their own constitutions, the right of free assembly, with legislative and administrative responsibilities. On the other hand, the welfare of every Decapolis member was wrapped up in the welfare of the others.

It was, accordingly, a confederacy of independent city-states patterned after the fashion of the Greek idea. In turn each city-state in the Decapolis was definitely charged with the interests of dependent towns and villages within its territory.

Third, the league was characterized by economic considerations; reciprocity in trade was the order of the day. High tariffs probably operated to the exclusion of undesirable competitions and commodities.

Fourth, great significance was necessarily attached to the military aspects of the Decapolis. Each city was not only definitely allied with the others in the matter of offensive and defensive warfare, but all were at the bidding of Rome with reference to providing contingent units for the Roman foreign legions and for harboring Roman armies in their campaigns.

Fifth, in matters of religion there was a unifying bond; the Greco-Roman gods and goddesses, from the highest to the lowest, were found in every portion of the Decapolis. Their temples attest the thoroughness with which the gods of Greece and Rome invaded even the remotest sections of the Near East.

Sixth, the connection between the various member cities was made quick and effective by means of the Roman highway system. There is no difficulty in following some of these roads today after the lapse of two thousand years. The business of every highway was to make possible effective communication in the interest of order. In no other manner could Rome have imposed its will upon the scattered thousands in all these open spaces.

And, *finally,* throughout the region of the Decapolis, Greek was the common language. Gadarenes, Gerasenes, Philadelphians, and Hippenes, all conversed

53. Arch on the street called "Straight" in Damascus.

in the language of Hellenism, the immediate gift of Alexander to Palestine, Syria, and Transjordan.

There is no record that Jesus or the disciples visited any of these outstanding centers, but the reference to his presence in the Decapolis carries with it probably more than we have been accustomed to allow, and we may well be assured that the great region was not passed by when the good news was being proclaimed.

Significant Cities of the Gospels and the Acts

Until A.D. 70 Palestine was essentially the country of Herod the Great. All of the activities of Jesus and the early activities of the apostles were confined to this small corner of the Roman world, and even then only a surprisingly small part of the land of Palestine was actually involved in their travels and ministry. Some of the significant cities have been mentioned already, but there are a few which need special mention now.

Bethlehem, the town in which Jesus was born, is well known. It is located in the hill country of Judea, six miles south of Jerusalem. The name of the town signifies "house of bread."

The modern town with a predominantly Christian population stands over the beautiful fields where shepherds guarded their flocks. The center of Bethlehem is the Church of the Nativity, which was originally built by order of the emperor Constantine in A.D. 330. The church was placed over a cave which was the supposed place of Jesus' birth. The church has been destroyed and rebuilt several times, but parts of the ancient structures still lie under the massive buildings which the tourist sees today. In a portion of the complex of buildings is

54. The Roman theatre at Amman, present capital of Jordan, ancient Decapolis city of Philadelphia.

a chapel dedicated to the memory of Jerome who is said to have labored here in the production of the Latin Vulgate from the Greek and Hebrew scriptures. There is no evidence that the ministry of Jesus and the disciples included Bethlehem or that the gospel was ever proclaimed in the city of his nativity apart from the announcement by the angels.

Nazareth, the boyhood home of Jesus, does not occur in the Old Testament nor in the writings of Josephus. It is mentioned, however, repeatedly in the Gospels. The earliest extra-biblical mention of the town is found in an inscription from the excavations at Caesarea in 1960. This inscription has been dated to the third century A.D. The present town of Nazareth is on the site of the New Testament village, located in an upland hollow formed by several of the lower Galilean hills at an elevation of about fifteen hundred feet above the Mediterranean. The population of Nazareth today is considerable, owing to its association with Jesus, but it is probable that it was a small insignificant village during the days of Jesus' boyhood.

The general setting of Nazareth is one of the most beautiful in Palestine. From the heights of surrounding hills one may obtain a panoramic view of great extent. The present highway from Nazareth to Cana and the Sea of Galilee runs along an old caravan route connecting with upper Galilee, Damascus, and the East. Jesus and the disciples certainly traveled this road.

From Nazareth across Esdraelon and Jezreel crawled the pilgrim route to Jerusalem. Situated at the heart of lower Galilee, Nazareth was near every movement involving the social, commercial, religious, and military interests of the people. It was in this setting that Jesus spent twenty years of his early life. The modern town boasts many traditional places, including the Carpenter's Shop,

The Holy Land
TODAY

Scale of Miles
0 10 20 30 40 50

LEBANON

DAMASCUS

Mount
Hermon

SYRIA

CAPERNAUM

HAIFA

TIBERIUS

Sea of
Galilee

NAZARETH

CAESAREA

Mediterranean
Sea

JERASH

NABLUS

TEL AVIV

JORDAN

AMMAN

JERUSALEM

JERICHO

ASHDOD

BETHLEHEM

MADEBA

GAZA

Dead Sea

GAZA
STRIP

HEBRON

BEER-SHEBA

J O R D A N

ISRAEL

SEDOM

NEGEV

UNITED
ARAB
REPUBLIC
(EGYPT)

PETRA

EILAT

AQABA

GULF OF AQABA

the Synagogue, the Church of the An-
nunciation, and the Mount of Precipitation, but none has any genuine claim to
authenticity except possibly the Well of
Mary which has always been the only water supply within the city.

Capernaum, the headquarters of Jesus
after the rejection at Nazareth, is referred to sixteen times in the Gospels.
The ancient town is to be associated
with modern Tell Hum, the ruins of
which indicate a Roman town of considerable importance. Particularly significant is the synagogue which archaeologists now believe to be dated about
A.D. 200, long after the time of Jesus. It
is quite possible that earlier ruins of the
first century may be beneath the present
synagogue or elsewhere on the site. If
an earlier structure is under the one
which has been exposed by excavation,
then it is probable that we have located one of the places in which Jesus
preached.

Capernaum was an important military
and political center, since it is here that
one meets the Roman centurion who
gave the synagogue to the Jews and also
Matthew, the tax collector at the customs house. We know nothing of the
population of Capernaum, but references to the city indicate that it was one
of the chief places in Galilee, surpassing
even Tiberius, the capitol of Herod
Antipas. The city was within the territory of Antipas, about ten miles from
Tiberius on the Sea of Galilee.

Cana of Galilee, the native city of Na-
thaniel and the scene of Jesus' first miracle, lies about four miles from Nazareth
on the road to Tiberius. Though occupying a splendid site on the slopes of the
low Galilean hills, the town is unattractive. In the churches of the modern village are numerous evidences bearing
upon Jesus' visits to the place and traditions associated with these visits. Since
the principal highway from the Sea of

Galilee to the coast passed through this
village, it is likely that Jesus frequently
saw it as he went about his ministry in
Galilee. The town is mentioned four
times in the Gospel of John.

Jericho, the Old Testament city of
palm trees, appears during the ministry
of Jesus as a favorite Herodian resort.
The old mound-city of Jericho, whose
walls fell down before the Israelites and
Joshua, lay in desolation to the north of
the New Testament city. Herod the
Great rebuilt the city along the banks of
the Wady Kelt which flowed down from
the Judean hills to the west. New Testament Jericho stood about six miles from
the Jordan River and was a connecting
point for all roads out of central Palestine for the districts of Gilead, Moab,
and the East. Through Jericho ran the
great pilgrim highway from Galilee to
Jerusalem by way of Perea. The city is
mentioned six times in the Gospels. Special attention is called to its association
with Zacchaeus, Bartimaeus, and the
good Samaritan. Josephus informs us
that Herod the Great's death occurred at
Jericho and that the burial was at Herodium.

The seaport city of *Joppa* is one of the
interesting Old Testament cities and is
also mentioned ten times in the Acts. It
was known during the early Egyptian
period. Joppa appears in the age of the
Amarna Letters and is referred to from
the time of the Israelite invasion to the
destruction of Jerusalem in A.D. 70.

The earliest connections of Joppa
were likely with the Phoenicians, and
later with the Philistines, but at no period of Old Testament history was it vitally connected with Israel. Like other
Palestinian seacoast cities, Joppa had no
natural harbor. The Old Testament
phrase, "the sea at Joppa," is literally
correct. To this point were brought the
cedars of Lebanon for the temple of
Solomon. It was here that Jonah pur-

chased passage for Tarshish, and here in the Roman period occurred bitter reactions and rebellion against the Roman lordship in Palestine.

In this old metropolis of Palestine, where representatives from all places met on quaint and narrow streets, Simon Peter had the vision of the worldwide scope of the new faith which he was soon to announce to Cornelius at Caesarea. Joppa was the home of Dorcas and of Simon the tanner whose house stood by the sea. Modern tanneries are still found on the beach by the sea where skins are cleansed by the pounding waves. The town itself is very picturesque, occupying a commanding position on a headland one hundred and twenty-five feet above the Mediterranean. It is, of course, on the great highway which cuts through the Plains of Sharon and Philistia north to Syria and south to Egypt. Immediately to the north of the ancient site of Joppa is the modern capitol of Israel, Tel Aviv, a growing metropolis of the young nation.

Created by Herod the Great, the city of *Caesarea* on the shores of the Mediterranean is referred to fifteen times in the Acts. It was built on an ancient foundation called Strato's Tower and was named in honor of the emperor Augustus. Strato's Tower was a minor port along the Mediterranean associated with the Phoenicians, but it was made one of the major ports of Palestine under Herod who converted it into one of the finest cities of the land. He doubtless intended that it should supersede Jerusalem as the center of his kingdom and surpass Joppa as the principal commercial point along the coast.

Caesarea is described in glowing terms by Josephus, and archaeological excavations of the ancient site by an Italian

55. The Forum of Jerash (Gerasa), one of the Transjordan cities of the Decapolis.

team working there since 1960 have largely supported Josephus' description of the city. It was fortified by a circular wall extending inward from the seacoast, enclosing a city about three miles long with principal gates located on the east and west. Within the enclosure there were all the characteristic features of a Greco-Roman city, including theaters, hippodrome, public baths, temples, paved streets, and colonnaded thoroughfares. The water supply was obtained by aqueducts from the neighboring Nahr Zerka and from Mount Carmel, thirty miles away. The chief glory of Caesarea was the magnificent harbor which Herod constructed at tremendous expense. It featured a tremendous mole of large stones which provided an artificial breakwater which would protect ships from the wind and waves of the sea. Josephus described it as of equal splendor with the Piraeus of Athens.

Caesarea's connections with the Acts bring to attention the labors of Philip the evangelist, Cornelius, and Simon Peter, the horrible death of Agrippa, the visits of Paul and his imprisonment here for two years. At Caesarea Paul made his defense before Felix, Festus, and Agrippa II. From this city he was taken in custody to Rome to appear before Nero Caesar. Luke made Caesarea his headquarters when searching out accurately the facts concerning the ministry of Jesus. The town figured conspicuously in the Jewish rebellion which issued in the destruction of Jerusalem in A.D. 70. Located thirty miles north of Joppa, twenty-three miles from Samaria, and about sixty-five miles from Jerusalem, Caesarea was in easy communication with every part of the West Jordan country. Due to the recent opening of archaeological excavations at the site it is being visited increasingly by pilgrims and tourists in Palestine who find it resting quietly amid the scenes of ancient grandeur.

11
New Testament Jerusalem

Ancient Jerusalem has been described with regard to its original site and limits, its natural and artificial defenses, its conversion into the capital of the Hebrews, its expansion under Solomon and the kings of Judah, and finally its reconstruction under Nehemiah. A general reference to these discussions is perhaps all that is needed to give the student an opportunity to review the orderly development of the city from its founding to the Christian era. Thus, in the following description our inquiry will be concerned chiefly with Jerusalem * under Herod the Great and his immediate successors.

In general Herodian Jerusalem enclosed four principal hills which were situated in various parts of the town: southeast, the *hill of Ophel*, the original site of Urusalim; southwest, called by Josephus the Upper City; northeast, *Bezetha;* and, east, *Mount Moriah,* the sacred area of the town. Now, while these hills were incorporated within the city of Jerusalem, their contour practically de-

termined the city's fortifications on all sides. The strength of these natural hills, reinforced by construction of formidable walls, converted the city into a mountain fortress.

The beginning of the town was on the hill of Ophel, just above the present Virgin's Fountain, or Gihon, which offered to the early inhabitants their only water supply. As the population increased, the walls of the city were expanded to include the other hills, the order of inclusion being Mount Moriah, the southwest hill, and then Bezetha. There was a later expansion which enclosed more territory to the northwest, but this was not a part of Jerusalem during the ministry of Jesus.

With the passing of the centuries great changes have come over all of this area; the surface has been so altered as to render almost indistinguishable the original topographical features. The accumulation of debris has practically obliterated the valleys, and the construction

* The conclusions reached in this chapter are based upon new information from the Jerusalem Excavations of 1961–63. Reports are published in the *Palestine Exploration Quarterly,* 1962–64.

56. Jerusalem, seen from the Mount of Olives with the temple area in the foreground.

of numerous buildings and streets has defaced nearly all the features of the Jerusalem of yesterday. In spite of these changes, however, it is possible on close observation to follow the main outlines of the original hills, to mark the depressions which were formerly deep valleys, and to reconstruct some of the features of Jerusalem in the days of Jesus.

Our study of the city in New Testament times is organized as follows: *first*, Jerusalem during the reign of Herod the Great; *second*, the city during the ministry of Jesus; and *third*, the apostolic period to A.D. 70.

The Reign of Herod the Great

In sheer physical magnitude the building enterprises of Herod the Great exceeded those of any ruler of Jerusalem, including Solomon. One of the first projects was to rebuild and enlarge a strategic fortress at the northwest corner of the Temple area which guarded the north approach to the Temple. The fortress was built foursquare with massive towers at each corner ranging from sixty to one hundred feet in height. A central courtyard was paved with large flat stones and probably became the arena for semipublic pronouncements by the local rulers. It is thought that Jesus appeared before Pilate (John 19:13) in this courtyard. Herod named the fortress Antonia in honor of Mark Antony and made it his residence before he built a palace on the western hill.

The western hill was strongly fortified on its northern approach by the erection of massive towers which Herod named Hippicus, Phasael, and Mariamne. Herodian masonry can be seen today in the three towers which still guard the western approach to the old city at the Jaffa Gate. On the western hill south of the

57. The pool of Siloam in Jerusalem, at the lower end of Hezekiah's Tunnel.

fortress towers Herod built a palace which became the residence of later Roman rulers of Jerusalem when they visited the city. The palace was supplied with water by an aqueduct from a source near Bethlehem, possibly "Solomon's Pools" south of the city.

Also inside the city Herod built a xystus or arena for athletic contests, as well as an amphitheater and a theater. These may have been located in the Tyropoeon Valley where the terrain would lend itself to the building of structures with elevated spectator seats, but no remains have been identified.

Herod's most notable building enterprise was the reconstruction of the Temple, which he never finished. The sacred enclosure was enlarged to about twice its former size and new walls of characteristic Herodian masonry were built from bedrock. The stones were exceedingly large but closely fitted together without mortar. One massive block high in the wall at the southeast corner of the enclosure today is estimated to weigh nearly ninety tons.

By filling in the edge of the Kidron Valley at the southeast corner and constructing stone supporting pillars and arches, the courtyard area was extended both south and east. Underneath the paved area which lies on top of the pillars is a spacious ground level called "Solomon's Stables" today. At the southwest corner of the enclosure the Tyropoeon Valley was also partially filled in to allow extension of the paved courtyard on this side equal to that on the Kidron side. The so-called "Wailing Wall" along the west boundary of the sacred enclosure was built by Herod and can be seen today. Apparently a bridge across the Tyropoeon to the western hill was connected with the southwest corner of the enclosure at the point of "Robinson's Arch," an anchor stone for an arch set in the massive wall.

The Temple area was extended northward by filling in the ravine that once bounded the north side of the Temple mount. At the northwest corner, the Tower of Antonia guarded and overlooked the vast enclosure.

Only two stones known today can be related to the Temple structure built by Herod. Both contain inscriptions forbidding the entry of Gentiles into the inner court of the Temple upon pain of death, and they must have been set in the walls of the inner court near entrances. Thus it must be stated that no archaeological evidence of the Temple building itself is known.

In addition to the impressive structures noted above, Herod rebuilt the remaining walls of Jerusalem. The western hill, where his palace was located, was occupied on the summit possibly as a royal quarter. A wall of debatable course ran from a point near the towers Hippicus, Phasaelus, and Mariamne, bounding the north side of the palace in a northeasterly direction to the tower of Antonia. Josephus notes that the wall began at the "Gennath Gate" on the west side of the city, a point not yet identified by archaeologists. This wall is significant because of its bearing upon the location of Golgotha and the garden tomb, discussed below.

The Ministry of Jesus

Surprisingly few of the places in Jerusalem associated with the ministry of Jesus have been reliably located by archaeologists. Jesus knew the city that Herod built, and that city was destroyed by the Romans in A.D. 70 and again in A.D. 132–35, after which it was radically replanned and rebuilt as Aelia Capitolina. Only in the fourth century did interest arise in locating the sacred places associated with the ministry of Jesus, and by that time the topography of the city had changed. Consequently we are largely dependent upon church traditions of uncertain value dating from the fourth century for most of the sites pointed out to pilgrims today. Archaeological investigation of some sites has been quite thorough, but in most cases excavation has been either impossible or quite superficial and unsatisfactory. To illustrate the difficulties of identifying places, the present Via Dolorosa with its fourteen stations of the cross is as much as twenty feet above the first-century levels of the authentic Via Dolorosa.

Two pools of Jerusalem mentioned by John prior to the last week of Jesus' ministry may be located with some certainty. The pool called Bethesda, or Bethzatha (RSV), where Jesus healed the lame man (John 5:1–6) has possibly been located by excavations at the Church of St. Anne, just north of the Temple enclosure. Twin pools separated by a rock partition about twenty feet thick have been found, supporting early church traditions of twin pools in the area called Bezeth by Josephus. The biblical account suggests a water source of intermittent flow, but the source has not been located.

The man born blind (John 9:1–7) was instructed by Jesus to go and wash in the pool of Siloam. There is a pool of Siloam located today at the lower end of Hezekiah's tunnel from Gihon spring. The present pool structure is of more recent construction, but it is likely that the New Testament pool of Siloam was in the same vicinity.

The garden of Gethsemane where Jesus agonized over the prospect of his impending crucifixion and death is traditionally located on the slope of the Mount of Olives facing Jerusalem and the Temple area. The principal areas now associated with Gethsemane are the

58. The Garden of Gethsemane, on the slope of the Mount of Olives.

gardens of the Roman Catholics at the foot of Olivet, and those of the Greek Orthodox Church higher up the slope. Olive trees, some quite ancient, are found in the gardens. One cannot tell the exact place among these sites where Jesus was betrayed after his nocturnal vigil in prayer, but it is fairly certain that either in the gardens or not far away on the same slope of Olivet he was greeted on that fateful night by Judas with a kiss.

Overlooking the Hinnom Valley which circles the southwest hill of Jerusalem is the Greek Orthodox Monastery of St. Onuphrius. It stands on the border of the traditional Akeldama or potter's field. Adjoining the monastery property to the west is a large area abounding in rock-cut tombs and artificial caves, evidently designed for burials. Akeldama is regarded traditionally as coextensive with a large part of this territory. The origin of the potter's field dates from the perfidy of Judas Iscariot who betrayed Jesus for thirty pieces of silver. The money was used to purchase the field whose identity may be preserved to this day in the Arabic name *Hakk ed-Dum,* the Field of Blood.

Jesus appeared before Pilate at the praetorium which has been located by tradition at Herod's palace on the southwest hill and also at Antonia adjoining the Temple enclosure walls. Most authorities accept the location at Antonia, mainly on the basis of French excavations under the convent of the Sisters of Zion. A large stone pavement more than 150 feet square has been found in what was probably the courtyard of Antonia. Scratched in the stones of the pavement are the diagrams of what must have been Roman games played by the idle soldiers. Here then is quite likely the place of

which John 19:13 speaks: "Pilate . . . brought Jesus forth, and sat down in the judgment seat in a place that is called the Pavement, but in the Hebrew, Gabbatha." The sentence of death may have been pronounced on Jesus here.

The present Via Dolorosa, from the site of Antonia where Jesus was sentenced to the Church of the Holy Sepulcher where tradition holds that he was crucified, is of more emotional than historical value. The real Via Dolorosa is deep beneath the present one and probably follows a different course. However, this is a technicality of little consequence to the thousands of fervent pilgrims who annually bear crosses in processionals from the site of the judgment seat of Pilate, by way of the stations of the cross, to the Church of the Holy Sepulcher and traditional Golgotha.

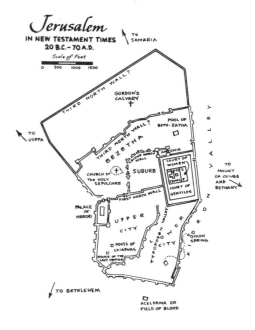

59. Gordon's Calvary, a suggested site of Golgotha where Jesus was crucified.

According to Eusebius, the Roman emperor Constantine in the fourth century directed Bishop Macarius to locate the places of the crucifixion and burial of Jesus. Reportedly he was led to the site through a vision of the Queen Mother, Helena. Constantine erected two churches: Golgotha at the site of the crucifixion and Anastasis at the site of the tomb. The sprawling Church of the Holy Sepulcher covers today the sites of both the ancient structures. Traditions of the site cannot be carried back earlier than the early fourth century. Nevertheless there must have been a strong tradition associated with the site in the fourth century because it was located then within the city walls, and Hadrian's Temple of Aphrodite was demolished to make room for Constantine's Church of the Anastasis. It is likely that a strong tradition, as well as visionary guidance, influenced the identification of the site. In the present Church of the Holy Sepulcher, the elevated rock pointed out as Golgotha and the tomb under the rotunda of the ancient structure almost lose the interest of the western pilgrim because of garish adornments of gold, crosses, relics, lights, and the unrealistic stories told to tourists.

A second site has been promoted as the site of Golgotha and the garden tomb. General Charles Gordon claimed that a rocky hill about 250 yards northeast of the Damascus Gate, previously pointed out by Otto Thenius of Dresden, was the place of the skull. He was aided in the identification by an active imagination, because cavities in the side of the hill did in fact suggest the appearance of a skull. A rock-cut tomb is located nearby. It is complete with a large stone shaped like a solid wheel which can be rolled in its hewn track to close the tomb entrance.

60. The Garden Tomb near Gordon's Calvary.

However the tomb seems to be postapostolic and perhaps is Byzantine in origin. No tradition earlier than the nineteenth century supports the authenticity of Gordon's Calvary or the tomb. It is true, nevertheless, that the devout pilgrim may find more of a sense of reverence in the quiet simple outdoor surroundings of Gordon's Calvary and the associated sepulcher than in the cluttered confines of the Church of the Holy Sepulcher, even though the latter has more claim to authenticity.

Location of Golgotha and the garden tomb is affected by the course of the "second wall" reported by Josephus. The first wall on the north seems to have run east from the towers of Herod at the present Jaffa Gate to the Temple enclosure walls. Josephus said the second wall began at the Gennath (or garden) Gate, of the first wall presumably, and that it enclosed the north quarter of the city and ended at the fortress Antonia. If the Gennath Gate was near the middle of the first wall, the second wall could have run northward on the east side of the Church of the Holy Sepulcher, then eastward to Antonia. A sounding ten meters square has been excavated in the courtyard of the Lutheran school which is a few yards north of a point near the middle of the first wall. There is evidence of filling beneath the Byzantine levels, but no evidence of a city wall or even architecture of the Herodian city.

If the Gennath Gate was near the west end of the first wall, the second wall could have turned to the east either north or south of the Church of the Holy Sepulcher. In either case there is the unusual situation of a fortification wall standing on lower ground than the surface outside it. The absence of positive archaeological evidence of the course of the second wall leaves the site of the traditional Golgotha dependent mainly on traditions dating to the fourth century. This may be just as well for the devout pilgrim because of the tendency to make sacred places almost objects of idol worship. It is possibly more conducive to reverence to know only that somewhere in the vicinity Jesus was crucified, buried, and rose again the third day.

The Apostolic Period to A.D. 70

Healing and preaching were done in the precincts of the Temple by the apostles, and clashes with Temple officials occurred there. It was the same Temple begun by Herod the Great and known to Jesus in his ministry.

One incident in Acts 6:9–15 (RSV) involving Stephen has possible amplification from archaeological discovery. It is said that some of those who belonged to "the synagogue of the Freedmen" (v. 9) disputed with Stephen. A possible reference to this synagogue is contained in the Theodotus inscription found near the tip of the southeast hill of Jerusalem in 1913–14. The text reads in part: "Theodotus son of Vettenus, priest and synagogue president . . . has built the synagogue . . . and the hostelry and the chambers and the cisterns of water in order to provide lodgings for those from abroad who need them." Theodotus' family name is thought to be derived from the Roman family of Vetteni, which suggests that he or an ancestor was a freedman from Italy. The inscription is believed to date prior to A.D. 70, and could refer to the synagogue of the Freedmen of Acts 6:9.

Stephen was stoned to death outside the city (7:58). The Dominican Church of St. Stephen just north of the Damascus Gate, built on the foundation of a fifth-century basilica, is one traditional site of his martyrdom. Another is the Greek Chapel of St. Stephen in the Kidron Valley, outside St. Stephen's Gate in the east wall of Jerusalem.

About A.D. 42, Herod Agrippa I began

what Josephus called the "third wall," but he quickly abandoned it to avoid incurring the displeasure of Emperor Claudius. The wall was intended to enclose the suburb Bezeth north of the Herodian "second wall." Foundations of an ancient wall have been found in the garden of the American School of Oriental Research and at points to the east and west of the school, several hundred yards north of the Damascus Gate. These may be remains of Agrippa's "third wall," but evidence is not conclusive and the wall has not been traced to its junction with the known walls of the Herodian city.

The "third wall," found first by Sukenik and Mayer, may be a post-New Testament period fortification. The actual "third wall" of Herod Agrippa I may have followed near the course of the present north wall of the old city. Excavations in 1962 indicate that Herod Agrippa extended the city to the south and completely enclosed the southwest hill, the Tyropoeon Valley, and the southeast hill with fortifications. Bliss and Dickie first located this line of walls and erroneously ascribed it to preexilic Jerusalem. Present evidence indicates that the first complete enclosure of the southwest hill and mouth of the Tyropoeon was in mid-first century A.D., probably by Agrippa I.

Jerusalem revolted against the Romans in A.D. 66, and the city became a hotbed of intrigue and revolution. Intramural strife among the people and leaders prepared the way for defeat by the Romans. The north wall of Agrippa I, now completed, was breached by the battering rams of the Romans with the aid of their siege towers, and the fortress Antonia was captured and occupied. The Temple area became the scene of a massacre followed by destruction of the Temple itself. The entire city was plundered and burned in A.D. 70, and it must have seemed that not one stone remained upon another (cf. Luke 19:43–44). Christians in the city are reported to have escaped to Pella. Tens of thousands of Jews perished and were thrown outside the wall into the valley of Hinnom. Jerusalem ceased to play a significant role in either Jewish or Christian history, because a curse seemed to have fallen upon it with the coming of the Roman legions.

12
Asia Minor:

Bridge to Europe

Asia Minor sustained very important relations to other portions of the biblical world. It was a great causeway whose geographical span connected continents. At the tip end of the peninsula, the shore lines of Europe and Asia almost touched. Here stood the natural gateway to and from the four quarters of the earth.

It was most appropriate that the scene of Paul's enlarged missionary activity should have been laid at Troas, the outpost of the old world. Here, where Europe joined hands with Asia, a vision appeared to Paul in the night—a man standing, beseeching, and saying come over into Europe and help us (cf. Acts 16:8–9). The answer of Paul and his friends to that vision of changing horizons was in full keeping with an expanding campaign designed sooner or later to touch all borderlands of the Mediterranean and beyond. Regarded in this manner, Asia Minor stood at a great turning point in the world course. Turning then to a consideration of this strategic territory as a vital part of the biblical backgrounds, we present the following: (1) the geographical characteristics of Asia Minor, (2) connections with the East and West, (3) contacts of Paul with the chief cities, and (4) Asia Minor in the book of Revelation.

Geographical Characteristics

The territory comprising Asia Minor lies between the Hellespont and the Euxine Sea (Black Sea) on the north and the great Mediterranean basin on the south. It has an average width of about 340 miles. Its western borders are marked by the Aegean Sea, while on the eastern frontier stands the massive range of the Armenian Taurus Mountains, perilous and forbidding. The total area embraced, roughly estimated, is approximately 200,000 square miles, which is equivalent to a section of the United States consisting of the New England states, New York, Pennsylvania, Maryland, New Jersey, and West Virginia. The whole of this territory, plus Istanbul and Thrace on the European side, constitutes the Republic of Turkey whose capital is now at Ankara in the interior. Interesting is the fact that the political center of modern Turkey is situated only eighty miles from the ancient stronghold of the Hittites at Bogazköy.

We are perhaps justified in holding that the most important divisions of Asia Minor lay within the central and western sections, that is, the territory situated west of a line drawn from Tarsus on the south to Sinope on the Euxine Sea. Here again, if one had to choose between the central and western areas, the Aegean coasts, by virtue of their continuous importance from 1500 B.C. down to the present, would have to be regarded as the heart of the country. Within this latter section, during the Greco-Roman era, was the flowering of some of the finest aspects of Hellenistic civilization disseminated by Alexander the Great.

Significant is the fact that, of the seven marvels of the ancient world, three, the Mausoleum at Halicarnassus, the Colossus at Rhodes, and the Temple of Artemis at Ephesus, stood in this immediate sector, to which might be added innumerable additional evidences showing the primacy of the Aegean coast country in cultural attainment. But both sections were highly developed in the first Christian century, having some of the most illustrious examples of municipal life in the empire. The most casual survey of outstanding centers coming within the scope of the New Testament reveals an astonishing list of places whose influence, in many instances, was decisive in early Christian activities: Antioch in Pisidia, Troas, Ephesus, Assos, Miletus, Patara, Rhodes, Myra, Colossae, Pergamum, Thyatira, Sardis, Smyrna, Lystra, Derbe, Philadelphia, Laodicea, Perga, Attalia, Iconium, and Tarsus. To this summary might be added other cities of importance in Asia Minor, great provincial areas, urban and rural territories which were completely under the sway of the Greco-Roman culture. The contacts created by these thriving communities brought the whole of Asia Minor into vital relation with contiguous territories.

Some of the physical characteristics of Asia Minor are extremely interesting. Approaching the country from any direction, it has the appearance of a massive mountain range banked up against the horizon. While this massive aspect is most conspicuous on the south and east, it applies equally to the north and west, where the ranges are frequently broken by abrupt passes issuing in extensive lowland areas, as along the coasts of Sicily and southern Italy. In the territory of the Carian, Lydian, and Mysian provinces on the Aegean littoral, particularly in the vicinity of Miletus, Ephesus, Sardis, Thyatira, Pergamum, and Troas, the hills recede to create fertile basins extending into the interior from twenty to one hundred miles.

Along the Hellespont, the Sea of Marmara, and the Bosporus, there is a comparatively wide fringe of cultivable land flanked in the interior by the bulking hills. The coasts of the Euxine area are marked by rugged and forbidding contour; in the background the hills rise to considerable elevation. On the Mediterranean seaboard the contrast is even more pronounced, with the exception of two beautiful plains centering around Perga in Pamphylia and Tarsus in Cilicia. In the Tarsian area the hills withdraw for an average distance of about thirty-five miles, while in the Pergan district they are much nearer.

Apart from these exceptional lowlands, the entire coast country is dominated by the towering heights of the Taurus Range. Occasionally there looms a massive hill or peak, wonderfully beautiful when the last rays of sunshine break into a riot of colors on its slopes or summit. The Taurus Range, the chief mountain of Asia Minor, extending from the Aegean to northern Mesopotamia, offers some of the most fascinating scenery. Its elevation varies from 7,000 to 10,000 feet. Slightly north of the Taurus Mountains run two other parallel ranges, the Bulgar Daglari and the Ala Shan, whose principal peaks reach practically the same elevation. Mount Argaeus in the vicinity of Caesarea is over 13,100 feet, the highest point in Asia Minor.

On the other hand, a journey into the interior of Asia Minor proves very quickly that the massive backgrounds are more than appearances. Proceeding inland from any direction, one is impressed with the marked change in elevation, which reaches, on the average, about 3,000 feet above the Mediterranean. While the greater part of this ascent is gradual, at some points, especially the narrow mountain passes, it becomes sharp and tortuous. This is an indirect way of stating that the whole of interior Asia Minor is an immense plateau with a variety of topographical features—open spaces, fields, upland levels, and a few valleys originally characterized by great fertility.

Even now, by proper conservation of water in these uplands, hundreds of thousands of acres could be reclaimed, for it is one of the peculiar marks of Asia Minor that, with no great rivers reaching the seas, only a limited proportion of rain and snow falling in the interior escapes the hills. For the most part, the mountain streams lose themselves in arid plateaus, or flow into many isolated lakes which in turn allow rapid evaporation. In some districts, as in the Tuz Salt Lake area north of Iconium, great stretches of water-soaked territory are formed. The elevation of Tuz is 3,100 feet above the Mediterranean. In seasons of severe drought the lake completely dries up. During seasons of heavy precipitation these lakes become very large, but normally they remain as follows: Tuz, sixty miles in length; Kirili, thirty miles; Egridir, thirty miles; and Lake Van, eighty miles.

As stated above, the waterways of Asia Minor are not of considerable importance, either from the standpoint of size or function. There are no navigable streams penetrating the interior. The bulk of water reaching the seas is from the seaward slopes of the great ranges of the uplands. On the other hand, along the courses of these various streams one may observe beautiful valleys or lowlands which have played a prominent part in providing some of the necessities of life for a group of flourishing cities.

A survey of the Euxine area, for example, shows the *Lycus* and the *Halys* (Kizil Irmak), both of which take their sources in the Armenian mountains, flowing into the Euxine near the important cities of Samsun and Sinope. The Halys, with a length of 520 miles, is the largest river in Asia Minor proper. The *Sangarius* (Sakarya), whose upper reaches touch ancient Gordium and modern Ankara, flows into the Euxine slightly east of the Bosporus. Three streams, the *Macestus, Rhyndacus* (Atranos), and *Granicus,* empty into the Sea of Marmara through the Phrygian lowlands. Of these the most important is the Granicus, the scene of Alexander's triumph over Darius in 334 B.C.

No large river empties into the Aegean Sea, though several waterways on the west coast have great associations. At the mouth of the *Hermus* [Gediz or Sarabat] River stood Smyrna, one of the outstanding cities of the Aegean coastal area. Ephesus, the greatest center in Asia Minor during the New Testament era, was located at the sea end of the *Cayster River.* In view of the fact that the city piers are still *in situ,* the river at one time was navigable from Ephesus to the sea. Through the valley of the *Maeander* (Menderes) ran the old highway between the East and West by way of the Cilician Gates. Following through the Province of Caria, the *Indus* reached the Aegean opposite Rhodes.

On the southern coasts of Asia Minor five streams of importance are mentioned. In the vicinity of Perga and Attalia, the *Kestrus* reaches the Mediterranean after a comparatively easy descent from the Taurus Mountains. Along the course of the Kestrus was one of the approaches into the interior. At the mouth of the *Calycadnus* (Göksu) was located the important seaport of Seleucia. From the Plains of Seleucia the valley of the Calycadnus provided also a passage through the Taurus, reaching the fringe of the interior in the vicinity of Derbe and Lystra.

The *Cydnus River* bursts from the Taurus Mountains with alluvial deposits to replenish the fertile plains of Tarsus. In the days of Paul the Cydnus was navigable as far as Tarsus to the sea, a distance of about 12 miles. Of equal importance is the river *Sarus* (Seyhan), 780 miles long, which, after creating the important junction point of Adana, reaches the Gulf of Alexandretta (Gulf of Iskendaron) slightly southeast of Tarsus. About 10 miles east of the Sarus is a parallel stream, the *Pyramus* (Ceyhan), which flows through the plains of Issus at the foothills of Amanus mountains to reach the sea. In this area was Alexander's second victory over the Persians.

Finally, in the eastern hills of Asia Minor two other rivers, the *Euphrates* and the *Tigris,* take their sources only to slip away quickly through the lowlands of Mesopotamia to the Persian Gulf. The Euphrates, rising on the northern slopes of the Armenian Taurus range, flows in a winding course for 1,780 miles, while the Tigris, issuing from the southern foothills of the same range, hastens on for 1,060 miles in a comparatively direct course. These two great waterways combine to form the Arabian River, which empties into the Persian Gulf 125 miles from Ur of the Chaldees.

Connections with East and West

Travel in Asia Minor was not by way of the watercourses; "argosies with portly sail" formed no part of an interior landscape, as in Egypt. Communication was effected by means of an interminable network of ancient highways penetrating every section of the country. These open roads, improved and fortified, were at the point of their greatest efficiency during the Roman period, thus providing part of the material framework necessary for the extension of Christianity. Many of these progressive trails defied nature's barriers in reaching their objectives.

But the Romans were not responsible for the original highway program of Asia Minor, since some of these roads and passes antedate the Roman era by thousands of years. For example, from early centuries the highway out of northern Mesopotamia, leaving Carchemish or Aleppo and crossing the Amanus (Alma Dagh) and Taurus ranges to reach the interior at Bogazköy, has served as a most important line of travel. This route passes through Marash, Caesarea in the interior, and Bogazköy to the Euxine Sea. An alternative northern pass comes up from Nineveh on the Tigris to Malatya to join the preceding route in the vicinity of Caesarea.

Among these approaches to the interior, the most picturesque and historic is the narrow Cilician Gates, whose southern entrance into the Taurus Mountains is almost within sight of Tarsus, hardly forty miles away. This pass constitutes the principal approach into the interior from the Plains of Tarsus and Adana. Countless thousands have rushed into its narrow defiles, bent on meeting all demands growing out of trade and war.

Down this famous pass poured the early Hattian peoples from Cappadocia to establish themselves in the attractive

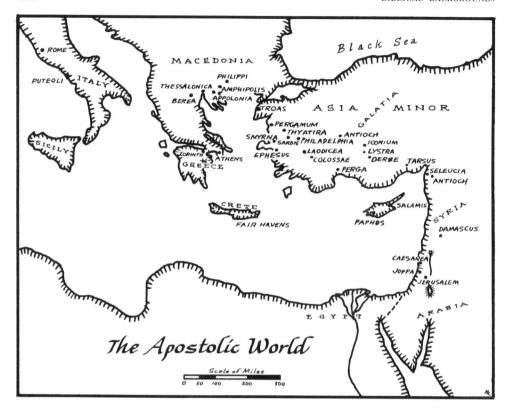

The Apostolic World

Scale of Miles

0   50   100   200   300

region lying between the Euphrates and
the Orontes, there to hold in check the
ferocious Babylonians and Assyrians on
the one hand and the Egyptians on the
other. Up through the Cilician Gates
went the Babylonians and Assyrians in
marauding campaigns. Up through the
tortuous defile pressed the Persians to
overrun the whole of Asia Minor. Down
this route came Alexander the Great
from Gordium to meet Darius in a decisive engagement on the Plains of Issus.
Down through the Cilician Gates Roman
legions pressed on, to lay in the Middle
East solid foundations of law and order
for the oriental section of the Roman
Empire, to hold it intact, and to admin-
ister it effectively.

Greatly improved by the Romans, who
left here the marks of their road-building

genius, the pass became the most important project in communication between
East and West. Caravans with wealth of
the Orient continued to journey through
its portals to reach the interior. Arabs
and Crusaders did not overlook it in
their mad rush for conquest and dominion. Nor is it without significance that
modern railroad engineers could find no
better route over which to send the Ana-
tolian express trains from Berlin, Constantinople, Ankara, and Adana on to
the heart of Mesopotamia. Finally, up
this pass went Paul from his native Tarsus to reach the thriving centers of the
Lycaonian plains with the good news.

**61. The Cilician Gates north of Tarsus,
through which Paul probably traveled
on his second missionary journey.**

One of the famous highways of the Roman Empire was the Old Way to the East. Its beginning may be placed at Babylon, in the heart of the Middle East. From there it proceeded progressively to touch Aleppo, Antioch in Syria, Adana, Tarsus, the Cilician Gates, Derbe, Lystra, Iconium, Antioch in Pisidia, Hierapolis, Colossae, Laodicea, Ephesus, Smyrna, and Troas at the end of the Asiatic trail. A shorter branch of this great arterial connection extended northwest from Antioch in Pisidia to reach Troas by way of Philadelphia, Sardis, Thyatira, and Pergamum.

Across the Aegean Sea, following the maritime shipping lanes by way of Samothracia, the way to the East was supplemented by the great Egnatian Way which extended from Neapolis to the Adriatic Sea. Beyond the low hills separating the seaboard and the interior, the road proceeded to Philippi, then by way of Amphipolis, Apollonia, Thessalonica, Pella, and the province of Illyricum to Dyrrachium on the Adriatic. On the southeast coast of Italy, the final section, the Appian Way, took up the trail at Brundisium and proceeded directly to Rome.

These highways are some of the finest examples of Roman engineering skill; their remains indicate the excellent manner in which the work was done. The construction of such roads, however, was a necessity in order to sustain contacts with all portions of the dominion, and to bring within quick and easy communication widely separated regions. Consequently, the Romans regarded their highway system as the most vital part of imperial defenses. Apart from these roads, the Empire could not have been held intact nor administered so efficiently. Across these highways passed the heralds of the Christian movement, protected by Roman outposts, to proclaim the gospel in the remotest sections.

Paul's Contacts with Chief Cities

A geographical survey of points in Asia Minor mentioned in the book of Acts shows that Paul's missionary movements followed in general the great overland trails. The *first journey* (Acts 13:1 to 14:28), for example, beginning at Antioch in Syria, proceeded to the important seaport of Seleucia. This maritime city was located five miles north of the Orontes outlet into the Mediterranean, a total distance of about twenty-one miles from Antioch. Embarking at Seleucia, Barnabas, Saul, and Mark made a quick passage to the island of Cyprus, seventy miles southwest, touching first at Salamis and then going overland to the seaport of Paphos, the administrative center of the province.

Although having a coast line of approximately four hundred miles, with important centers maintaining commercial and political connections with numerous points in the Levant, Cyprus was hardly more than a point of departure for Asia Minor and its challenging cities. Consequently, Paul and his company passed over the Sea of Lycia (Mediterranean Sea) to arrive at Attalia and Pamphylia, one hundred and eighty miles to the northwest. From there they traveled to the interior city of Perga, twelve miles to the northeast.

Situated in a plain of great fertility, well-watered by the Cestrus River issuing from the Pisidian uplands, Perga was practically self-supporting. Politically, it was the capital of the province of Pamphylia, the recognized metropolis of this section of Asia Minor. Here are ruins of a Roman theater capable of seating more than thirteen thousand people. Splendid baths, colonnaded streets, the stadium, temples, and other characteristics of the Greco-Roman centers indicate a city of considerable population. Dominating the backgrounds of the whole district are the commanding peaks and massive walls of the Taurus Range.

Two passes went up from the Pergan Plain into the interior. The first, the northwestern branch, followed the Cestrus valley to join the Old Way to the East in the vicinity of Laodicea. From there it moved by way of the Maeander (Menderes) lowlands to Ephesus and other Aegean centers, or continuing from Laodicea as a junction point, extending by way of Philadelphia, Sardis, and Pergamum to Troas. The second branch, the northeastern, followed by Paul and Barnabas, extended across the Taurus mountains from Perga to arrive at Pisidian Antioch. Here was a network of roads penetrating in all directions.

Founded by the Seleucid rulers, probably on an older Phrygian foundation, Antioch was quickly converted into a city of outstanding importance—the military, political, and business center for the whole Phrygian territory. Colonists who settled here, following the Macedonian victories, included Greeks, Phrygians, and Jews, the presence of the last named being sufficiently explained on the basis of Antioch's central position with reference to all overland roads.

Proceeding from Pisidian Antioch, the apostle needed only to follow the great oriental trade route to reach in quick succession the cities of Iconium, Lystra, and Derbe. Iconium, represented by the modern town of Konya, stands in the midst of an upland plain of rare beauty and fertility, and is regarded as one of the important cities of interior Asia Minor. It was clearly a border town, situated in the southeastern region of Phrygia, only a few miles from the Lycaonian boundary. The presence of a large number of Jews suggests that the city was commercially important, a position which it maintains in the modern period. On the other hand, the neighboring cities of Lystra, eighteen miles southwest

of Iconium, and Derbe, forty-five miles southeast of the same point, being situated at the foothills of Taurus Mountains, were more provincial. Their importance as great centers was not on a par with that of Iconium or Antioch.

According to the book of Acts, Lystra and Derbe belonged to the geographical territory of Lycaonia. Both were on the great imperial road running east and west through the Cilician Gates. Lystra was honored by Augustus who converted it into a Roman colony, a distinction carrying great responsibility with reference to safeguarding Roman interests from hostile incursions and of preserving law and order. Under Roman auspices Lystra became an important military and cultural center, though retaining native customs and language.

Derbe, a frontier town located in the extreme southeastern section of the Lycaonian plateau, was a town of considerable importance by virtue of its strategic location, though it does not seem to have enjoyed the same prominence as that attached to Lystra, Iconium, and Pisidian Antioch. No reference is made to any Jewish synagogue at Derbe. The absence of any large number of his countrymen probably explains also why no persecution took place at Derbe, and that the apostle's ministry here was apparently successful. While at Derbe Paul was only 125 miles from Tarsus, his native city, but, instead of returning to Syrian Antioch by the eastern passage, he retraced his steps through Lycaonia, Pisidia, and Pamphylia to the Orontes capital.

The *second journey* (Acts 15:36 to 18:22), on the other hand, was along the famous overland trail from Antioch in Syria to Troas at the northwest tip of Asia Minor. Intermediate points included Tarsus, the Cilician Pass, Derbe, Lystra, Iconium, and Pisidian Antioch. As previously indicated, Antioch stood at the crossroads of all commercial, social, political, and military interests affecting the interior of Asia Minor. The northern route out of Antioch passed through the populous districts of upper Galatia, following largely the winding courses of the Halys (Kizil Irmak) and Sangarius (Sarkaya) rivers, to reach the thriving centers of Pontus, on the one hand, and Bithynia, on the other. All of this marvelous territory, strategic then as now, looked straight into the region of the Golden Horn beyond which lay the shore lines of Europe.

If Paul had any expectation of making this northern passage from Antioch in Pisidia, it would have been in full keeping with innumerable Oriental travelers and traders who followed this line from northern Mesopotamia to the Hellespont. The narratives suggest, however, that Paul was apparently determined on striking at Ephesus, the chief city in Asia Minor, which lay to the west. But being prevented from speaking the word in the province of Asia, he proceeded to the northwest, going through the Phrygian and Galatian country to come over against Mysia. Arriving in this section, there was an alternative proposal to penetrate the northeastern province of Bithynia, but it was rejected. The apostle continued on the great highway along the borders of Mysia, to arrive at Troas overlooking the Aegean.

There is no agreement regarding the limits of these provincial units. Since boundaries were frequently shifted, both on ethnological and ethnographical grounds, it is practically impossible to mark the exact line of Paul's advance to Troas.

In all likelihood the missionaries followed the imperial highways whenever it was possible. The principal road from Pisidian Antioch to Troas proceeded over the Old Way to the West through the Phrygian-Galatian country to Phila-

delphia, Sardis, and Thyatira. In the vicinity of this latter place probably occurred the attempted journey into the region of Bithynia. Being frustrated in this, the missionaries continued their advance along the borders of Mysia to Troas.

Ancient Troy was situated on a prominence almost at the junction of the Aegean and the Hellespont, the Bridge of Hellas (Greece). The ruins of the great Trojan stronghold lie only a short distance above the modern village of Ezine. These were excavated by Schliemann with astonishing results. Here was the scene of the Greco-Trojan wars which raged for ten years before the walls of Troy. About five miles south of the Trojan capital, the Lydian kings founded another Troy, also uncovered by Schliemann. Still farther south, about twelve miles, opposite the island of Tenedos (Bozcaada), lay a third city by the same name. This was the Troy of the New Testament period.

Troas was a great center, a watchtower from which one could observe the changing currents of business, politics, and social conventions. Across its streets went a continuous cross section of European and Asian life. Connected with coastwise trade, vessels frequently anchored at its improvised harbor, sailing at regular intervals. Embarking at Troas the voyage to Neapolis and Macedonia required only two days, the passage being broken by a night's stay on the island of Samothracia. Here then, on the threshold of Europe, was heard the Macedonian call for help.

As subsequent events show, Paul's response involved a larger area, affecting not only Philippi but Amphipolis, Apollonia, Thessalonica, Berea, Athens, Corinth, and Cenchreae. Sailing from

62. The port of Puteoli, where Paul was brought on his way to Rome.

Cenchreae the apostle came to Ephesus, and from Ephesus he proceeded to Caesarea on the Palestinian coast. Having saluted the church, the overland journey was made to Antioch in Syria.

The *third journey* (Acts 18:23 to 21:17) offers no special problems regarding the highways traversed, it being assumed that the departure from Antioch in Syria was followed by passage through the Cilician Gates by way of Lystra, Iconium, to Antioch in Pisidia. Two passages led through the Pisidian territory to Ephesus, the first by way of Laodicea and the Maeander lowlands, and the second by the upper highroad—the old overland road through Philadelphia and the Caÿster Valley to the Aegean coasts. In all probability he followed the latter passage. After the uproar at Ephesus, Paul proceeded into Macedonia along the main highroad through Smyrna, Pergamum, Adramyttium, and Troas to Neapolis. Returning from Greece and Macedonia, the apostle once again touched the mainland and islands of Asia Minor at Troas, Assos, Mitylene, Chios, Samos, Miletus, Cos, Rhodes, and Patara, on his last visit to Jerusalem.

Finally, on his *voyage to Rome* (Acts 27:1 to 28:16), Paul came into contact with Asia Minor only at isolated points. Sailing from Caesarea in the company of his freinds, the apostle touched first at ancient Sidon, then traveled to Asia Minor across the Cilicia Sea (the Gulf of Alexandretta) and the Pamphylian Sea (Sea of Lycia or Mediterranean Sea). Arriving at Myra, an important port of call for Egyptian-Syrian coastwise vessels, Paul was transferred to an Alexandrian grain ship bound for Italy. From Myra the regular shipping lane included Cnidus then westward to Rome. However, because of contrary winds, the course of the vessel was changed to the southwest.

The open port of Fair Havens, under the lee of Crete, was made with safety, but a further attempt to reach the winter harbor of Phoenix was followed by the disasters of fourteen days and nights on the Mediterranean. The progress of the vessel is narrated in connection with Syrtis, Cauda, the Adriatic, and Melita. Continuing the voyage on another Alexandrian vessel, the apostle came to Rome by way of Syracuse in Sicily, Rhegium on the Strait of Messina, Puteoli at Naples, and then on the great Appian Way from Brundisium to the capital.

Churches of the Revelation

The seven churches in the province of Asia, namely, Ephesus, Smyrna, Pergamum, Thyatira, Sardis, Philadelphia, and Laodicea, were all closely grouped in the vicinity of Ephesus, while the island of Patmos, the scene of John's vision, was off the shores of Asia Minor not more than seventy miles from the city of Ephesus. With the exception of Ephesus, which will be discussed in a later connection, we present here a few details regarding these pivotal centers.

The *island of Patmos,* the scene of John's banishment, lay along the coast of Asia Minor about fifty miles west of Miletus and seventy miles southwest of Ephesus. Although one of the smallest of the hundreds of islands that dot the Greek Archipelago, its association with the beloved disciple has given it a special place in history. One might describe the physical features of the island as a treeless area rising abruptly from a massive stone wall encompassing the whole region. Against this volcanic heap the waves of the Aegean dash themselves continually. It was here, however, that on one occasion the writer saw the Aegean in a state of perfect calm, not

63. Amphitheatre and acropolis at Pergamum, one of the cities of the seven churches in the book of Revelation.

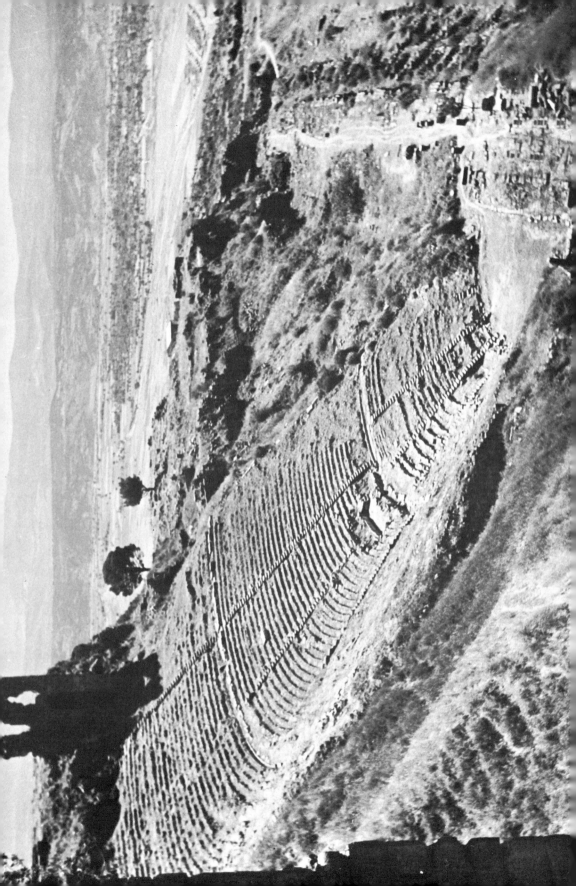

even a ripple was on the water, resembling indeed a sea of glass.

But whether boisterous or calm, it was that which separated him from the mainland, thus giving rise to an exiled prisoner's aspiration for the time when there would "be no more sea." While the date of John's confinement to this bleak waste of Patmos is disputed, there is no question regarding the place of his imprisonment nor of the lower type of prisoners banished with him. The entire area, ten mies long and six miles broad, was given over by the Romans as one of the principal regions for incarceration of undesirables.

Smyrna is now one of the most attractive cities in Asia Minor. Because of its repeated catastrophes of earthquake, fire, and flood, it has been called the "hardluck" city of the Levant. It is significant, however, that with its long and honorable history through three thousand years, Smyrna is today witnessing its greatest period of development. Located, from the seaward side, at the end of a bay of remarkable beauty, the city continues its ancient supremacy in maritime interests, enjoying a flourishing trade with Levantine countries.

On the other hand, from the landward side Smyrna maintained a position of envied leadership as one of the great points on overland trade routes. Though claiming to be "the first city" in Asia Minor, Smyrna was not allowed this distinction without protest by two other cities of outstanding importance, Pergamum and Ephesus. In point of time, however, it has justified its claim, seeing that it survives and grows.

In the Revelation letter are found probable allusions bearing on the various aspects of the city's checkered history—its tribulations, prestige, and wealth. In this metropolitan center one would expect to find the Jews numerically and economically very strong. They

are referred to in connection with the blasphemies of the Jews and with the synagogue of Satan. Furthermore, here in this city of material splendor, hybrid philosophy, and Hellenistic culture, the early Christians were evidently constantly on the defensive, though, according to tradition, Polycarp's death (*ca.* A.D. 155) in the stadium above the city was probably typical of their loyalty to the Christ instead of Caesar.

Pergamum was located on the Smyrna inland highway which reached to Troas. Although there is no statement that Paul was ever in the city, it is likely that he passed through its borders on his way from the Phrygian-Galatian country to the Aegean. Pergamum disputed with Ephesus and Smyrna the headship of Asia Minor—a boast which was not ungrounded, seeing that it alone became the seat of a kingdom which, during the period 283–133 B.C., embraced the later provincial areas of Mysia, Lydia, Caria, Phrygia, and Pamphylia. It is likely that the city was the capital of Asia during the early part of the Christian era.

Under a succession of illustrious kings Pergamum became one of the most beautiful cities of the East. It was distinctively a Greek city, one of that brilliant group of cultural centers whose influence was so decisive in preparing the East for the advent of Christianity. Pergamum probably surpassed its rival neighbors of Sardis and Ephesus in art, in sculpture, and in religious innovations. From the latter standpoint Pergamum was an outstanding promoter of the cult of Aesculapius, god of medicine, while in the matter of emperor-cult worship, Pergamum was the first provincial territory to acknowledge the divinity of the Roman ruler. This religiopolitical cult was the most potent and insidious foe of Christianity during the first century.

Thyatira, one of Asia's famous cities, appears first in the New Testament in connection with Paul's visit to Philippi where he met "Lydia, a seller of purple, of the city of Thyatira" (Acts 16:14), who invited the missionaries into her home. We may well be assured that this noble merchant-woman was not the least of Thyatira's gifts to the ancient world. It is of interest to observe here, however, that the accuracy of Luke in circumstantial details regarding various cities is supported by that which we now know concerning Thyatira's leadership in dyeing interests. In like manner the inhabitants attained marked proficiency in the making and working of bronze. Aside from these peaceful aspects of the city's life, Thyatira was situated on the principal highway connecting East and West, and was well fortified to defend its strategic position.

Sardis was the only one of the seven churches of which it was written, "Thou hast a name that thou livest, and art dead" (Rev. 3:1). That is now literally true, though the imposing ruins along the slopes of Mount Tmolus (Boz Dagh), illustrative of many centuries of cultural progress, stare at the visitor on all sides. The situation of the city was selected with almost prophetic insight as to its future importance. As one leaves Smyrna on the way to ancient Sardis, he passes through some of the most beautiful lowland scenery in western Asia, particularly the valley area created by the winding course of the Pactolus River.

Along the fringe of hills, but soon to spread into the valley, Sardis was founded. Prominence was early achieved, principally because of the city's vital connection with the important highways to and from the East. In its marts were shown the wares of the world; through its streets slowly trudged the dromedaries toward all points. In the prosperity of its merchants Sardis maintained its prestige as one of the first cities of Asia, boasting of its wealth. Situated only about seventy miles from Ephesus, it was one of the keenest rivals of that metropolis in the honor paid to Artemis.

Laodicea lay near to the headwaters of the Meander and Lycus rivers, approximately one hundred miles from Ephesus, the queen city of Asia Minor. Laodicea was an interior point of exceptional importance by virtue of its connection with the four quarters of Asia. To the southeast was the mountain pass issuing at Perga in the foothills of the Taurus Range; to the east went the great highroad penetrating the Lycaonian plains and the Cilician Gates to reach the Mesopotamian sector by way of Tarsus, Antioch, and Aleppo. To the west lay Ephesus at the shore line of the Aegean, while northwest were the fine centers of Philadelphia, Sardis, and neighboring cities, all located on the same military and commercial highways.

Although a continuous stream of wealth was poured into the lap of Laodicea on account of these connections, the town regarded itself as practically self-supporting by virtue of the industries common to the region. This boasted sufficiency is specifically mentioned in the letter addressed to the Laodiceans. In the vicinity of Laodicea were two other important cities, Hierapolis and Colossae, whose development was restricted by their more powerful neighbor. All three centers were situated in the beautiful valley of the Lycus River, a Phrygian mountain stream flowing into the upper reaches of the Maeander.

Hierapolis is mentioned only once in the New Testament. Its exact location was five miles north of Laodicea on the road to Philadelphia. Early tradition connects the city with the labors of Philip and two of his daughters. Here was born Epictetus, one of the choicest spirits among Roman Stoics, and his fellow townsman, Papias, about ten years later (A.D. 70–130).

Colossae, on the other hand, stood slightly southeast of Laodicea, about six miles, being located on the overland trail from the East to the Aegean seaboard. The city has the distinction of being mentioned in connection with Onesimus, Philemon, Epaphras, Archippus, and others. It is clear that Epaphras was the agent in its evangelization (Col. 1:7). Paul, when writing the Colossian epistle, stated that he had not visited the town.

Finally, *Philadelphia,* hardly more than forty-five miles northwest of Laodicea, was situated in the heart of the Cogamis River Valley, flanked in the interior by the foothills of the Maeonian Plateau. The Hermus (Gediz), flowing to the northwest, produced with its tributaries the delightful locations of Sardis, Thyatira, and Smyrna. The city of Philadelphia was distinguished in its role as the "Little Athens" of Asia Minor. This indicated perhaps a cultural mission of prime importance among other outstanding Hellenistic cities. Its period of greatest prosperity may be placed during the first and second Christian centuries, though retaining a commanding position as late as the seventh century when it was converted into a principal Byzantine center. A small town, Alasehir, occupies the site of ancient Philadelphia. It is significant that of these seven cities hardly anything remains except at Smyrna and Philadelphia, both of which were commended in an unusual manner in the letters addressed to them.

13
Greco-Roman Centers

The most decisive factor in the political and economic backgrounds of the Greco-Roman world was the highly developed life of a score of representative cities strategically located in various parts of the Empire. It may be fairly said that since the inception of the city-state idea, particularly by the Greeks at Athens, Sparta, and Thebes, there prevailed a wholesome rivalry among flourishing centers to excel in matters affecting every aspect of city planning and improvement. While it may be admitted that the city-state was a definite part of the Sumerian and Philistine organization, centuries prior to the Hellenic development, no one would contend that the earlier centers ever attained, or even approximated, the perfection achieved by the Greek cities, especially Athens.

Indeed, it now appears that Athens, because of its brilliant success in municipal building, provided a norm for aspiring centers such as Rome, Alexandria, Antioch in Syria, and Ephesus. It is granted that, in the case of Rome and Alexandria, we have subsequent development and expansion of municipal life probably surpassing that of Athens, but,

considering the model after which they planned, the glory belonging originally to the mother city is thereby enhanced.

At the dawn of the Christian era, scattered throughout the Roman world was this group of metropolitan centers whose leadership was acknowledged in provincial territories. In some cases their influence was determinative even in imperial affairs. To strike and win these pivotal points was equivalent to the evangelization of greatly enlarged areas. Now in the campaigns of Paul, for example, waiving here the question regarding a definite plan of missionary activity, it is clear that he struck the great cultural centers almost exclusively. We do not need to charge the apostle, however, with having chosen deliberately these conspicuous urban points on the ground that he was averse to visiting rural sections, or that he felt himself better qualified by virtue of life in Tarsus and in Jerusalem.

It is evident that the selection of strategic points was attended by strategy of the first order. It is significant that, wherever the apostle was led, there was a great center of cultural influence involving provincial territories. In a word, these great points, already at hand, were converted into sources from which the gospel was progressively heralded into all parts of contiguous regions.

A list of the representative cities might be made almost at random, but in keeping with our primary interest in biblical backgrounds we have selected eight outstanding centers whose contacts, for the most part, contributed to the progress of the Christian movement: *Tarsus, Antioch in Syria, Ephesus, Philippi, Thessalonica, Athens, Corinth,* and *Rome.* Expressed in terms of social, political, commercial, and religious influence, they formed an encircling network which vitally affected all parts of the Mediterranean borderlands.

All of these might be designated Pauline cities, so intimate were their relations with the great Apostle to the Gentiles. This of course is the fundamental aspect in which we are interested. But the fact that they were so closely related to the missionary activities of Paul raises a further question regarding the probable grounds on which they were chosen as strategic points. If there was any expectation of an enlarged area of Christian influence growing out of the evangelization of urban communities, what was the basis of that expectation? Obviously the question is not difficult to answer, particularly in view of the fact that the vital relations existing between these cities and other parts of the world were not only well known but definitely cultivated. In summing up the leading characteristics of this group of cities, we make the following observations.

The importance of these cities related, in the *first* instance, to their political status. Without exception every city named here occupied the position of an administrative center for surrounding territory. In the cases of Antioch in Syria, Tarsus, Ephesus, and Corinth, we are actually dealing with provincial capitals. Rome, of course, stands out as the imperial center, the mistress of the world. On the other hand, Philippi was regarded as a leading city of its district, Thessalonica was the administrative center of the second Macedonian division, and Athens was the chief city of Attica, surpassing its neighbors in many particulars. These cities set the pace for the observance of Roman rights and privileges, the dignity of citizenship, and the maintenance of law and order. Although there were some exceptions, Paul's experiences in these political centers clearly reflect the operation of Roman law and convention, as at Philippi, Thessalonica, Corinth, and Ephesus. One recalls the frequent contacts of the apostle with Roman officials, both local and provincial, in these regions. It is well known that Christianity, in common with other religions of the Roman Empire, first received its legal standing in these foremost centers of the world.

In the *second* place, the group of cities under consideration represented the best qualities in the cultural backgrounds of the early Christian era. Each center expressed the highest form of social organization and institutions. Here were brought to realization or approximation the great civic ideals so characteristic of the period; here was the process of mental growth and discipline which reached its culmination in some of the greatest philosophers of antiquity. In the eastern division of the Empire were found the great educational institutions which enjoyed world reputation; students came from remotest sections to be instructed in the arts and sciences. It was inevitable that the Christian message and claims should be subjected to the keenest criticism that the Greco-Roman world had to offer, and that in this process of searching inquiry it must prove itself not alien to but compatible with the highest

aspects of contemporary life. Furthermore, if Christianity was to justify its
claim as a universal religion, its fold had
to include the learned and unlearned,
cultured and uncultured, the common
man and the intellectuals. Its ability to
attract, to win, and to hold all classes
within these great cultural centers was
the final proof of its genius and its
grace.

Third, all of these cities were important from a commercial or business
standpoint. It is true that the trade activities of Athens and Philippi were not as
pronounced as those of the remaining
centers, but this is entirely a relative
matter. Even Philippi, distinctively a
military outpost, was situated near the
Egnatian Way, the great trade route
to the Orient, while Athens stood in
close proximity to Piraeus, one of the
outstanding ports of the world. The commercial interests of all these cities involved both maritime and overland connections. Antioch in Syria, Tarsus, and
Rome were all situated in the interior
along the courses of beautiful rivers, but
except for very small boats none had
strict maritime connections; their thriving seaports in each case stood about
fifteen miles away. But Antioch was one
of the most important inland points between East and West. Tarsus guarded
the Cilician Gates, and Rome was strictly
the terminus for every shipping lane and
overland trail. Ephesus was strategic in
all Asia Minor interests, particularly
those relating to caravan connections,
while Thessalonica, located at the head
of a great gulf, looked to the Aegean
borderlands by the sea and to Rome by
the Egnatian Way. Corinth, finally, overlooking the Corinthian Gulf, was the
chief point in Adriatic coastwise trade,
while from the landward side it stood at
the center of highways linking together
the Peloponnesus and northern provinces of Greece and Macedonia.

Fourth, the religious interests of these
outstanding communities were pronounced. Here one meets all the famous
shrines of the Greco-Roman world, ranging from Bacchus and Daphne in
Antioch, Artemis in Ephesus, Athena in
Athens, to the whole motley brood
safely housed in the Pantheon at Rome.
Everywhere was the pervasive influence
of the mystery religions and emperor
worship. The material expression of religious life at Ephesus, Rome, and Athens
was extravagant. The introduction of
Christianity into such environments was
deliberate and confident. Sooner or later
these cults must yield the field to the
great evangel which offered a reasonable
answer to every legitimate call of the
human heart and life. To attack these
pagan strongholds was certainly a great
venture of faith, but the Christian
triumph is the proof of its justification.

Finally, every city in this group, being
intimately connected with dependent
territory, was a pivotal point from which
radiated influences affecting the whole
social order. These dependencies were in
the nature of daughter cities whose main
source of civic idealism and activity was
found in the principal center. Here was a
factor of tremendous importance. News
always traveled quickly from the capitals: urbanites and provincials crowded
the streets and marketplaces "either to
tell or to hear some new thing." Here
was the great clearing house, the
sounding boards which echoed into
adjacent regions the headline features
of each day. The evangelization of
one of these centers carried far-reaching
consequences; it was the leaven that
would affect ultimately the surrounding
country. That was the natural working
of the gospel and the natural expectation
attending its publication everywhere.
We are not surprised to learn that its
normal course was realized at Thessalon-

ica, that its success elsewhere was no less conspicuous.

Tarsus

Tarsus, the chief city in Cilicia, was situated about ten miles from the Mediterranean seaboard. It lay along the east and west banks of the Cydnus River in a plain of rare beauty and fertility. The entire area of Tarsus and its environs is composed of alluvial deposits brought down from the Taurus Mountains by the three principal rivers of the regions—the Cydnus, Sarus (Seyhan), and Pyramus (Ceyhan). All of these streams, being very small, are navigable only to light boats. Plutarch describes a voyage made by Cleopatra, queen of Egypt, from the Mediterranean to Tarsus. Although this incident indicates that the city had maritime connections, they were certainly not of any great importance since the city was too far inland.

On the other hand, its overland contacts were of the first rank. The natural position of Tarsus was that of a gateway to the Cilician Pass, thirty-five miles to the north, through which ran the inland highways. The existence of a city at this particular point was practically inevitable. Its strategic location was fittingly crowned by its rapid development in the Greco-Roman world, when Tarsus became a metropolitan center vying with Athens, Antioch, and Alexandria as a seat of affluence and enlightenment.

Of special interest is the statement of the Roman poet Juvenal who, in tracing the history of Tarsus, remarks that the city derived its name from the fact that the wing of Pegasus fell there. But apart from this mythological reference, it is on the reputation of Saul of Tarsus, its most illustrious son, that the fame of the city has been winged to the modern period. One is reminded of the apostle's reply to Lysias in Jerusalem when, suspected of being an Egyptian, he said with much

feeling: "I am a Jew, from Tarsus in Cilicia, a citizen of no mean city" (Acts 21:39, RSV).

The impression made here is that of deep civic pride as well as ancestral feeling. In this he was amply justified. It was the home of a great university where eminent teachers discoursed on some of the finest aspects of Stoic philosophy and other branches of human inquiry. According to Strabo, the Tarsians, in their pursuit of knowledge, were peculiar in that "the learners are all natives, and that hardly any strangers sojourn there; nor do the natives remain at home, but seek the completion of their education abroad, and then seldom return."

Paul's relations with Tarsus put him at the heart of the Greco-Roman East. Out of this environment he came, a Hellenistic Jew and Roman citizen, characterized by a cosmopolitan spirit which entered so largely into the heritage of Alexander the Great, to fulfil the mission of Christianity both to Jew and to Greek.

Antioch in Syria

The ornate capital of the Seleucid rulers was situated in one of the most attractive regions of northern Syria. Towering above the city was the Silpius Mountain Range, forming a natural defense, while through the heart of the town flowed the beautiful Orontes River. It was one of the few outstanding Hellenistic centers whose origin or development was not definitely attributed to Alexander the Great, though it is said the Macedonian paused here, after the Battle of Issus, to offer sacrifice on the altar of Jupiter. Antioch was founded in 300 B.C. by Seleucus Nicator who named it in honor of his father Antiochus. It was designed by the Syrian kings as a capital city to compete with Alexandria of the Ptolemies. Although Antoich never succeeded in surpassing the Egyptian metropolis, it achieved great distinction as the third city of the Greco-Roman world. Its greatness rested on political, commercial, cultural, and religious considerations of extraordinary importance.

Politically, it was the capital of the whole Syrian littoral, the administrative center for a vast territory which, at one time, included the whole of the Near and Middle East. This was, of course, immediately after the death of Alexander the Great, when the eastern portion of his empire was divided between Ptolemy and Seleucus, the principal seat of the former being at Alexandria while the latter reigned at Antioch. In all probability, Antiochus Epiphanes contributed most to its magnificence by the creation of temples, bridges, colonnades, and municipal gardens, thus converting it into one of the most beautiful cities. To Epiphanes also goes the credit for having extended Antioch from the southern and western sections to border on the infamous groves of Daphne five miles to the west.

With the advent of the Romans who took over the Seleucid dominions in the East, Antioch was further beautified, particularly by Pompey, who in 63 B.C. bargained for its military support against Julius Caesar by granting a considerable degree of independence to the city. On the other hand, after the Battle of Pharsalus (48 B.C.) Caesar expressed his appreciation of their disloyalty to Pompey by erecting the Caesareum, theater, amphitheater, and other public works. Tiberius Ceasar extended the walls of the city on the south. Although visited frequently by disastrous earthquakes, because of its political importance Antioch was repeatedly rebuilt out of funds provided both by rulers and citizens. Each emergence was on a greater and more magnificent scale.

Commercially, Antioch was regarded as one of the principal business centers of the East. It was connected with the Roman highway system which linked Mesopotamia and the Orient to the Mediterranean coasts. Portions of these roadways are still visible, while modern engineers have utilized foundations made by the Romans two thousand years ago. Caravans continue to follow the ancient trails to arrive in the marts of Antioch for bargain and exchange. Twenty-one miles to the west of the city was Seleucia, the principal seaport of Antioch, which flourished by virtue of its connection with the capital. Finally, as a consequence of these business interests thousands of Jews moved to Antioch where, according to Josephus, they had "privileges equal to those of the Macedonians and Greeks who were the inhabitants, insomuch that these privileges continue to this very day."

But it was from the cultural standpoint that the city achieved its greatest importance. It was one of the chief centers of influence in the scheme of Hellenizing the East. Its population, consisting mostly of Greeks and Macedonians, was in full sympathy with the promotion of Greek culture as applied to the material expression of religious life, civic splendor, and modes of thought. In this respect Antioch was as conspicuously successful as any other Hellenistic city in the East. It is recalled that the Maccabean struggles headed up in this special phase of Antioch's cultural activities. Later, during the Roman period, the influence of Antioch was powerful throughout the Mediterranean world, though the special phase of its influence related to vice and corruption. It was currently said that the Orontes had overflowed the Tiber, so great was the appeal of the groves of Daphne and its hideous orgies of shame to the Roman world.

Unlike Alexandria, Antioch stands out in the forefront of New Testament centers, its prominence, of course, being based on its vital connection with Gentile evangelization (Acts 13:1–3). It became the main center of Christian activity at an early period. Here, also, Christianity made its greatest impression. Mentioned repeatedly in the Acts, in each instance it is definitely associated with some phase of the Christian movement.

Its first appearance is in connection with Nicolaus, a proselyte of Antioch, who was one of the seven chosen for special service in the Jerusalem church. Antioch was visited by dispersed Christians who came by way of Phoenicia and Cyprus, preaching only to Jews; later it was evangelized by those who proceeded from Cyprus and Cyrene, preaching also to the Greeks. Barnabas came here on an important mission from Jerusalem, subsequently to remain with Saul of Tarsus and, finally, to proceed on the first mission campaign. Antioch was likewise the scene of the inauguration of the second and third missionary journeys, which touched great areas of the Roman world.

Aside from traditions which associate Luke and Theophilus with Antioch, the city was invested with pronounced religious significance through subsequent centuries. The great patristic school, whose fundamental approach to the Scriptures was historical and grammatical and whose chosen province was the defense of the truth *contra mundum*, flourished here. Finally, it is estimated that between the third and sixth centuries, thirty ecclesiastical councils were held in Antioch, thus attesting the prominence of the city in Christian deliberation and leadership.

Ephesus

Although several neighboring cities disputed with Ephesus the civic leadership of western Asia Minor, the Lydian metropolis probably had no difficulty in defending its primacy. It was the capital of the province of Asia during the New Testament period. Apart from its political importance, Ephesus was easily the ranking city in commercial and religious interests, these being perhaps its most significant connections.

Situated at the confluence of the Maeander and Caÿster valleys, Ephesus was easily approached by all interior highways headed for the Aegean. Its natural position converted the city into an open marketplace where native and foreign wares were bought and sold. Into this emporium of land trade came merchants from the ends of the earth. All roads reached Ephesus ultimately, but it was in a special sense the objective for the great trunk lines East and West. On the other hand, located only three miles from the Aegean Sea, its maritime connections were correspondingly important.

It is highly significant that, in the absence of harbor facilities for seagoing vessels, the Ephesians converted the Caÿster watercourse into a navigable stream at least for small vessels. Evidences of the city piers may yet be seen in a marsh area immediately before the ancient town. Foundation stones of the municipal wharf, where vessels received their cargoes, are still *in situ,* while the dim outlines of ancient canals from the city and temple area can be followed to the channel of the Caÿster River.

Large vessels with passengers and cargoes bound for Ephesus drew up at Miletus, the principal seaport, located about thirty miles to the south. Between Ephesus and Miletus was a connecting highway of Roman construction. While it is true that Miletus was an important

64. The marble street at Ephesus which leads from the theatre where Paul and his companions were dragged by the mob of Ephesians.

city on its own account, being regarded as one of the main cities of western Asia prior to the rise of Ephesus, during the Roman period it generally slipped into a secondary position looking to the Ephesian metropolis. In the New Testament this relationship is intimated particularly in connection with the farewell scene between Paul and the Ephesian elders (Acts 20:15–38).

The religious interests of Ephesus, however, constituted its chief claim for preeminence among Asia Minor cities. It was the "temple keeper of the great Artemis, and of the sacred stone that fell from the sky" (Acts 19:35, RSV). Marked now by a scene of complete desolation, it is difficult to realize that the sacred area at Ephesus once sustained a temple which took its rank as one of the seven marvels of the ancient world. On the night that Alexander the Great was born the temple of the Ephesian Artemis was destroyed by fire. The whole of Asia Minor and other sections contributed with liberality to rebuild it and to make it one of the architectural splendors of the age. This reconstructed sanctuary was standing throughout the New Testament period. It was located on an undulating plain about a mile and a half northeast of the city, but it was connected with the metropolis by a roadway paved with marble. This magnificent street, leading out of Ephesus by the South or Magnesian Gate, was, on the average, about thirty-five feet wide.

No doubt Paul, through his long residence in the city, was familiar with the religious precessions from Ephesus to the temple. Since the temple and the image were the chief items connected with the pagan Artemis, it is likely that the manufacturing interests which Paul's preaching interrupted were concerned with making not only imitations of the sanctuary but of the goddess herself. On some coins the temple and the image are shown together. Gold and silver were probably the chief metals used in producing these objects.

It is possible to reconstruct the physical features of Ephesus along fairly accurate lines. To the northeast, as already indicated, stood the temple of Artemis. Following the marble roadway from the temple we enter the Magnesian Gate—a stately portal having two openings for horses and horse-drawn vehicles and one for pedestrians. We do not know the exact appearance of the street from the gate to the theater, but in all probability it was colonnaded. Ruins along the way show hundreds of foundations formerly mounted by statues in the Greco-Roman style, dedicated to gods, goddesses, rulers, and, perhaps, one to "an unknown god" as at Athens.

The above illustration shows the nature of the street and its original ornamentation. It was the principal avenue of the city. Although bearing the marks of ages, abandoned to the destructive forces of nature and of man, it continues to reflect something of its ancient glory. The illustration shows also the exact location of the theater, the main place of assembly, which stood at the end of the street, a stone structure with ascending aisles and tiers of seats capable of accommodating twenty-five thousand people. This was the scene of the great Ephesian riot instigated against Paul by Demetrius and his fellow craftsmen (Acts 19:33–41).

Sitting in the rear of the theater one may get a splendid view of the central section of the ancient city, including the ruins of the forum area, the outline of streets now obstructed by debris, the harbor arrangements and canal looking toward the Aegean, and the colossal remains of old buildings, particularly of churches, which flourished here in the third and fourth centuries. A short distance to the north of the theater is a massive pile of ruins where once stood the magnificent stadium. Its main outlines are easily followed. One recalls here the familiar metaphor of Paul regarding combats between men and beasts at Ephesus. To the west of the stadium was the shrine of Serapis, an Egyptian divinity introduced at Ephesus in Hellenistic dress.

A pagan city of the first rank, Ephesus lost nothing in the early Christian era but maintained her leadership as one of the most conspicuous centers of Christian activity in the apostolic period. The thrilling events which occurred here in connection with the labors of Paul, Aquila, Priscilla, Apollos, and Timothy about the middle of the first century were possibly crowned by the presence and martyrdom of John the beloved disciple.

Philippi

The province of Macedonia was divided into four governmental districts with Amphipolis and Thessalonica, two outstanding cities, being classified as capitals of the first and second districts respectively. Philippi was located in the first division. In the case of Amphipolis, however, though considered as the administrative center for the whole area, it was clearly surpassed by Philippi, whose geographical location made it a vital point in the defense of the empire, and whose colonial status converted the city into a dignified representative of Roman life and thought. The reference in Acts 16:12 to Philippi as "the leading city of the district of Macedonia" (RSV) denotes either its status as the most important city, since Amphipolis was the capital although an inferior city, or the passage is an obscure reference to Philippi as a city of the first district of Macedonia, and a Roman colony, which was its actual status.

Geographically, Philippi was an inland town situated about ten miles north of the Aegean seaport of Neapolis (modern Kavalla), from which it was separated by a continuous range of low-lying hills. Its maritime interests, centering at Neapolis, were safeguarded by the construction of a Roman highway, a spur of the great Egnatian Way, which intersected the trunk line about four miles south of Philippi.

Situated at the base of an acropolis, with a copious water supply derived from the Gangites River which encompassed the town on the north and west, and with an exceptional agricultural background provided by the fertile valley running northeast and southwest, the economic outlook of Philippi was promising. In addition to these advantages, Rome showered its largess on the colonial stronghold. Actually, however, the position of Philippi was that of an outpost or fortress whose principal business was to ward off barbarian hordes and to preserve the Roman peace on the edges of the empire. The military atmosphere may have kept away Jewish settlers, thus preventing the establishment of a synagogue, or the Jews may have been required to hold their meetings "by the riverside" (Acts 16:13) or outside the pomerium, a line enclosing empty space around the city wall within which burials were prohibited and strange cults were not allowed.

Thessalonica

Following the Egnatian Way through Amphipolis and Apollonia we come to Thessalonica, the chief commercial center of Macedonia, situated eighty-five miles southwest of Philippi. Its land and maritime interests converted it into an emporium of the first rank, while its political status as the real capital of Macedonia elevated the city in provincial administration. Thronged by caravans overland, its harbor reeking with old bottoms from overseas, Thessalonica presented every feature of a cosmopolitan center, its portals opened wide to strangers from the ends of the earth. Suggestive is the passage that describes the group of world-topplers, represented by Paul and his co-workers, who inevitably reach Thessalonica in the course of their world mission.

But prior to Paul's arrival, thousands of Jews were already in the city, having been led by characteristic business judgment to settle in thriving centers. Nor were these representatives of the great western dispersion deceived in the selection of Thessalonica. Here they established themselves to become, in time, a decisive factor in Thessalonian affairs, both by virtue of their numerical strength and material prosperity.

Ancient Thessalonica occupied the same site as that of the present city, at the headwaters of the Thermaic Gulf (Gulf of Salonika). It was a strongly fortified town, as indicated by extensive ruins, with a considerable population. Our first glimpse of Thessalonica in the New Testament shows a city of no little significance, clearly loyal to the Roman emperor and easily stirred by religious prejudices (Acts 17:2–8). In all likelihood the loyalty here intimated was largely the product of Thessalonica's regional headship in the Roman administrative system, in the first instance, and of its prosperous commercial relations, in the second.

By virtue of its position at the halfway point on the Egnatian route between the Aegean and the Adriatic coasts, the city regarded itself not only as responsible to Rome but desirous of its patronage and good will. Furthermore, it was the official residence of the Roman governor in whom was vested the oversight of the entire region. The city enjoyed the status of a "free city," or autonomous city-state, possessed of its own politarchs and as-

sembly. If we may judge from the action taken in Paul's case, the rulers were apparently bent on justice, though greatly disturbed because of the tumult, and were determined to allow legal protection to Paul and his companions (Acts 17:9). At any rate, one observes here a procedure unlike that followed at Philippi, the difference between harsh military discipline on the one hand, and milder processes of civil law on the other.

Athens

Immediately after the outbreak at Thessalonica, Paul proceeded to the neighboring city of Berea and then on to Athens, the principal city of Attica and Greece, two hundred miles south of Thessalonica (Acts 17:10 ff.). We do not know the apostle's original intention regarding a visit to Athens, but his advent marked the highest point in his attack on Gentile strongholds of influence and culture. This, says Aristophanes, is "our Athens, violet-wreathed, brilliant, most enviable city." In some respects Athens was one of the world's great cities; its contribution to the enrichment of human civilization has never been surpassed. Actually, the modern age feels that it has not equaled the perfection of genius displayed at Athens in the period of Pericles and after. This is all the more remarkable when it is remembered that the glory of Greece sprang almost full grown from the Attic plains in the wake of the Athenian triumphs over Persia at Marathon (490 B.C.) and at Salamis (480 B.C.).

But long prior to this time Athens was an important center. Codrus, the last king of Athens, closed his reign just about the time that Samuel was choosing the first king of Israel. On the other

65. The Parthenon on the acropolis in Athens.

hand, hundreds of years earlier than Samuel and Saul, at the time that Abram was setting forth from Ur of Mesopotamia bound for a promised land, there was already a settlement on the Acropolis at Athens with a limited community in the plain below. From that remote period to the present the Acropolis has been the central point in life at Athens. Its commanding elevation above the plain converted the hill into a natural fortress, a place of refuge in times of danger. This aspect of the Acropolis persisted as late as the Turko-Venetian struggles in the seventeenth century, when the Turks utilized the hill as a heavily armed fort.

But the importance of the Acropolis does not pertain in the first instance to its military significance; religion provided the foundation of its greatness. The erection of every public building in ancient Athens was in some manner connected with the gods of Hellas. On the other hand, while the whole Hellenic Pantheon was represented in the capital, Athena, the virgin goddess, was the special ward and custodian of the metropolis to which she gave her name. The center of her worship was of course the Acropolis, the hill of Athena. Over this site destruction has stalked pitilessly, leveling to dust and ashes the most wonderful examples of architectural and sculptural perfection. Sufficient evidence is left, however, to justify the now proverbial expression, "the glory that was Greece."

Study the picture of the Acropolis as it now stands, never to be restored. The beautiful entrance to the sacred enclosure looked to the west. The Propylaea of Mnesicles, a magnificent marble portal, constituted the only way of approach for worshipers and sacrifices. To the rear of the Propylaea stood a statue of Athena sixty-six feet in height, said to have been produced by Phidias from the bronze in-

cluded in the spoils of the Marathon battle. Beyond the statue was the Erechtheum, probably the oldest temple on the Acropolis, dedicated to Athena and to Poseidon, god of the sea. The exquisite porch of the Caryatids with its graceful figures in marble constituted one of the great creations in Greek sculpture. In the same classification was the little Temple of Athena Victorious which stood overlooking the Acropolis entrance. Originally it was constructed of Pentelic marble, its date going back to 440 B.C. One never ceases to admire this building whose reconstruction is more complete than that of any other shrine on the hill.

Greater than all, however, was the Parthenon, which was not only the outstanding triumph of Hellenic genius but the most beautiful building ever constructed. Standing on the highest point of the Acropolis, its elevation was slightly more than five hundred feet above the sea. It was composed entirely of Pentelic marble with the most ornate embellishments. A period of ten years was required for its completion, it being dedicated in the era of Athens' greatest splendor, the age of Pericles. It was, of course, one of the great wonders of antiquity. Special attention is called to the wooden statue of the goddess Athena, overlaid with plates of ivory and of gold, forty-two and a half feet in height. Finally, the Parthenon was in a state of perfect preservation, not only when Paul visited Athens, but stood in magnificence until 1687 when it was wrecked by a Venetian shell igniting a Turkish powder magazine in the interior.

At the base of the Acropolis were other outstanding structures which graced the Athens of Paul's day. The Theater of

66. Mars Hill, viewed from the acropolis in Athens. The outcropping of rock in the left center is the traditional location.

Dionysus, where the comedies and trage-
dies of the great playwrights Aristophanes, Euripides, and Sophocles were
presented, was located on the southeastern side, an open-air structure with seating capacity for sixteen thousand people.
Not far to the west was the Temple of
Aesculapius and beyond that the Odeum
of Herodes Atticus seating five thousand
people. On the northeast, in the midst of
the plain, was the Temple of Zeus,
counted as the eighth wonder of the
world. Nearby was the Stadium, now perfectly restored along its original lines,
the gift of an Alexandrian Greek to his
native city. In this structure, with a capacity of sixty thousand spectators, the
modern Olympic games were inaugurated in 1906.

On the northern side of the Acropolis
stood the Tower of the Winds, a fascinating piece of work which has lost nothing
of its charm, while to the west was the
Temple of Theseus, the most perfectly
preserved of the Greek edifices. Between
the Tower and the Theseum was the
marketplace, or Forum of the Roman
period, while to the north of the Forum
was the Agora area visited by Paul,
where Athenians leisurely conversed on
topics of the day, and where the apostle
came to grips with the Epicurean and
Stoic philosophers.

From the Agora, Paul was conducted
to the Areopagus, or hill of Ares, which
was located immediately to the west of
the Acropolis. Here Paul made his defense in full view of the most spectacular
environment of pagan idolatry the world
has known. How unintelligible to these
splendor-loving Athenians was the announcement concerning a Lord of
heaven and earth who "dwelleth not in
temples made with hands; neither is he
served by men's hands, as though he
needed anything" (Acts 17:24–25, ASV) !
To Athenians, the godhead was associated with gold, silver, and stone graven

by art and device of man. From the
magnificence of these earthly sanctuaries
we can well believe that Athenians regarded their divinities as wanting everything and that they, as a very religious
people, denied them nothing.

Finally, the retirement of Paul from
Athens was probably by the great connecting highway between the capital city
and Piraeus, the chief seaport, about five
miles to the southwest. During the reign
of Themistocles this roadway was between formidable walls two hundred and
fifty feet apart. Ruins of the old fortifications may still be seen. In true Greek
fashion the boulevard was lined with
statuary dedicated to all the divinities of
the Athenians and one altar "to an unknown god."

Corinth

From Athens to Corinth it was a distance of only fifty miles either by land or
water. It is not known whether Paul
went toward Corinth from the seaport of
Piraeus to land at Cenchreae, a Corinthian seaport on the Aegean seven miles
from the metropolis, or followed the
overland route from Athens by way of
Eleusis, the seat of the Eleusinian mystery cult. In either event he would have
crossed the Isthmus of Corinth which is
now cut by the Corinthian canal. It is
interesting to note that prior to Paul's
visit Caesar had planned a canal across
the narrow strip, and that almost syn-
chronizing with the apostle's arrival was
the proposal of Nero to accomplish the
same work. Nothing was ever done, however, until the modern period. The present canal, about four miles in length, was
completed in 1893.

The building of the canal was a
significant achievement in engineering,

**67. The Lechaion Road leading out of
Corinth. Paul traveled this road on his
second missionary journey.**

but the necessity of a waterway connection between the Aegean and the Adriatic serves to show the strategic position of Corinth as a flourishing center of trade and culture. The city stood on the great commercial routes between the Orient and the Occident both by land and sea, while it was also the main point between the Peloponnesus and northern Greece. Its two principal seaports, Cenchreae on the Aegean and Lechaeum on the Gulf, indicate its importance in maritime interests.

The ancient city stood in the midst of a plain of matchless beauty and fertility, extending about four miles from the slopes of the Acropolis to the Gulf of Corinth. Corinth itself was practically midway of the two. It was surrounded by a strong wall about five miles in circumference. Corinth was accordingly a great city, the population being more than one hundred thousand during the Roman period.

The Acropolis stands 1,886 feet above sea level. A portion of the hill was fortified. On the summit was the great Temple of Aphrodite whose worship was so powerful among the Corinthians. Through excavations we are able to restore the general outlines of this metropolitan center and to identify particular places such as the Glauce, Temple of Apollo, theater, business section, streets, shops, and the possible location of a Jewish synagogue.

The position of Corinth in early Hellenic developments was largely involved with the fortunes of Sparta against Athens. The Acropolis at Athens is plainly in view from Acro-Corinth on a clear day, and in ancient relations there was never a day that Corinth was not watching the capital of Attica. Corinth was the chief power back of Sparta in the final

68. Ruins in the Apollo temple at Corinth, built before the time of Paul.

thrust which issued in the fall of Athens in 404 B.C. But Corinth also was in a perilous situation. Conquered in turn by Alexander the Great and the Romans, the city was finally reduced to an insignificant position. An act of rebellion against Rome was followed by its complete destruction in 146 B.C., the deportation of its inhabitants, and the actual abandonment of the site until Julius Caesar restored it in 44 B.C.

It then quickly grew into a prominent center, becoming the chief city in the Peloponnesus, and the capital of the province of Achaia. This was the Corinth of Paul's day, the official residence of Gallio, the proconsul, and the scene of a successful mission on the part of Paul, Aquila, Priscilla, Apollos, and others. It was accordingly a vital point in the Christian enterprise. Here Christianity was given a legal standing in the eastern portion of the empire by the decision of Gallio. Here, of course, in this thoroughly Greco-Roman stronghold, with its philosophical, religious, and moral background, the practical aspects of the Christian religion received not only a severe testing but, in the Corinthian epistles, a powerful vindication.

Rome

The capital of the Caesars easily justified its claim of being the chief city in the Roman Empire, greater than Athens, Alexandria, or Antioch. Indeed, Rome is one of the great cities of all time. Although situated in the western division of the Roman world it sustained intimate connections with the remotest regions, being at once the dominating figure in all imperial affairs—political, social, cultural, military, commercial, and religious. In the midst of its seven famed hills stood the Forum, the administrative center of a vast expanse of territory which included all borderlands of the Mediterranean, the ancient countries of the Near and Middle East, the hinterlands of Europe, Britannia, and interior portions of northeast Africa. The imperial organization outlined here equaled in extensiveness the world empire of Alexander the Great, while in wealth, population, and effectiveness of administration it was greater.

It is reasonable to suppose that the unitary nature of this great political system presented to Paul a challenge with respect to the immediate scope of the gospel, though it is not necessary to claim that it constituted the ultimate of the apostle's thought, which included the whole world regardless of its political complexion then, or at any other time. The ends of the earth always lay at the heart of the Christian message. It is clear, however, that the administrative center of the empire made a tremendous appeal to the apostle, apparently from the beginning of his career, and that he thought of it in some respects as the culminating point in his mission to the Gentile world. If he entertained any such thought of Rome, he was eminently justified on the ground that a conquest of Rome meant the establishment of Christianity in the most conspicuous cultural and political center of the day. Accordingly, we can understand why the apostle longed to visit Rome, and why his deferred journeys were regarded as keeping him from a larger usefulness (cf. Rom. 1:13 ff.) .

The beginnings of Rome are shrouded in mystery. Although now regarded as one of the world's old cities, Rome was comparatively young in the company of Jerusalem, Thebes, Memphis, Babylon, and Damascus. A city whose legendary founding dates only from 753 B.C. falls far short of Ur whose cultural apex was reached thirteen centuries earlier. This statement is made, however, not to disparage the antiquity of Rome but to emphasize its phenomenal development.

In all probability, its geographical setting was a significant factor in this amazing progress.

Situated in a plentifully watered plain, twelve miles from the seacoast, it was sufficiently removed from maritime incursions to develop unhindered, while its interior setting gave promise of substantial agricultural support for a considerable population. Through the midst of this upland plain flowed the historic Tiber which, in antiquity, was supposed to have been navigable for some distance. Clustered in this valley were the low hills of the Quirinal, Esquiline, Viminal, Palatine, Capitoline, Caelian, and Aventine. Chief among these were the Capitoline and the Palatine between which was located the Forum, the scene of some of the most dazzling displays of pagan splendor ever witnessed. In this environment stood the palatial residences of the Caesars, temples, arches of triumph, theaters, amphitheaters, colossal public baths, altars, statues, colonnaded streets, memorial columns, and gardens.

With the gradual expanse of Rome, suburban areas came into existence under the patronage of royalty and nobility, and great places of amusement, such as the Circus Maximus and the Colosseum were built. Ornate monuments were scattered throughout the city; scores of temples and shrines expressive of the religious life of Rome in the first century were established. The early consummation of this municipal development was reached in the age of Augustus Caesar who boasted that, having inherited a city of brick, he was leaving a city of stone. It is likely, however, that after the destruction of Rome by fire in A.D. 64 the imperial city rose to new heights of magnificence and in wealth. Its population was certainly in excess of 1,000,000 people at the time of Paul's arrival, while subsequently it reached the high figure of 1,500,000, including approximately 800,000 slaves.

It is of interest to note here that in the early days of Rome a city wall enclosed all of the area marked by the outlines of the "seven hills," but the phenomenal growth of the town soon took in considerable territory beyond. From 146 B.C. to Aurelian in A.D. 270, Rome was practically an unwalled city. When defenses were erected against encroaching barbarians, it is estimated that the circumference of the walls was about thirteen miles. Relatively, this circuit was less than the course of the walls either at Alexandria or Antioch in Syria, which were approximately fourteen miles in circumference. The contour of the land at Rome determined the outlines of the city, necessitating a more compact settlement in a restricted area. Consequently, the streets of Rome were not, as a rule, of the boulevard type as at Antioch and Alexandria where city planning was undertaken on unoccupied sites. It followed also in Rome that because of the congested population the elite of the city chose the suburban areas for construction of attractive villas. In all respects, however, Rome surpassed every other center of the Roman world, being at once the ruler and example of competing municipalities.

The relations which Rome sustained to the backgrounds of the New Testament were more vital and determinative than those of any other city, except Jerusalem. Fundamentally, one was the producer, while the other was the propagator of the Christian faith. By this it meant that Jerusalem stands at the threshold of the beginnings of Christianity, while Rome, through its significant preparation for the fulness of time, paved the way for its worldwide application. If the prevalence of world peace marked the advent of Jesus in a Near East dependency, the maintenance of

law and order in world administration made possible the unhindered movements and activities of his apostles in provincial areas scattered throughout the empire.

Rome provided the external or material framework within which the new religion operated with relative security and effectiveness. The phenomenal progress of Christianity was due in part to this great aristocrat of orderly processes. Courts of law, offering impartial justice, were designed by Rome; unsurpassed highways—the great Appian, Flaminian, and Ostian—connecting the remotest sections with the center of the empire reached their central point at the bronze mile post in the Forum. Roman legions preserved order to the very edges of the empire, and Roman officials governed with unexampled proficiency.

But in addition to these external aspects of efficient government, probably the chief contribution of Rome was to conserve, perhaps to improve, all of those cultural marks produced by the genius of the Greeks. It is true that the early environment of Christianity from the Gentile standpoint was Greco-Roman, but the Roman aspect of those cultural backgrounds was largely a duplication of the Greek life and thought. On the other hand, even though Rome is not to be considered primarily as a producer, it is doubtful whether it could have assumed a role more beneficial to the world than that of a great conservator of human culture and social progress.

Here, then, was the great arena of Mediterranean borderlands where Christianity won its greatest triumphs. Its conquests included the whole domain of the Roman Empire. Although Rome itself is not mentioned frequently in the New Testament, its towering figure is seen throughout the Gospels as in other portions of the narratives and Epistles, from the decree of Augustus Caesar that brought Joseph and Mary to Bethlehem, to the edict of Claudius that banished Aquila and Priscilla from Rome. Even John, the beloved, came under imperial disfavor in the Patmos exile.

Indeed, the Roman power was seen standing at the crossroads of all Christian purposes and activities. Particularly was this true in the decisive struggles between the deification of Caesar and the deity of Jesus, between emperor worship and Christianity. Polycarp, burned at the stake in the stadium above Smyrna, steadfastly claimed the lordship of Jesus, but thousands of others preceded him just as loyally during the Neronian and Domitianic persecutions. Tradition has it that Simon Peter was crucified in Rome head downward, though we have no record that Peter visited Rome. But Paul was there, finally to make the supreme sacrifice as a good soldier of Jesus Christ, keeping the faith.

The burning of Rome in A.D. 64 was probably associated with the Christians. The Colosseum echoed with the frenzied cries of sixty thousand people exulting in Christian martyrdom; public highways witnessed the hideous spectacle of crucifixions and funeral pyres. Cast out of ordinary relations as respectable members of the community, the Chris-

tians burrowed into mother earth, leaving miles of catacombs as the mute witness of their unchanging fidelity.

As in another setting, they

were tortured, not accepting their deliverance; that they might obtain a better resurrection: and others had trial of mockings and scourgings, yea, moreover of bonds and imprisonment: they were stoned, they were sawn asunder, they were tempted, they were slain with the sword: they went about in sheepskins, in goatskins; being destitute, afflicted, ill-treated (of whom the world was not worthy), wandering in deserts and mountains and caves, and the holes of the earth (Heb. 11:35–38, ASV).

But radiant above all this sordid treatment and undeserved martyrdom was the emblem of the cross by which was offered life in the midst of death. Succeeding centuries would tell a different story regarding the triumphs of the saints, even in the city of the Caesars, but the heroic struggles of these early Christians were continuous and simultaneous in every part of the Roman world. Triumphs were not withheld as Christians wrestled with principalities and powers, but it was reserved for later years to see the consummation of abiding peace.

Index

Place Names

215

Personal Names

Personal Names

Subjects

Names of Deities

Scripture References